Silhouette of Beethoven by Neesen, 1786

(Courtesy Beethovenhaus, Bonn)

BEETHOVEN

Impressions
by his
Contemporaries

Edited by
O. G. SONNECK

DOVER PUBLICATIONS, INC.
NEW YORK

Published in Canada by General Publishing Company, Ltd., 30 Lesmill Road, Don Mills, Toronto, Ontario.

This Dover edition, first published in 1967, is an unabridged and unaltered republication of the work originally published by G. Schirmer, Inc., in 1926 under the title *Beethoven: Impressions of Contemporaries.*
This edition is published by special arrangement with G. Schirmer, Inc., New York.

International Standard Book Number: 0-486-21770-1
Library of Congress Catalog Card Number: 66-30379

Manufactured in the United States of America
Dover Publications, Inc.
180 Varick Street
New York, N.Y. 10014

PREFACE

Anton Schindler first seems to have suggested in his Beethoven biography (1845) that a collection of contemporary impressions of the composer would form a very interesting volume. This idea appealed to Ludwig Nohl who, in 1877, published his book "Beethoven as Seen by Contemporaries." That pioneer-attempt has definitely been superseded by the practically exhaustive compilations of Friedrich Kerst (first edition, 1913) and Albert Leitzmann (1914), whose research and interest in their task placed all future books of similar purport under heavy obligation. Indeed, without Kerst and Leitzmann, this commemorative volume, too, would have become, if not impossible, at least improbable as a contribution to the Beethoven Centenary on March 26, 1927.

Recently a liberal selection of Beethoven's letters has again been made available in English to students of Beethoven's personality. Hence, there was no need for duplicating the enterprise of a fellow-publisher. Furthermore, the honor of printing in the author's native language what is likely to remain for many years the authoritative biography of the master, fell to us: Alexander Wheelock Thayer's "Life of Beethoven," published in 1921 by The Beethoven Association. This monumental work includes many letters of Beethoven and a considerable number of recollections of his personality by contemporaries, but no book is available in English which devotes itself exclusively to such impressions. Hence, we accepted the suggestion of our Vice-President, Mr. O. G. Sonneck, that he plan, compile and annotate for the Beethoven Centenary a book of moderate size to fill that gap.

The book was not planned as a contribution to Beethoven's biography. For that reason, practically no attempt was made to "edit" the reminiscences of the contemporaries in whose company, as it were, the reader

iii

visits the composer. That is to say, no attempt to reconcile errors of memory, time, etc., with the conflicting facts. Of such errors many could be pointed out, but they do not conflict with the impressions of the master's personality which visitors carried away with them and it seemed preferable not to mar their narratives by editorial comment unessential for the real purpose of this volume.

Of the one hundred and fifty or more recorded reminiscences of contemporaries who visited Beethoven, slightly more than thirty were selected. Such a selection, of course, will vary with every compiler, but the present selection was arrived at only after a good deal of comparative valuation of the available material in the interest of the general reader in America. Naturally, he will find much repetition, but that lies in the nature of the subject and could not be avoided. Indeed, it ought not be avoided, since it acquires the force of accumulative corroborative evidence. Beethoven, being what he was, could not very well appear in a different light to every visitor—and yet, how amusingly at times the impressions of him contradict one another. Even so, the differences are not nearly so extraordinary as those between the existing contemporary likenesses of Beethoven!

In only rare instances were these impressions of contemporaries originally written in English. All others called for translation. By courtesy of Mrs. Krehbiel a few translations were borrowed from Henry Edward Krehbiel's edition of Thayer's "Life of Beethoven," mentioned above. A few were made by Dr. Theodore Baker, our former Literary Editor, and others were made by Mr. Sonneck himself, but the majority were entrusted to Dr. Baker's successor, Mr. Frederick H. Martens.

G. SCHIRMER, INC.

New York, December, 1926.

CONTENTS

ILLUSTRATIONS

BEETHOVEN :

IMPRESSIONS OF CONTEMPORARIES

GOTTFRIED FISCHER'S STORY

The date of Beethoven's birth at the "Beethoven Haus" in the Bonngasse, Bonn, is not known with certainty. He was baptized on December 17, 1770. Therefore, the probability is that Ludwig van Beethoven was born on December sixteenth. For many years Beethoven shared the belief that he was born in 1772. The supposition is that his father—as other fathers of prodigies have done before and after—desired him to appear younger than he was. At any rate, when his juvenile "Drei Sonaten für Klavier" were published in 1783, the dedication to the Elector of Cologne, Maximilian Friedrich, read "composed by Ludwig van Beethoven, age eleven years."

Some time after Beethoven's birth, his family moved to the house of the Fischer family in the Rheingasse. This gave rise to a further legend: the Fischer house in the Rheingasse came to be considered the house in which the composer of "Fidelio" and the "Ninth Symphony" was born and where thousands upon thousands in the course of time paid homage to his memory, until the indisputable claim of the "Beethoven Haus" in the Bonngasse was established.

In the Fischer house Gottfried Fischer was born in 1780 and died there in 1864. When about sixty years old, master-baker Gottfried, at the request of many pilgrims to his house, the supposed birth-house of Beethoven, began to write down his and his older sister's Cäcilie reminiscences of Ludwig, adding to them until about 1857. Under the circumstances, the Fischer reminiscences are a curious jumble of essential and unessential things, in awkward language, but they shed important and entertaining light on Beethoven's boyhood.

When Ludwig van Beethoven had grown a bit he attended the elementary school, taught by Herr Huppert, at house No. 1091 in the Neugasse, which connects with the Rheingasse; later he went to the Münsterschule.

According to his father he did not learn much in school; for this reason his father set him down so early before the piano and kept him hard at work.

Cäcilie Fischer testifies how his father instructed him at the piano; he would have to stand on a little bench and play. That our former Oberbürgermeister Windeck has seen, too.

Ludwig van Beethoven also had daily lessons on the violin. Once he was playing without notes; his father happened in, and said: "What silly trash are you scratching together again now? You know that I can't bear that; scratch by note, otherwise your scratching won't amount to much."—When Johann van Beethoven happened to have visitors and Ludwig came into the room, he was wont to edge up to the piano and play chords with his right hand. Then his father would say: "What are you splashing around for? Go away, or I'll box your ears."—In time his father grew attentive when he heard him play the violin. He was again playing after his own fashion, without notes, when his father came in: "Won't you ever stop, after all I've told you?" He played again, and said to his father: "Now isn't that beautiful?" His father said: "That is something else, you made it up yourself. You are not to do that yet; apply yourself to the piano and violin, strike the notes quickly and correctly, that is more important. When you have once got so far, then you can and must work enough with your head; but don't concern yourself with that now—you are not to do that yet."—Afterwards, Ludwig van Beethoven also took daily lessons on the viola.

When Ludwig van Beethoven had grown a bit more, often dirty, negligent, Cäcilie Fischer said to him: "How dirty you are looking again—you ought to keep yourself clean!" Said he: "What's the odds? When I'm once a gentleman (*Herr*) no one will take any notice of that."

When Ludwig van Beethoven had been well trained

on the piano by his father, and began to feel himself master of the notes and the piano, he was emboldened to play on the organ and take lessons. And so he went for a trial to Brother Willibald in our local Franciscan monastery, a masterly teacher who knew his father, Johann van Beethoven, well. He very obligingly accepted him, with permission of the Father Superior, and gave him instruction, including training in the Church ritual, and made such progress that he could often make use of him as a substitute, so that he was greatly liked and esteemed by Brother Willibald.

As Ludwig van Beethoven became more and more venturesome on the organ, he had a mind to play on a larger organ, and made an essay in the Minorite monastery. Here he won such a friendly footing with the organist, that he was taken on to play the organ regularly every morning at 6 at Holy Mass. The bench on which he often sat is still to be seen there. There was a certain Father Hanzmann in the monastery who was likewise a good organist, and who also, when he cared to, played the organ. When the Beethovens had a concert at home, Father Hanzmann was always there. Ludwig could not bear him, and said to Cäcilie: "That monk, he always has to come here; he might as well stay in his monastery and read his prayer-book."

In Bonn there was a middle-aged man by the name of Stommb, who had formerly been a musician and learned to compose. Thereby, it was said, he had become insane; he used to wander through the town with a conductor's wand in his right hand and a music-roll in his left; not a word would he say. When he came into the ground floor at Rheinstrasse No. 934, where no one had thought to see him, he would strike with his wand on the table in the ground floor and point up towards the Beethoven home as if to indicate that musicians were there, too, and then beat time with the conductor's wand on the music-roll, not saying one word.

Ludwig van Beethoven often laughed about it, and once said: "We can see by that how it goes with musicians; music has already made this one mad—what may happen to us?"

It seems as if this scatterbrained musician must have felt this. For when he had gone out, and was on the street, he would point at Beethoven's lodgings and strike the music with his wand, and go away.

If the old saying be accepted: Children and fools speak truth, one might suppose he wished to say that Ludwig van Beethoven would become a great man, and would make a noise in the world.

Cäcilie Fischer was often much vexed that the fool always came into this house only, and frightened the servants.

The three sons of Herr Johann van Beethoven, namely, Ludwig, Kaspar and Nikola, were very jealous of their parents' honor. On occasions when their papa was in company and (what did not often happen) had drunk a trifle too much, and his sons noticed it, all three were straightway on the spot, worried, and tried in the most winning way to induce their papa to go quietly home with them, so as not to make a scene; they would say soothingly, "O Papächen, Papächen!" and then he would comply. He was not quarrelsome in his cups, but merry and lively, so we in the house would hardly notice anything.

Ludwig now thought himself his father's equal in music; his brother Kaspar had learned what was required of him in school, and the same in his study of herbs, so that in time he could be received as an apprentice by an apothecary. Both were bold and adventurous; when they could play mischievous tricks they were overjoyed and laughed heartily, and Ludwig would arch his back like a cat, as was his wont.

At that time Goodwife Fischer kept hens, and had long wondered why her hens were laying so few eggs.

She kept watch, but caught nobody. Till it happened that she went into the yard quite unsuspectingly and saw that Ludwig van Beethoven had crept through the fence into the henhouse. Frau Fischer said: "Ha, ha, Ludwig, what are you up to there?" He said: "My brother Kaspar threw my handkerchief in here and I came in to get it." Frau Fischer said: "Yes, yes, that may well be why I am getting so few eggs." Ludwig said: "Oh, Frau Fischer, the hens often hide their eggs; then, when you come across them, you will be all the gladder. And then there are foxes, they say, and they steal eggs, too." Frau Fischer said: "I think you are one of those same sly foxes. What will ever become of you!" Ludwig said: "Oh, heaven only knows! From what you say, up to date I am still a foxy player!" (*Notenfuchs.*) Says Frau Fischer: "Yes, and an egg-fox, too!" (*Eierfuchs*).

Then the two boys ran off laughing like rogues. Frau Fischer had to laugh with them, and could not find it in her heart to call them to account for their monkey trick.—

Early on a summer morning a cock had flown out of another yard and lighted on the roof of Fischers' rear building where Ludwig's father and mamma slept, toward the street.

The three boys slept on the side toward the yard, and Ludwig spied the cock directly. The Fischer boys also slept toward the yard, and had seen the cock; so they watched quietly to see how the fun would end.

Ludwig said: "That cock looks to me like a fat young rider; he has no spurs yet. Just see, just see how respectfully the cock is commending himself to us! If I could catch him, I'd soon beat the time for him!"

Ludwig and Kaspar sneaked out into the yard, and tempted and coaxed the cock with bread until they caught him. Then they squeezed his throat so that he could not scream, ran upstairs to their attic, and laughed. Now they probably had planned with the maid that she should prepare the cock when papa and mamma had gone out.

Next day the house-owner's son, Johann Fischer, said to Ludwig: "The cock must have become a musician; for I heard how he sang an alto-part." They laughed; Ludwig said: "That alto-part, when he was roasted enough, made me tired, too. But you surely won't say anything to papa or mamma about it, else we three boys would have to run out of the house."

The other said: "Oh, what does the cock matter to me? He might have stayed in his yard." Ludwig said, that formerly it was the law that one might keep whatever one found early in the morning that had flown into the yard. "And that is right, and folks ought to take better care of their livestock, for great mischief can be done by livestock."

Later one could not say that Ludwig cared much for companions or society. And then, when he had to turn his mind to music or set to work by himself, he assumed quite another demeanor and insisted on due respect. His happiest hours were those when he was free from the company of his parents, which was seldom the case— when all the family were away and he was alone by himself. So he got so far that in his twelfth year he already came forward as a composer, and in his fifteenth was appointed organist, and in token of rank wore a sword on his left side when he went up to the rood-loft in the court-church with his father.

Gala dress for court musicians: Sea-green frock coat, green knee-breeches with buckles, stockings of white or black silk, shoes with black bow-knots, embroidered vest with pocket-flaps, the vest bound with real gold cord, hair curled and with queue, crush hat under the left arm, sword on the left side with silver belt.

Former physique of Herr Ludwig van Beethoven: Short and thick-set, broad across the shoulders, short neck, large head, rounded nose, dark-brown complexion;

always leaned forward a little in walking. When still a boy they used to call him "der Spagnol" (the Spaniard) in our house.

One morning Ludwig van Beethoven was in his chamber overlooking the yard, leaning in the window with his head in both hands and staring fixedly at one spot. Cäcilie Fischer came over the yard and said to him: "How does it look, Ludwig?" but got no answer. Afterwards she asked him, what he meant by it: "No answer is an answer, too." He said: "O no, not that; excuse me; I was just occupied with such a lovely, deep thought, I couldn't bear to be disturbed."

From his attic Beethoven had the beautiful view over the Rhine and the other side, the view of the Seven Mountains like that from the old toll-house. In the attic were two telescopes, a small one and a large one; with them one could see twenty miles. That was Herr Ludwig van Beethoven's delight, for the Beethovens loved the Rhine.

As Ludwig van Beethoven advanced from day to day in music and composition, and sold his compositions to strangers, he thereby became so famous far and wide that many music-lovers came to visit him from distant foreign parts out of curiosity, and requested Herr Ludwig van Beethoven that he allow them to hear him play in a little concert. Then Herr Johann van Beethoven, when it was possible, sent out for musicians and gave a concert in his room. Most likely the gentlemen paid him well for it—we do not know.

As the disturbance through the strangers grew worse and worse, Herr Fischer said to Herr Johann van Beethoven: "If I were not a baker, all this disturbance from outsiders would not worry me; one has the night for rest. But as I am a baker, and must stay up at night to bake, I must sleep in the daytime; I cannot stand it—it would make me sick. Herr van Beethoven, I am sorry to tell you that you must look around for other lodgings."

Johann van Beethoven often said: "My son Ludwig, he is now my only joy; he is getting on so well in music and composition, everyone observes him with admiration. My Ludwig, my Ludwig, I can see that in time he will become a great man in the world.   You who are gathered together here, and live to see it, remember my words!"

CHRISTIAN GOTTLOB NEEFE
(1783)

At the tender age of twelve Beethoven had begun to assist his teacher at the organ and as *cembalist* in the opera orchestra, when Christian Gottlob Neefe (1748-1798), Court organist at Bonn to the Elector of Cologne and a composer of once popular "Singspiele," contributed on March 2, 1783 to "Cramer's Magazine" the following prophetic communication (The translation here used is that in Thayer I, 69):

Louis van Beethoven, son of the tenor singer mentioned, a boy of eleven years and of most promising talent.   He plays the clavier very skilfully and with power, reads at sight very well, and—to put it in a nutshell—he plays chiefly "The Well-Tempered Clavichord" of Sebastian Bach, which Herr Neefe put into his hands. Whoever knows this collection of preludes and fugues in all the keys—which might almost be called the *non plus ultra* of our art—will know what this means.   So far as his duties permitted, Herr Neefe has also given him instruction in thorough-bass.   He is now training him in composition and for his encouragement has had nine variations for the pianoforte, written by him on a march [by Ernst Christoph Dressler] engraved at Mannheim. This youthful genius is deserving of help to enable him to travel.   He would surely become a second Wolfgang Amadeus Mozart were he to continue as he has begun.

Mozart
(1787)

When the "youthful genius" was at last, in the springtime of 1787, enabled to travel, he naturally betook himself to Mozart in Vienna, but the news of his mother's serious illness compelled him to return to Bonn after a few lessons with the master. "My journey cost me a great deal," Beethoven wrote to a friend in September, 1787, "and I have not the smallest hope of earning anything here. Fate is not propitious to me in Bonn." His introduction to Mozart is narrated by Mozart's biographer Jahn as follows (Thayer, I, 90):

Beethoven, who as a youth of great promise came to Vienna in 1786 [really in 1787], but was obliged to return to Bonn after a brief sojourn, was taken to Mozart and at that musician's request played something for him which he, taking it for granted that it was a show-piece prepared for the occasion, praised in a rather cool manner. Beethoven observing this, begged Mozart to give him a theme for improvisation. He always played admirably when excited and now he was inspired, too, by the presence of the master whom he reverenced greatly; he played in such a style that Mozart, whose attention and interest grew more and more, finally went silently to some friends who were sitting in an adjoining room, and said, vivaciously, "Keep your eyes on him; some day he will give the world something to talk about."

Carl Ludwig Junker
(1791)

In the autumn of 1791 the Elector, the music-loving Maximilian Francis, took with him to Mergentheim, the capital of the Teutonic Order, his court musicians for the entertainment of the assembled Commanders and Knights of the order. Junker, better known as a writer on music than as a composer, visited the musicians at Mergentheim. In his letter to Bossler's "Correspondenz" on November 23, 1791 he overflowed with admiration for his "friend Bethofen" in these enthusiastic terms (Thayer, I, 115-116):

Here I was also an eye-witness to the esteem and respect in which this chapel stands with the Elector. Just as the rehearsal was to begin Ries was sent for by the Prince, and upon his return brought a bag of gold. "Gentlemen," said he, "this being the Elector's name-day he sends you a present of a thousand thalers." And again, I was eye-witness of this orchestra's surpassing excellence. Herr Winneberger, Kapellmeister at Wallenstein, laid before it a symphony of his own composition, which was by no means easy of execution, especially for the wind-instruments, which had several solos *concertante*. It went finely, however, at the first trial, to the great surprise of the composer. An hour after the dinner-music the concert began. It was opened with a symphony of Mozart; then followed a recitative and air sung by Simonetti; next, a violoncello concerto played by Herr Romberger [Bernhard Romberg]; fourthly, a symphony by Pleyel; fifthly, an air by Righini, sung by Simonetti; sixthly, a double concerto for violin and violoncello played by the two Rombergs; and the closing piece was the symphony of Winneberger, which had very many brilliant passages. The opinion already expressed as to the performance of this orchestra was confirmed. It was not possible to attain a higher degree of exactness. Such perfection in the pianos, fortes, rinforzandos—such a swelling and gradual increase of tone and then such an almost imperceptible dying away, from the most powerful to the lightest accents—all this was formerly to be heard only in Mannheim. It would be difficult to find another orchestra in which the violins and basses are throughout in such excellent hands. . . . The members of the chapel, almost without exception, are in their best years, glowing with health, men of culture and fine personal appearance. They form truly a fine sight, when one adds the splendid uniform in which the Elector has clothed them—red, and richly trimmed with gold.

I heard also one of the greatest of pianists—the dear, good Bethofen, some compositions by whom appeared in the Spires' "Blumenlese" in 1783, written in his eleventh year. True, he did not perform in public, probably the instrument here was not to his mind. It is one of Spath's make, and at Bonn he plays upon one by Steiner. But, what was infinitely preferable to me, I heard him extemporize in private; yes, I was even invited to propose a theme for him to vary. The greatness of this amiable, light-hearted man, as a virtuoso, may in my opinion be safely estimated from his almost inexhaustible wealth of ideas, the altogether characteristic style of expression in his playing, and the great execution which he displays. I know, therefore, no one thing which he lacks, that conduces to the greatness of an artist. I have heard Vogler upon the pianoforte—of his organ playing I say nothing, not having heard him upon that instrument—have often heard him, heard him by the hour together, and never failed to wonder at his astonishing execution; but Bethofen, in addition to the execution, has greater clearness and weight of idea, and more expression—in short, he is more for the heart—equally great, therefore, as an *adagio* or *allegro* player. Even the members of this remarkable orchestra are, without exception, his admirers, and all ears when he plays. Yet he is exceedingly modest and free from all pretension. He, however, acknowledged to me, that, upon the journeys which the Elector had enabled him to make, he had seldom found in the playing of the most distinguished virtuosos that excellence which he supposed he had a right to expect. His style of treating his instrument is so different from that usually adopted, that it impresses one with the idea, that by a path of his own discovery he has attained that height of excellence whereon he now stands.

Had I acceded to the pressing entreaties of my friend Bethofen, to which Herr Winneberger added his own,

and remained another day in Mergentheim, I have no
doubt he would have played to me for hours; and the day,
thus spent in the society of these two great artists, would
have been transformed into a day of the highest bliss.

Johann Schenk
(1792)

Johann Schenk (1761-1836) died in poverty, though his "Singspiele" enjoyed an extraordinary popularity. His "Der Dorfbar-
bier," for instance, held the stage for decades. How he became
Beethoven's teacher in counterpoint, he narrated in his autobiography. Of course, it must not be supposed that Beethoven, when
he left Bonn in 1792 to settle in Vienna, was ignorant of the technique
of composition; his fairly numerous early works of the Bonn period
would disprove such a notion. What he needed was a thorough
schooling in academic counterpoint. Unfortunately for him Mozart
had died in 1791 and Joseph Haydn possessed little talent as a
teacher. The studies with Haydn *via* Schenk continued until early
in 1794 when the famous theoretician Albrechtsberger superseded
both and brought Beethoven's studies to a competent conclusion.
(Thayer, I, 153-154.)

In 1792, His Royal Highness Archduke Maximilian,
Elector of Cologne, was pleased to send his charge Louis
van Beethoven to Vienna to study musical composition
with Haydn. Towards the end of July, Abbé Gelinek
informed me that he had made the acquaintance of a
young man who displayed extraordinary virtuosity on
the pianoforte, such, indeed, as he had not observed since
Mozart. In passing he said that Beethoven had been
studying counterpoint with Haydn for more than six
months and was still at work on the first exercise; also
that His Excellency Baron van Swieten had earnestly
recommended the study of counterpoint and frequently
inquired of him how far he had advanced in his studies.
As a result of these frequent incitations and the fact
that he was still in the first stages of his instruction,
Beethoven, eager to learn, became discontented and
often gave expression to his dissatisfaction to his friend.

Gelinek took the matter much to heart and came to me with the question whether I felt disposed to become better acquainted with Beethoven as soon as possible, and a day was fixed for me to meet him in Gelinek's lodgings and hear him play on the pianoforte.

Thus I saw the composer, now so famous, for the first time and heard him play. After the customary courtesies he offered to improvise on the pianoforte. He asked me to sit beside him. Having struck a few chords and tossed off a few figures as if they were of no significance, the creative genius gradually unveiled his profound psychological pictures. My ear was continually charmed by the beauty of the many and varied motives which he wove with wonderful clarity and loveliness into each other, and I surrendered my heart to the impressions made upon it while he gave himself wholly up to his creative imagination, and anon, leaving the field of mere tonal charm, boldly stormed the most distant keys in order to give expression to violent passions. . . .

The first thing that I did the next day was to visit the still unknown artist who had so brilliantly disclosed his mastership. On his writing-desk I found a few passages from his first lesson in counterpoint. A cursory glance disclosed the fact that, brief as it was, there were mistakes in every key. Gelinek's utterances were thus verified. Feeling sure that my pupil was unfamiliar with the preliminary rules of counterpoint, I gave him the familiar text-book of Joseph Fux, "Gradus ad Parnassum," and asked him to look at the exercises that followed. Joseph Haydn, who had returned to Vienna towards the end of the preceding year, was intent on utilizing his muse in the composition of large masterworks, and thus laudably occupied could not well devote himself to the rules of grammar. I was now eagerly desirous to become the helper of the zealous student. But before beginning the instruction I made him understand that our coöperation would have to be kept secret. In view of this

I recommended that he copy every exercise which I
corrected in order that Haydn should not recognize the
handwriting of a stranger when the exercise was submitted to him.   After a year, Beethoven and Gelinek
had a falling out for a reason that has escaped me;
both, it seemed to me, were at fault.   As a result Gelinek
got angry and betrayed my secret.   Beethoven and his
brothers made no secret of it longer.

I began my honorable office with my good Louis in
the beginning of August, 1792, and filled it uninterruptedly until May, 1793, by which time he finished double
counterpoint in the octave and went to Eisenstadt.   If
his Royal Highness had sent his charge at once to Albrechtsberger his studies would never have been interrupted and he would have completed them.

Franz Gerhard Wegeler
(1794–1796)

In the literature about Beethoven the "Biographical Notices"
(1838) by Franz Gerhard Wegeler and Ferdinand Ries occupy a
prominent position.   Wegeler, five years older than Beethoven, was
one of Beethoven's most intimate friends at Bonn.   When the
victorious French army occupied the Rhineland in 1794, Wegeler,
then the Rector of the University of Bonn, though only twenty-
nine years old, fled to Vienna where he renewed his intimate friendship with Beethoven during the next two years.   The following
reminiscences of Wegeler (Thayer, I, 180-181) relate to the years
1794-1796, when Beethoven's financial affairs had taken a turn for
the better.

Carl, Prince of Lichnowsky, Count Werdenberg,
Dynast Granson, was a very great patron, yes, a friend
of Beethoven's, who took him into his house as a guest,
where he remained at least a few years.   I found him
there toward the end of the year 1794, and left him there
in the middle of 1796.   Meanwhile, however, Beethoven
had almost always a home in the country.

The Prince was a great lover and connoisseur of music. He played the pianoforte, and by studying Beethoven's pieces and playing them more or less well, sought to convince him that there was no need of changing anything in his style of composition, though the composer's attention was often called to the difficulties of his works. There were performances at his house every Friday morning, participated in by four hired musicians— Schuppanzigh, Weiss, Kraft and another (Link?), besides our friend; generally also an amateur, Zmeskall. Beethoven always listened with pleasure to the observations of these gentlemen. Thus, to cite a single instance, the famous violoncellist Kraft in my presence called his attention to a passage in the finale of the Trio, Op. 1, No. 3, to the fact that it ought to be marked "sulla corda G," and the indication 4-4 time which Beethoven had marked in the finale of the second Trio, changed to 2-4. Here the new compositions of Beethoven, so far as was feasible, were first performed. Here there were generally present several great musicians and music-lovers. I, too, as long as I lived in Vienna, was present, if not every time, at least most of the time.

Here a Hungarian count once placed a difficult composition by Bach in manuscript before him which he played *a vista* exactly as Bach would have played it, according to the testimony of the owner. Here the Viennese author Förster once brought him a quartet of which he had made a clean copy only that morning. In the second portion of the first movement the violoncello got out. Beethoven stood up, and still playing his own part sang the bass accompaniment. When I spoke about it to him as a proof of acquirements, he replied with a smile: "The bass part had to be so, else the author would have known nothing about composition." To the remark that he had played a *presto* which he had never seen before so rapidly that it must have been impossible to see the individual notes, he answered: "Nor is that necessary; if you read rapidly there may be a multitude of typographical errors, but you neither see nor give heed to them, so long as the language is a familiar one."

After the concert the musicians generally stayed to dine. Here there gathered, in addition, artists and savants without regard to social position. The Princess Christiane was the highly cultivated daughter of Count Franz Joseph von Thun, who, a very philanthropic and respectable gentleman, was disposed to extravagant enthusiasm by his intercourse with Lavater, and believed himself capable of healing diseases through the power of his right hand.

Beethoven, brought up in the most straitened circumstances and always, so to say, under tutelage, even though it might only be that of his friends, had no idea of the value of money and was anything but economical. Thus, to cite an instance, four o'clock was the dinner hour in Prince Lichnowsky's palace. "And so," said Beethoven, "I must get home every day at three-thirty, put on a better suit, shave, and so on. . . . I can't stand that." For this reason he often went to the taverns, where incidentally, as in all matters economic, he fared the worse because, as already said, he knew nothing of the value of things themselves or of money. The Prince, who had a loud, metallic voice, once commanded one of his servants that should he and Beethoven ring at the same time, the latter was first to be served. Beethoven overheard him and hired a servant of his own the very next day. In the same way, though the Prince placed his stables at his disposal, he bought a horse for himself when seized by a passing fancy for learning how to ride.

Among the biographical notices with which Ignaz, Ritter von Seyfried, has provided his study of Beethoven, we find the following sentence, on p. 13: "Beethoven never married nor, strange to say, did he ever have a love affair." The truth of the matter, as my brother-in-law, Stephan von Breuning, Ferdinand Ries, Bernhard Romberg and I myself came to know it, is that Beethoven never was out of love, and usually was much affected by the love he was in at the time. . . . In Vienna Beethoven, at least so long as I was living there, always had some love affair in hand, and on occasion he made conquests which many an Adonis would have found it difficult, if not impossible, to encompass.

FRAU VON BERNHARD
(1796–1800)

In 1867 Ludwig Nohl published the Beethoven reminiscences of Frau von Bernhard. She was the daughter of a Herr von Kissow who lived for many years at Reval, Esthonia and, then moved to Augsburg where his daughter was born in 1783. At an early age she showed a pronounced musical talent and her father sent her to Vienna to be educated as a pianist by Beethoven's friends Nanette Streicher and her husband Andreas Streicher, the latter best known in history as a piano-manufacturer. Little Miss von Kissow was introduced by Nanette Streicher to Herr von Klüpfeld, Secretary of the Russian Legation and became a member of his household.

One day Streicher laid before her some pieces by Beethoven; these were the piano sonatas Op. 2, which had just been published [1796] by Artaria. He observed that they were new things that the ladies did not care to play because they were too unintelligible and too difficult for them; would she like to learn them? The girl felt sure that she would, and soon performed these and other piano-works by Beethoven so skilfully that she was invited to the private musical entertainments at the homes of Lichnowsky and Rasumowsky. Beethoven himself, who then was still often to be seen here, heard how well the girl played his pieces, and speedily made her acquaintance; indeed, he prized her talent so highly that thenceforward, up to the year 1800 (when she left Vienna), he as a rule sent her a copy of each of his newest piano-pieces as soon as they appeared in print, together with a brief and friendly, usually jocular, note. None of these notes, unhappily, are extant; for at that time so many handsome Russian officers frequented Herr von Klüpfell's house that the ill-favored Beethoven made no impression whatever on her. For that matter, she saw the young artist very frequently.

For Herr von Klüpfell was likewise very musical, and Beethoven was a frequent visitor at his house, where he would often play the piano for hours, but always "without notes." Everybody thought this wonderful, and went into ecstasies over it. One day it happened that the well-known pianist Franz Krommer was there, too, and performed a new composition of his own. Beethoven at first sat next her on the sofa, but soon wandered about, went up to the piano to look over some music, and paid not the slightest attention to the playing. This irritated Herr von Klüpfell, and he requested a friend of the young nonchalant to tell him that this was unseemly; that a young man, still a nobody, should always show respect when an older, deserving composer was playing something. From that moment Beethoven never again set foot in the house of Herr Klüpfell.

Frau von Bernhard is full of reminiscences concerning the young man's irrepressible idiosyncrasies. "When he came to us, he would usually stick his head through the door to make sure that no one was present whom he disliked. He was short and insignificant, with an ugly red face full of pockmarks. His hair was very dark and hung fairly tousled about his face. His attire was very ordinary and not remotely of the choiceness that was customary in those days and particularly in our circles. Besides, he spoke in a pronounced dialect and had a rather common way of expressing himself, indeed, his entire deportment showed no signs of exterior polish; on the contrary, he was unmannerly both in demeanor and behavior. He was very proud; I have seen Countess Thun, the mother of Princess Lichnowsky, lying on her knees before him (who was seated on the sofa) and begging him to play something—and Beethoven would not do it. But then, Countess Thun was a very eccentric woman.

"I was often invited to the Lichnowskys, to play there. He was kindly and a perfect gentleman; she was a very lovely lady. But they did not seem to live happily together; her face always bore such a melancholy expression, and I heard that he spent money lavishly, more than his income would warrant. Her sister, even more beautiful, was also married to a patron of Beethoven.[1] She was almost invariably present when they were making music."

Here she also saw Haydn and Salieri, who were then very famous, whereas even then no one cared to say a good word for Beethoven. "I still remember distinctly how both Haydn and Salieri sat on the sofa on one side of the little music-room, both most carefully dressed in the old-fashioned style with bag-wig, shoes and silk stockings, while Beethoven used to appear even here in the freer ultra-Rhenish garb, almost carelessly dressed."

JOHANN WENZEL TOMASCHEK
(1798)

This excellent Bohemian organist, teacher and composer (1774-1850) published his autobiography in the "Libussa" year-book of 1845. It contained the following independent and valuable discussion of Beethoven's powers and characteristics as a pianoforte virtuoso. Thayer, I, 217, in quoting most of it, reminds his readers that Tomaschek down to 1840 had heard all the greatest virtuosos from Mozart on, and calls attention to Beethoven's own claim three years later that he had greatly perfected his playing.

In the year 1798, in which I continued my juridical studies, Beethoven, the giant among pianoforte players,

---

[1] Elizabeth was married to Count Rasumowsky.

came to Prague. He gave a largely attended concert in the Konviktssaal, at which he played his Concerto in C major, Op. 15, and the Adagio and graceful Rondo in A major from Op. 2, and concluded with an improvisation on a theme given him by Countess Sch. . . [Schlick?], "Ah tu fosti il primo oggetto," from Mozart's "Titus" (duet No. 7). Beethoven's magnificent playing and particularly the daring flights in his improvisation stirred me strangely to the depths of my soul; indeed I found myself so profoundly bowed down that I did not touch my pianoforte for several days. . . . I heard Beethoven at his second concert, which neither in performance nor in composition renewed again the first powerful impression. This time he played the Concerto in B-flat which he had just composed in Prague.   Then I heard him a third time at the home of Count C., where he played, besides the graceful Rondo from the A major Sonata, an improvisation on the theme: "Ah! vous dirai-je, Maman."   This time I listened to Beethoven's artistic work with more composure. I admired his powerful and brilliant playing, but his frequent daring deviations from one motive to another, whereby the organic connection, the gradual development of idea was put aside, did not escape me. Evils of this nature frequently weaken his greatest compositions, those which sprang from a too exuberant conception.   It is not seldom that the unbiased listener is rudely awakened from his transport. The singular and original seemed to be his chief aim in composition, as is confirmed by the answer which he made to a lady who asked him if he often attended Mozart's operas. "I do not know them," he replied, "and do not care to hear the music of others lest I forfeit some of my originality."   As a composer I am competent enough here to express my opinion of Beethoven's artistic career without hesitation.

I consider him one of the most gifted composers, but only for instrumental music, not for vocal music, in which he did not fare very happily. Harmony, counterpoint, eurhythm, and particularly musical esthetics, he did not seem to have overly much at heart; hence his larger works are defaced by occasional trivialities.

CARL CZERNY
(about 1800)

An ironical Fate decreed that the indefatigable productivity of Carl Czerny (1791-1857) as a composer should leave no traces, but that he should hold the centre of the pædagogical stage for more than a century. How many millions, more or less with rebellion in their hearts, have worshipped at Czerny's shrine of velocity, dexterity, etc., it would be difficult to estimate. For this enormous popularity (or unpopularity) Beethoven is indirectly responsible, since it was he who prepared at the beginning of the nineteenth century Czerny for his career as pianist and piano teacher. Czerny, in turn, became the teacher of Liszt and he the teacher of Siloti, Friedheim, Liebling, Rosenthal and others who are still active in our midst,—in a sense, the direct descendants as pianists of Beethoven.

I still can remember Gelinek's telling my father, one day, that he had been asked to spend the evening at a gathering where he was to break a lance with an unknown pianist. "We will give him a first-class drubbing," Gelinek added. The following day my father asked Gelinek how the battle of the preceding night had turned out.

"Oh," said Gelinek, quite downcast, "I shall think back on last night many a time! That young fellow was full of the very devil! Never have I heard of such playing! He improvised on a theme I had given him as I never have heard Mozart himself improvise. Then he played compositions of his own which are in the highest degree astonishing and grandiose and he displayed difficulties and effects on the piano beyond anything of which we might have dreamed."

"Why," said my father, astonished, "what is the man's name?"

"He is a young man, small, homely, dark and obstinate-looking," replied Gelinek, "whom Prince Lichnowski brought here from Germany a few years ago, so that he might study composition with Haydn, Albrechtsberger and Salieri, and he is called Beethoven."

It was the first time I had ever heard this name and I at once importuned my father to procure Beethoven's compositions for me. Soon I had everything by him which had appeared in print: the three first trios and sonatas, some variations, the "Adelaïde," etc.; and just as I already had learned a number of fine things by other masters, I now soon learned to appreciate the beauty and originality of Beethoven's works, so far as the limitations of my age allowed, a fact to which one circumstance, in particular, contributed.

At that time an old man named Krumpholz (brother of the inventor of the pedal-harp) visited us nearly every evening. He was a violinist and as such had a position in the orchestra of the Court Theatre; yet at the same time he was a musical enthusiast whose passion for music was carried to the most extravagant lengths. Nature had endowed him to a high degree with a just and delicate feeling for the beautiful in tonal art, and though he possessed no great fund of technical knowledge, he was able to criticize every composition with much acumen, and, so to say, anticipate the judgments of the musical world.

As soon as young Beethoven appeared for the first time, Krumpholz attached himself to him with a persistence and devotion which soon made him a familiar figure in his home, so that he practically spent nearly the whole day with him and Beethoven, who ordinarily was most reticent with every one regarding his musical projects, told Krumpholz about all his ideas, played every new composition for him time and again, and improvised for him every day. Although Beethoven often poked fun at the unfeigned ecstasies into which Krumpholz invariably fell, and never called him anything but his jester; yet he was touched by his attachment, which led him to affront the bitterest enmities in order to defend his cause against its adversaries, so numerous in those days. For at that time Beethoven's compositions were totally misunderstood by the general public, and all the followers of the old Mozart-Haydn school opposed them with the most intense animosity.

This was the man for whom, day by day, I had to play Beethoven's works, and although he knew nothing of piano playing, he was, quite naturally, able to tell me a great deal about their tempo, interpretation, effects, characteristics, etc., since he often had heard them played by Beethoven himself, and in most cases had been present when they came into being. His enthusiasm soon infected me and before long I, in turn, was a Beethoven worshipper like himself, learned all that Beethoven had written by heart, and, considering my years, played it with skill and enthusiasm. Krumpholz also invariably told me about the new things Beethoven had "under pen," and would sing or play on his violin the themes he had heard in Beethoven's home during the forenoon. Owing to this circumstance I always was informed at a much earlier date than others with regard to what Beethoven had under way. Later this made it possible for me to realize how long, often for years at a time, Beethoven polished his compositions before they were published, and how in new works he used motives which had occurred to him many years before, because our friendly relations with Krumpholz were maintained over a long period of years up to his death, which took place in 1817.

I was about ten years old when Krumpholz took me to see Beethoven. With what joy and terror I greeted the day on which I was to meet the admired master! Even now this moment is still vividly present in my memory. It was a winter's day when my father, Krumpholz, and I took our way from Leopoldstadt (where we still were living) to Vienna proper, to a street called *der tiefe Graben* (the Deep Ditch), and climbed endless flights to the fifth and sixth story, where a rather untidy-looking servant announced us to Beethoven and then admitted us. The room presented a most disorderly appearance; papers and articles of clothing were scattered about everywhere, some trunks, bare walls, hardly a chair, save the wobbly one at the Walter fortepiano (then the best), and in this room was gathered a company of from six to eight persons, among them the two Wranitzky brothers, Süssmayr, Schuppanzigh and one of Beethoven's brothers.

Beethoven himself wore a morning-coat of some long-haired, dark-gray material and trousers to match, so that he at once recalled to me the picture in Campe's "Robinson Crusoe," which I was reading at the time. His coal-black hair, cut *à la Titus*, bristled shaggily about his head. His beard—he had not been shaved for several days—made the lower part of his already brown face still darker. I also noticed with that visual quickness peculiar to children that he had cotton which seemed to have been steeped in a yellowish liquid, in his ears.

At that time, however, he did not give the least evidence of deafness. I was at once told to play something, and since I did not dare begin with one of his own compositions, played Mozart's great C major Concerto, the one beginning with chords. Beethoven soon gave me his attention, drew near my chair, and in those places where I had only accompanying passages played the orchestral melody with me, using his left hand. His hands were overgrown with hair and his fingers, especially at the ends, were very broad. The satisfaction he expressed gave me the courage to play his *Sonata pathétique*, which had just appeared, and, finally, his "Adelaïde," which my father sang in his very passable tenor. When he had ended Beethoven turned to him and said: "The boy has talent. I will teach him myself and accept him as my pupil. Send him to me several times a week. First of all, however, get him a copy of Emanuel Bach's book on the true art of piano playing, for he must bring it with him the next time he comes."

Then all those present congratulated my father on this favorable verdict, Krumpholz in particular being quite delighted, and my father at once hurried off to hunt up Bach's book.

During the first lessons Beethoven kept me altogether on scales in all the keys, and showed me (something at the time still unknown to most players) the only correct position of the hands and fingers and, in particular, how to use the thumb, rules whose usefulness I did not learn fully to appreciate until a much later date. Then he went over the studies belonging to this method with me and, especially, called my attention to the *legato*, which he himself controlled to such an incomparable degree, and which at that time all other pianists regarded as impossible of execution on the fortepiano, for even after Mozart's day, the choppy, short, detached manner of playing was the fashion.[1] In later years Beethoven himself told me that he had heard Mozart play on various occasions and that Mozart, since at the time the invention of the fortepiano was still in its infancy, had accustomed himself to a mode of playing on the claviers then more frequently used, which was in no wise adapted to the fortepiano. In course of time I also made the acquaintance of several persons who had taken lessons from Mozart, and found this remark justified by their playing.

My father never was willing to have me take the long trip to the city alone, and hence always took me to Beethoven in person. In this way I lost so many lessons and, besides, it so often happened that Beethoven was

---

[1] Not with Mozart himself, whose letters of June 27, 1781, and January 17, 1782, show him to have demanded the very opposite, as Kerst points out.

composing at the moment, and I would be excused, that after a time my studies were interrupted for a longer period, and I was once more thrown back upon my own assiduity.

In the year 1802 Beethoven gave his first public concert at the Theatre, where he played his first Concerto in E flat major, and had his first and second symphonies performed with tremendous applause, and finally gave a free improvisation, choosing "Gott erhalte Franz den Kaiser" as his theme.

Once, at a social evening—it was at the home of Mozart's widow—the company was much larger and numerous than customary, and among the many elegant gentlemen and ladies present I noticed a young man whose appearance challenged my attention. He had an ordinary, unpleasant face which twitched continually, and his clothing, in the heighth of poor taste, suggested that he might be some sort of country schoolteacher. In curious contrast to his clothes were a number of valuable, glittering rings which he wore on nearly all his fingers. As usual there was music, and at length this young man—he may have been a little over twenty— was asked to play. What a master he showed himself to be! Although by that time I already had enjoyed so many opportunities of hearing Gelinek, Lipowsky, Wölffl and Beethoven himself, the playing of this insignificant looking individual seemed to open up a new world. Never before had I listened to such novel, brilliant feats of difficulty, to such clarity, elegance and delicacy of interpretation, and a fantasy coördinated with such excellent good taste. When later he interpreted some of Mozart's violin sonatas (Krommer accompanying him), these compositions which I knew so well became filled with new meaning. And then I learned that this was young Hummel, formerly Mozart's pupil, who had just returned from London where he had been taking lessons of Clementi. Hummel's playing already at that time—in so far as the instruments then existing made possible—had reached that high plane which later made him so famous.

If Beethoven's playing was notable for its tremendous power, character, unheard-of bravura and facility, Hummel's performance, on the other hand, was a model of all that is clean and distinct, of the most charming elegance and delicacy, and its difficulties were invariably calculated to produce the greatest, most astonishing effect, since he combined Mozart's manner with the Clementi school so wisely adapted to the instrument. It was therefore quite natural that in the world at large he should have been reputed the better player, and that soon the adherents of the two masters formed two factions which assailed each other with all their might and main. Hummel's followers reproached Beethoven with maltreating the fortepiano, said his playing was devoid of purity and distinctness, that his employ of the pedal produced only a confused noise, and that his compositions were labored, artificial, unmelodious, and in addition irregular in form. Beethoven's partisans, on the other hand, asserted that Hummel lacked all real imagination, declared his playing was as monotonous as that of a hurdy-gurdy, that he held his fingers clawed in, spider-fashion, and that his compositions were mere elaborations of Mozart and Haydn themes. Hummel's playing did not fail to influence me, since it spurred me on to play with greater purity and distinctness.

One morning Beethoven—who had not seen me for the past two years and who had taken amiss my father's having stopped my lessons—came to Prince Lichnowsky's and seemed to be well content with my progress. "I said at once," he remarked, "that the boy had talent, but," he added with a smile, "his father was not strict enough with him." "Ah, Mr. van Beethoven," replied my father, good-naturedly, "you must remember he is our only child."

He also was satisfied with my sight-reading, after he had given me the manuscript of his Sonata in C major, Op. 35, to play. From that time forward Beethoven was favorably inclined toward me and treated me in a friendly manner until the end of his days. I had to attend to all corrections in his new works as they were published, and when his opera "Fidelio" was performed in the year 1805 (November 20th), he allowed me to arrange it for the fortepiano. To his remarks in connection with this task I owe that facility in arranging which later I found so useful.

My friendly relations with Beethoven meanwhile were uninterrupted, and when in the year 1815 he entrusted the nephew whom he had adopted to me to teach, I saw him at my home nearly every day, and there, when he happened to be in good humor, often listened to him improvise in a manner I never can forget.

He had, as he often said, practiced day and night during his youth, and worked so hard that his health had suffered, and those bodily ills which produced a continual inclination toward hypochondria in him undoubtedly were due to this cause.

It was astonishing how he could take in compositions at a glance—even manuscripts and large scores—and how well he played them. In this respect he had no equal. His manner of interpreting them was always decisive, but sharp and hard. The same praise is due his presentation of the great masters' compositions: he played Handel's oratorios and Gluck's works wonderfully well, thereby earning the greatest applause; and this also holds good of Sebastian Bach's fugues.

He once told me that as a boy he had been negligent and not much taken to task, and that his musical training had been a poor one. "And yet," he continued, "I had a talent for music." It was touching to hear him utter these words with all seriousness, as though none otherwise would have suspected it. On another occasion the conversation turned on the fame which his name had gained throughout the world. "Nonsense," he said, "I never thought of writing for reputation and honors! What is in my heart must out and so I write it down." Aside from those times when he was in one of the melancholy moods which occasionally overtook him, and which resulted from his physical ailments, he always was merry, mischievous, full of witticisms and jokes, and cared not a whit what people said of him.

When Beethoven was a young man he found a good friend at Court. Had he wished he might have lived in the greatest style. In disposition he was much akin to Jean-Jacques Rousseau, but he was noble, great-hearted and pure in character.

About the year 1800,when Beethoven had composed his Op. 28, he said to his intimate friend Krumpholz: "I am not very well satisfied with the work I have thus far done. From this day on I shall take a new way." Shortly after this appeared his three sonatas, Op. 31, in which one may see that he had partially carried out his resolve.

His improvisation was brilliant and astonishing in the extreme; and no matter in what company he might be, he knew how to make such an impression on every listener that frequently there was not a single dry eye,while many broke out into loud sobs, for there was a certain magic in his expression, aside from the beauty and originality of his ideas and his genial way of presenting them. When he had concluded an improvisation of this kind, he was capable of breaking out into boisterous laughter and of mocking his listeners for yielding to the emotion he had called forth in them. He would even say to them: "You are fools!" At times he felt himself insulted by such manifestations of sympathy. "Who can continue to live among such spoiled children?" he would cry, and for that reason alone (so he told me), he declined to accept the invitation sent him by the King of Prussia after an improvisation of this kind.

Countess Giulietta Guicciardi and Countess Therese Brunswick
(about 1801)

As Beethoven's deafness progressed, it became more and more necessary to carry on conversation with him by means of conversation-books. That is to say, the visitor would write his questions or answers on sheets of paper, kept for the purpose by Beethoven. Under the circumstances, of course, these conversation-books of which not less than 138 are preserved at the National Library in Berlin, generally do not record what Beethoven asked or answered. Among the exceptions is one of the year 1823 in which Schindler and Beethoven conversed about Count Gallenberg, who married the Countess Giulietta Guicciardi (born 1784) in 1803. In the course of conversation and among other things Beethoven said (in poor French): "J'étois bien aimé d'elle et plus que jamais son époux." Presumably on the strength of this remark Schindler assumed and in his biography of the master concluded that the famous love-letters in the third of which occur the words "my immortal beloved" were intended for the charming Countess Giulietta Guicciardi. (These letters were found after Beethoven's death in a secret drawer and whoever the intended recipient was, Beethoven perhaps never mailed the passionate outpourings of his heart.) Unquestionably Beethoven became deeply attached to her in 1801, but, whether or no she was the "immortal beloved" is a different story. Indeed, to this day the riddle of the identity of Beethoven's "immortal beloved" remains unsolved, notwithstanding the penetrating researches of sundry Beethoven specialists. Some favor the Countess Guicciardi, others the Countess Therese Brunswick, again others Theresa von Malfatti (to whom Beethoven actually offered his hand) and again others Amalie Sebald, not to mention minor candidates.

In 1852 Otto Jahn called on the Countess Gallenberg, *née* Guicciardi and made the following brief notes of her remarks. Naturally, Jahn could not commit the *faux pas* of putting questions about the "immortal beloved" to Countess Gallenberg and, of course, she volunteered no information on the subject. Her description of Beethoven, under the circumstances, lacked every flavor of romance and might have been that of any of Beethoven's aristocratic pupils of long ago, who had befriended him.

This applies also to the brief entry about Beethoven in the diary of Countess Therese von Brunswick (1775-1861) published in 1909 by La Mara, one of her champions as the "immortal beloved." La Mara's arguments brought forth from Mr. de Gerando, a member

Engraved by Neidl after the Portrait-Drawing of Beethoven
by Stainhauser, 1801

(Courtesy Beethovenhaus, Bonn)

Miniature of Beethoven
by Horneman, 1803

(Courtesy Beethovenhaus, Bonn)

of the Brunswick family, a denial, but also the revelation that Countess Therese in her youth did passionately love a man whose Christian name was Louis.   Unfortunately Mr. de Gerando adduced reasons why he cannot have been identical with Louis van Beethoven, reasons which Mr. Philip Hale, however, in the New Music Review, July and September, 1909, did not consider conclusive.   The spelling Brunswick is the usual one, but Brunsvik (de Korompa) appears to be more correct.

COUNTESS GIULIETTA GUICCIARDI

Beethoven had been her teacher.—He had her play his things, and was extremely severe with her until she achieved an interpretation correct in its very least detail.—He made a point of playing without effort.   He was prone to excitement, flinging down music and tearing it up.—He would accept no payment, though he was very poor; but accepted linen under the pretext that it had been hand-sewn by the Countess.—In the same way he taught Princess Odescalchi and Baroness Ertmann; they came to him or he went to them.—He did not like to play his own compositions; but cared only to improvise.   At the least sound he would rise and go away.

Count Brunswick, who played the 'cello, adored him, as did his sister Therese and Countess Deym.

Beethoven had given the Countess [Guicciardi] the Rondo in G; then asked her to return it since he had to dedicate something to Countess Lichnowsky and then inscribed the sonata to her [Op. 27, No. 2].

Beethoven was very homely, but noble, delicately fibred, well educated.

As a rule, Beethoven went shabbily dressed.

COUNTESS THERESE BRUNSWICK

When we were in Vienna, my mother wished to secure for her daughters Therese and Josephine the priceless advantage of Beethoven's piano tuition.   Beethoven, so

Adalbert Rosti, one of my brother's schoolmates declared, could not be induced to accept a hapchance invitation; yet should Her Excellency so far discommode herself as to climb his three flights of winding stairs in St. Peter's Place and visit him, he could vouch for her success. This was done. Like a schoolgirl on her way to school, my copy of Beethoven's Sonata with violin and 'cello accompaniment under my arm, we entered. And dear, immortal Louis van Beethoven was very amiable and as polite as possible. After we had exchanged some conventional remarks he had me sit down at his piano, which was out of tune, and I at once led off by singing the violin and 'cello accompaniments, while I played quite decently. This so delighted him that he promised to come every day, to the Archduke Karl Hotel, then known as the Golden Dragon. It was in May, and the last year of the century just past.

He came assiduously, but instead of remaining for an hour, from 12 o'clock on, he would often stay until 4 or 5 and never wearied of holding down and bending my fingers, which I had learned to stretch up and hold flatly. The great man must have been well content; for sixteen days in succession he did not once fail to appear. Until it grew to be 5 o'clock we did not feel hungry; and my dear mother, though hungry, did not complain—to the great indignation of the innfolk, for at that time it had not yet become the custom to eat dinner at 5 o'clock in the evening.

It was at this time that I formed the warm, intimate friendship with Beethoven which endured to the end of his life. He came to Ofen; he came to Martonwásár; he was accepted by the circle of chosen spirits who formed our social republic. A circular place in the open was planted with tall linden-trees; each tree bore the name of a member of the society. Even when we mourned their absence we spoke with their symbols, conversed with them and let them teach us. Very often, after bidding the tree good-morning, I would question it regarding this and that, whatever I wished to know, and it never failed to make reply!

IGNAZ VON SEYFRIED
(1799–1806)

When Ignatz von Seyfried in March, 1797, at the age of twenty-one, assumed the responsible position of one of Schikaneder's opera conductors, he had already attracted attention as a promising composer. His intimacy with Beethoven seems to have begun in 1800 and to have lasted until about 1806. Many years later (1832) he issued under the title of "Beethoven's Studien" a book which is under a cloud among Beethoven scholars because of its arbitrary and unreliable statements about Beethoven's studies in the theory of composition. On the other hand, his personal reminiscences and impressions of Beethoven at the end of the book are accepted as authentic, though savoring somewhat of exaggerated self-esteem.

The first quotation printed below refers to the meeting in 1799 between Beethoven and his rival Josef Wölffl (1772-1812) which, according to Thayer whose translation of that episode is used, bears all the marks of being a faithful transcript of the writer's own memories. The absence of jealousy between the two rivals was proved on Wölffl's part by the dedication of his Pianoforte Sonatas, Op. 7, to Beethoven.

Beethoven had already attracted attention to himself by several compositions and was rated a first-class pianist in Vienna when he was confronted by a rival in the closing years of the last century. Thereupon there was, in a way, a revival of the old Parisian feud of the Gluckists and Piccinists, and the many friends of art in the Imperial City arrayed themselves in two parties. At the head of Beethoven's admirers stood the amiable Prince Lichnowsky; among the most zealous patrons of Wölffl was the broadly cultured Baron Raymond von Wetzlar, whose delightful villa (on the Grünberg near the Emperor's recreation-castle) offered to all artists, native and foreign, an asylum in the summer months, as pleasing as it was desirable, with true British loyalty.

There the interesting combats of the two athletes not infrequently offered an indescribable artistic treat to the numerous and thoroughly select gathering. Each brought forward the latest product of his mind. Now one and anon the other gave free rein to its glowing fancy; sometimes they would seat themselves at two pianofortes and improvise alternately on themes which they gave each other, and thus created many a four-hand Capriccio which if it could have been put upon paper at the moment would surely have bidden defiance to time. It would have been difficult, perhaps impossible, to award the palm of victory to either one of the gladiators in respect of technical skill. Nature had been a particularly kind mother to Wölffl in bestowing upon him a gigantic hand which could span a tenth as easily as other hands compass an octave, and permitted him to play passages of double notes in these intervals with the rapidity of lightning. In his improvisations even then Beethoven did not deny his tendency toward the mysterious and gloomy. When once he began to revel in the infinite world of tones, he was transported also above all earthly things;—his spirit had burst all restricting bonds, shaken off the yokes of servitude, and soared triumphantly and jubilantly into the luminous spaces of the higher æther. Now his playing tore along like a wildly foaming cataract, and the conjurer constrained his instrument to an utterance so forceful that the stoutest structure was scarcely able to withstand it; and anon he sank down, exhausted, exhaling gentle plaints, dissolving in melancholy. Again the spirit would soar aloft, triumphing over transitory terrestrial sufferings, turn its glance upward in reverent sounds and find rest and comfort on the innocent bosom of holy nature. But who shall sound the depths of the sea? It was the mystical Sanscrit language whose hieroglyphs can be read only by the initiated. Wölffl, on the contrary, trained in the school of Mozart, was always equable;

never superficial but always clear and thus more accessible to the multitude. He used art only as a means to an end, never to exhibit his acquirements. He always enlisted the interest of his hearers and inevitably compelled them to follow the progression of his well-ordered ideas. Whoever has heard Hummel will know what is meant by this. . . .

But for this (the attitude of their patrons) the protégés cared very little. They respected each other because they knew best how to appreciate each other, and as straightforward honest Germans followed the principle that the roadway of art is broad enough for many, and that it is not necessary to lose one's self in envy in pushing forward for the goal of fame!

Every year Beethoven spent the summer months in the country, where under skies of azure blue he liked best to compose, and composed most successfully. Once he took lodgings in romantic Mödling, in order to be able to enjoy the Lower Austrian Switzerland, the picturesque [Brühl], to his heart's content. So a four-horse wagon was freighted with a few articles of furniture and a tremendous load of music; the tower-like machine slowly got under way, and the owner of its treasures marched along ahead of it as happy as could be, *per pedes Apostolorum*. No sooner did he cross the city boundary and find himself among blossoming fields, where gentle zephyrs set the green corn swaying like waves, amid the jubilant song of fluttering larks, celebrating the longed-for coming of lovely spring with trills of raptured greeting, than his genius awoke; thoughts began to traverse his mind, were spun out, ranged in order, noted down in lead-pencil—and the aim and goal of his migration was entirely forgotten. The gods alone know whither our Master strayed during the whole long period which elapsed, but suffice to say it was not until dusk was falling that dripping with sweat, covered with dust, hungry, thirsty and tired to death, he arrived in his chosen

Tusculum. Yet, heaven be merciful, what a horrible spectacle awaited him there! The driver had made his snail-like way to his destination without misadventure, but had waited two full hours for the patron who had hired and already had paid him in advance. Since he did not know his name it was impossible to make inquiries; and in any event the cart-horse tamer wished to sleep at home. So he made short work of it, unloaded the whole contents of his wagon in the marketplace and drove off without further ado. Beethoven was at first very angry; then he broke into uproarious laughter, after a brief reflection hired half-a-dozen gaping street boys, and had all he could do before the cries of the watchmen announcing the midnight hour rang out on the air, to get the children of his brain safely under the shelter of a roof by the light of Luna's silver ray.

The more his hearing failed, and those intestinal troubles which in the last years of his life also afflicted him gained the upper hand, the more rapidly there also developed the ominous symptoms of a torturing hypochondria. He commenced to complain about a world which was all evil, intent only on delusion and deceit; about malice, betrayal and treachery. He insisted that there were no longer any honest men, saw the darkest side of everything, and at length even began to suspect his housekeeper, who had proven herself by many years of service. He suddenly decided to be quite independent, and this fantastic idea, like every other which took firm root in his mind, he at once proceeded to realize. He visited the market in person, chose, chaffered and bought, undoubtedly at anything but the most reasonable prices, and undertook to prepare his food with his own hands. This he continued to do for some little time, and when the few friends whom he still suffered about him made the most serious representations to him, he became quite angry and, as a valid proof of his own notable knowledge of the noble art of cooking, invited them to eat dinner with him the following day. There was nothing left for those invited but to appear punctually, full of expectation as to what would happen. They found their host in a short evening jacket, a stately nightcap on his bristly shock of hair, and his loins girded with a blue kitchen apron, very busily engaged at the hearth.

After waiting patiently for an hour and a half, while the turbulent demands of their stomachs were with increasing difficulty assuaged by cordial dialogue, the dinner was finally served. The soup recalled those charitable leavings distributed to beggars in the taverns; the beef was but half done and calculated to gratify only an ostrich; the vegetables floated in a mixture of water and grease; and the roast seemed to have been smoked in the chimney. Nevertheless the giver of the feast did full justice to every dish. And the applause which he anticipated put him in so rosy a humor that he called himself "Cook Mehlschoberl," after a character in the burlesque, "The Merry Nuptials," and tried by his own example and by extravagant praise of the dainties which still remained to animate his continent guests. They, however, found it barely possible to choke down a few morsels, and stuck to good bread, fresh fruit, sweet pastry and the unadulterated juice of the grape. Soon after this memorable banquet, fortunately, the master of tones grew weary of ruling the kitchen. Of his own free will he resigned the sceptre; his housekeeper once more entered upon her former honors and dignities, and her resigned Master returned to his writing-desk, which he was now not allowed to leave so frequently in order to procure himself an indigestion by means of his own culinary mixtures.

As a conductor our Master could in no wise be called a model, and the orchestra had to pay heed lest it be misled by its mentor, for he thought only of his tone-poems, and was ceaselessly engaged in calling attention to their authentic expression by means of the most manifold gesticulations. Thus he often struck *down* with his baton at a strong dynamic point, though it might occur on the weak beat of the measure. He was accustomed to indicate a *diminuendo* by trying to make himself smaller and smaller, and at the *pianissimo* slipped under the conductor's desk, so to say. As the tonal masses increased in volume, he too seemed to swell, as though out of a contraction, and with the entrance of the entire body of instrumental tone he rose on the tips of his toes, grew to well-nigh giant size, and swaying in the air with his arms, seemed to be trying to float up into the clouds. He was all active movement, no organic part of himself was idle, and the whole man might be compared to a *perpetuum mobile.* With increasing deafness, it is true, a rude disagreement often took place when the *maestro* was beating in arsis and the orchestra was accompanying him in thesis; then the conductor who had strayed from the path found his way back most easily in the soft movements, while the most powerful *forte* meant nothing to him. In these cases his eye also came to his assistance: he could observe the bow-stroke of the string instruments, guess from it the figure they were playing, and soon find his place again.

While Beethoven was not as yet burdened with his chronic infirmities he took pleasure in repeatedly attending opera performances, especially those given at the then splendidly flourishing *Theater an der Wien,* at times, no doubt, because he could do so in all comfort, since he practically had but to step out of his room to find himself in the parterre. There he was especially captivated by the creations of Cherubini and Méhul, which at that time had just begun to rouse the enthusiasm of all Vienna. There Beethoven would plant himself directly behind the orchestra-rail and remain, seemingly dumbfounded, to the very last bow-stroke. And this was the only visible sign he gave of being interested in the art-work. When, on the contrary, it did not appeal to him, he turned right about face at the end of the first act and made off. In general it was difficult and well-nigh impossible to read in his face any indication of approval or distaste; he remained ever the same, apparently unmoved, and was equally reticent in passing judgment on his artistic colleagues; his soul alone toiled unweariedly within him, its bodily covering seemed a soulless marble statue. Strangely enough, listening to wretched, execrable music appeared to cause him the utmost joy, which he at times proclaimed with roars of laughter. All who were better acquainted with him knew that in the art of laughter he also was a virtuoso of the first rank; it was a pity, however, that even those nearest him seldom learned the why and wherefore of an explosion of the kind, since as a rule he laughed at his own secret thoughts and imaginings without condescending to explain them.

Our Beethoven was by no means one of those pigheaded composers whom no orchestra in the world can satisfy; at times he was all too considerate, and did not even have passages which had gone amiss during first rehearsals repeated, saying: "The next time it will go as it should." He was very meticulous with regard to expression, the more delicate shadings, an equalized distribution of light and shade, and an effective *tempo rubato*, and without betraying the slightest impatience always took pleasure in discussing them individually with the various musicians. And then, when he saw that the musicians had grasped his ideas, and moved, carried away and filled with enthusiasm by the magic charm of his tonal creations, were playing together with increasing fervor, his face would be illumined with joy, all his features would radiate happiness and content, a satisfied smile would wreathe his lips, and a thundering *Bravi tutti!* would reward the successful artistic achievement. It was the first and most beautiful moment of triumph for this lofty genius, compared with which, as he himself admitted without reserve, even the stormy applause of a great receptive public was cast into the shade. When it was a matter of playing at first sight, the players often were obliged to stop to make corrections, and the thread of continuity was severed: even then, however, he was patient. But when, especially in the Scherzos of his symphonies, sudden, unexpected changes of tempo threw all into confusion, he would laugh tremendously, assure the men he had looked for nothing else, that he had been waiting for it to happen, and would take almost childish pleasure in the thought that he had been successful in unhorsing such routined orchestral knights.

Among his favorite dishes was a kind of bread-soup, cooked like mush, to which he looked forward with pleasure every Thursday. Together with it ten sizeable eggs had to be presented to him on a plate. Before they were stirred into the soup fluid he first separated and tested them by holding them against the light, then decapitated them with his own hand and anxiously sniffed them to see whether they were fresh. When fate decreed that some among them scented their straw, so to speak, the storm broke. In a voice of thunder the housekeeper was cited to court. She, however, well knowing what this meant, and between two fires, lent only half an ear to his raging and scolding, and held herself in readiness to beat a quick retreat before, as was customary, the cannonade was about to begin, and the decapitate batteries would begin to play upon her back and pour out their yellow-white, sticky intestines over her in veritable lava streams.

Beethoven never was seen in the street without a little note-book in which he jotted down his ideas of the moment. When by chance this was mentioned, he would parody the words of Joan of Arc: "I may not come unless I bear my flag!" With a steadiness without compare he stuck to this law he had laid down for himself, although in other respects a truly admirable confusion ruled in his household. Books and music were strewn about in every corner; here the fragments of a cold snack, there bottles, still sealed or half-emptied; on his standing desk was the hurried sketch of a new quartet; elsewhere were the débris of his breakfast; here on the piano, in the shape of scribbled-over pages, lay the material for a magnificent symphony, still slumbering as an embryo; there drooped a corrected proof waiting for release. The floor was covered with business and personal letters; between the windows stood a respectable loaf of *Strachino*, beside it the still notable ruins of a genuine Verona salami—and despite all this higgledy-piggledy our Master, quite contrary to the actual facts, had the habit of calling attention to his accuracy and love of order with Ciceronian eloquence on all occasions. Only when something he wanted had to be hunted for hours, days and even weeks, and all endeavors to find it remained fruitless, would he strike a new note as he looked about for a victim to blame: "Yes, yes," he would wail pitifully, "it is my misfortune! Nothing is left in the place where I put it; everything is moved about; everything is done to play me a trick. O these humans, these humans!" The servants, however, knew the good-natured growler; they let him grumble to his heart's content and—after a few minutes had passed— all was forgotten until a similar cause called forth a similar scene.

He himself often poked fun at his actually almost indecipherable handwriting and would add in extenuation: "Life is too short to paint letters or notes, and more beautiful notes would not help me out of my 'Nöten'" (troubles).

The whole forenoon, from the first ray of dawn up to dinner-time, was devoted to mechanical work, to actual note-writing; the remainder of the day was dedicated

to thought and to the arrangement of his ideas. No
sooner had Beethoven swallowed his last mouthful than,
unless he had some more extended excursion in mind, he
would set forth on his customary promenade, that is to
say, he would twice make the circuit of the city in double-
quick step, as though something had stung him. Did
it rain, snow or hail, did the thermometer stand at sixteen degrees below zero, did Boreas blow with icy breath
from puffed cheeks from across the Bohemian border,
did thunders roar, lightnings zigzag through the air,
winds howl or Phœbus' torrid rays fall vertically on
his head as in Lybia's seas of sand? How could any of
these things trouble this man filled with a sacred fire,
who bore his God in his heart, and in whose soul, perhaps, there blossomed forth a springtime of paradisiacal
mildness amid all this uproar of the elements.

Even in the presence of his intimate friends Beethoven
seldom permitted himself to judge any of his artistic
colleagues. What he thought of the following four
masters, however, his own words may testify:

"Among all living opera composers Cherubini is for
me the most deserving of respect. I am furthermore
entirely in accordance with his conception of the Requiem,
and, should I ever decide to write one myself, shall take
much from him as it stands.

"Karl Maria von Weber began to study too late; his art
could never develop in an altogether natural manner, and
it is evident he strove only to be recognized as a genius.

"Mozart's greatest work remains 'The Magic Flute';
for therein he for the first time reveals himself as a
German master. 'Don Juan' still is fashioned altogether in the Italian style and, besides, art, which is
sacred, should never be degraded to serve as a pretext
for so scandalous a subject.

"Handel is the unattained master of all masters. Go
to him and learn how to produce great effects with scant
deploy of means."

When he did not really feel in the mood, one had to ask him repeatedly in order to get him to sit down at the piano at all. Before he commenced to play he was in the habit of striking the keys with the palm of his hand, of running a finger along their length, in short, of indulging in all sorts of nonsense, laughing heartily at himself the while.

Once, while visiting at a patron's country estate in the summer, he was so importuned to play for the foreign visitors present, that he grew positively angry and firmly refused to perform what he scornfully termed a hireling's task. The threat to confine him to the house —it was, of course, not seriously meant—resulted in Beethoven running away in the dark and the dew to the nearest town, a distance of an hour, and thence hurrying to Vienna as though on the wings of the wind by extra post. His patron's bust supplied the expiatory victim for the insult offered him, and was cast from the closet on which it stood to smash on the floor.

One of Beethoven's curious manias was his passion for changing his lodgings, although moving with all his possessions always greatly discommoded him, and always was accompanied by a loss of belongings. No sooner had he taken possession of a new dwelling-place than he would find something objectionable about it, and then would run his feet sore trying to discover another. As a result it sometimes happened that he rented various lodgings at the same time and then, a second Hercules at the crossroads, found himself not a little embarrassed regarding their rights of priority in accordance with the claims of justice and cheapness.

Beethoven, in the truest sense of the word, was a real German, body and soul. Entirely at home in the Latin, French and Italian languages, he used by preference and whenever at all possible his native tongue. Had he been able to have his own way in the matter, all his works would have appeared in print with German title-pages. He even tried to delete the exotic word "piano-forte," and chose in its stead the expressive term *Hammerklavier* ("hammerpiano") as a suitable and appropriate substitute. As a relief from strenuous work, aside from poetry, for which he had a spiritual affinity, he turned to the study of universal history. Among German poets Goethe was and remained his favorite.

With regard to the other arts and sciences he also possessed, without making any show of it, a fund of more than surface knowledge; and took especial pleasure in discussing political matters with intimate friends. His summaries were so apt, his conceptions so correct, and his viewpoints so clear that none ever would have credited this diplomatic neophyte, who lived only in and for his art, with having formulated them.

Justice, personal decency, the moral code, a devout mind and religious purity meant more to him than all else; these virtues were enthroned in him and he demanded that others cultivate them. "A man is as good as his word" was his motto, and nothing angered him more than an unkept promise. He took pleasure in helping others out of pure love for his neighbor, only too often making considerable sacrifices, greatly to his own disadvantage. Anyone who turned to him in free and full confidence always could count upon certain, actual aid. He was neither avaricious nor yet extravagant; yet neither had he any idea of the real value of money, which he regarded merely as a means of procuring unavoidably required necessities. Only during his last years did he show signs of a worried thriftiness without, however, ever allowing it to interfere with his inborn propensity for doing good. While half the world reëchoed the illuminate singer's praises, only a few were capable of estimating his lofty human values to their full extent. Why was this? Because the majority were rebuffed by the rough outward shell and never even guessed at its noble inner kernel. Yet is not the most costly, well-nigh priceless diamond often concealed in a pallid, dull, colorless and unpolished wrapper?

FERDINAND RIES
(1801–1805)

The following impressions are quoted from the "Biographical Notices" of Wegeler and Ries (1838), to which reference has already been made. Ferdinand Ries (1784-1838), son of Franz Ries in Bonn, to whose family Beethoven owed a debt of gratitude, studied with Beethoven from 1801 to 1805. After very successful concert-tours as pianist through practically all of Europe, Ries in 1813 settled for several years in London. There he used all his influence to foster the art of his admired and beloved master, though his correspondence with Beethoven proves that it was not always easy to do so to Beethoven's satisfaction. As a composer Ferdinand Ries showed in his more than two hundred works skilful industry rather than originality and they are to-day practically forgotten.

My father gave me my first instruction in piano playing and in music in general, instruction which, fortunately for my future career, was thorough in the highest degree. When he decided, for Bonn had suffered deeply owing to the war, that it was time for me to continue my musical education elsewhere, I was sent at the age of fifteen, first to Munich and then to Vienna.

The friendly relations which my father had maintained uninterruptedly with Beethoven as a boy and as a youth, justified his expectation that the Master would receive me kindly. I carried a letter of recommendation with me. When I handed it over to Beethoven upon my arrival in Vienna, in 1800, he was extremely busy completing his oratorio "Christ on the Mount of Olives," since it was to be presented for his benefit under favorable auspices for the first time at a great *Academie* (concert) in the Vienna Theatre. He read the letter and said:

"I cannot answer your father now; but tell him that I have not forgotten how my mother died; that will content him." Later I discovered that when the Beethoven family had been in great want my father had helped them materially in every way.

In the course of the first few days Beethoven discovered that he could use me, and hence I often was sent for as early as five o'clock, something which also happened on the day the oratorio was to be given. I found him in bed, writing on single sheets of paper, and when I asked what they were, he answered: "Trombones." At the performance the trombones blew from these manuscript parts.

Among all composers Beethoven thought most of Mozart and Handel, and next came Bach. When I found him with music in his hand or saw some lying on his desk, it was sure to be a composition by one of these heroes. Haydn seldom escaped without a few digs in the ribs, for Beethoven cherished a grudge against him from earlier days. The following tale may account for one reason. Beethoven's three Trios, Op. 1, were to be introduced to the musical world at a *soirée* at Prince Lichnowsky's. Most of Vienna's artists and music lovers had been invited, in particular Haydn, whose verdict all were eager to hear. The trios were played and at once made an extraordinary impression. Haydn, too, said many fine things about them, but advised Beethoven not to publish the third one, in C minor. This surprised Beethoven greatly, for he thought it the best, and, in fact, to this day it is the one which always makes the greatest impression. Haydn's remark, therefore, made a bad impression on Beethoven, and left implanted in his mind the idea that Haydn was envious and jealous and wished him ill. I must admit that when Beethoven told me the story I did not put much faith in it. So I took occasion to ask Haydn himself about it. His answer, however, confirmed what

Beethoven had said, for he told me he had not imagined that the trio would be so rapidly and easily grasped, and so favorably taken up by the public.

It was Haydn's wish that Beethoven place on his earlier works: "Pupil of Haydn." This Beethoven refused to do because, as he said, though he had taken a few lessons from Haydn, he never had learned anything from him. (During his first stay in Vienna Beethoven took some lessons from Mozart, but complained that Mozart never played for him.) Beethoven also had studied counterpoint with Albrechtsberger and dramatic music with Salieri. I knew all of them well; but though all three had the highest esteem for Beethoven, they were agreed with regard to their opinion of him as a student. Each said that Beethoven was so obstinate and so bent on having his own way, that he had to learn much which he refused to accept as a matter for study through bitter personal experience. Albrechtsberger and Salieri, in particular, dwelt on this; the former's pedantic rules and the latter's unimportant ones with regard to dramatic composition (according to the older Italian school), did not appeal to Beethoven. Whether the studies issued by Ritter von Seyfried do "furnish the incontrovertible proof that Beethoven dedicated the two student years he spent under Albrechtsberger's eyes to following the study of theory with indefatigable endurance" is—in view of what has been said—open to question.

What follows may serve to corroborate the above: Once, while out walking with him, I mentioned two perfect fifths, which stand out by their beauty of sound in one of his earlier violin quartets, in C minor. Beethoven did not know of them and insisted it was wrong to call them fifths. Since he was in the habit of always carrying music-paper about him, I asked for some and set down the passage in all four parts. Then when he saw I was right he said: "Well, and who has forbidden them?" Since I did not know how I was to take his question, he repeated it several times until, much astonished, I replied: "It is one of the fundamental rules." Again he repeated his question, whereupon I said: "Marburg, Kirnberger, Fuchs, etc., etc., all the theoreticians!" "And *so I allow them!*" was his answer.

Beethoven had promised to give the three solo sonatas, Op. 31, to Nägeli in Zurich, while his brother Karl (Kaspar)[1] who—the more's the pity!—always meddled in Beethoven's affairs, wanted to sell them to a Leipzig publisher. The brothers often argued about the matter, since Beethoven wished to keep his promise, once he had made it. When the sonatas were about to be sent away Beethoven was living in Heiligenstadt. During a walk the brothers quarrelled again, and even passed from words to blows. The next day Beethoven gave me the sonatas, to send to Zurich at once, together with a letter to his brother, enclosed in another from Stephan von Bruening, for Kaspar to read. No one could have expounded a nobler moral in a more kind-hearted way than Beethoven in writing his brother anent the latter's behavior on the preceding day. First he showed its real contemptibility, then he forgave him completely; though he foretold a wretched future for him unless he completely mended his life and ways.

These same sonatas [Op. 31] were responsible for a curious occurrence. When proofs of them arrived I found Beethoven busy writing. "Run over the sonatas for me," he said, and remained sitting at his writing-desk. There were an uncommon number of mistakes in the proofs, which in itself made Beethoven very impatient. At the end of the first Allegro in the G major Sonata, moreover, Nägeli had even written in four measures of his own composition, that is to say, the four measures of the last hold:

---

[1] He died in Vienna in the winter of 1815. Beethoven became the guardian of his son Karl whom he later adopted as his foster-son, a relationship which was to cast dark shadows over the last years of Beethoven's life.

When I played them Beethoven leaped up in a rage, came running over to me and half-pushing me away from the piano, shouted: "Where the devil did you find that?" His astonishment and anger when he saw that the music was so printed were inconceivable. I was told to draw up a list of all the errors, and send back the sonatas to Simrock in Bonn at once. He was to have them reëngraved with the addition: *Edition très correcte.* And to this day the phrase is printed on the title-page. The four spurious measures, however, may still be found in some other reprint editions.

When Steibelt (1765-1823), the famous piano virtuoso, came from Paris to Vienna, in all the glory of his fame, several of Beethoven's friends were afraid the latter's reputation would be injured by the newcomer.

Steibelt did not visit Beethoven; they met for the first time in the home of Count Fries, where Beethoven gave his new Trio in B-flat major, Op. 11, for piano, clarinet and violoncello, its initial performance. It does not give the pianist much of an opportunity. Steibelt listened to it with a certain condescension, paid Beethoven a few compliments, and felt assured of his own victory. He played a quintet he had composed, and improvised; and his *tremulandos*, at that time an absolute novelty, made a great impression. Beethoven could not be induced to play again. Eight days later there was another concert at Count Fries' home. Steibelt again played a quintet with much success and besides (as was quite evident), had practiced a brilliant fantasy for which he had chosen the identical theme developed in the variations of Beethoven's trio. This roused the indignation of Beethoven and his admirers; he had to seat himself at the piano to improvise, which he did in his usual, I might say unmannerly fashion, flinging himself down at the instrument as though half-pushed. As he moved toward it he took up the violoncello part of Steibelt's quintet, purposely put it on the piano-rack upside-down, and drummed out a theme from its first measures with his fingers. Then, now that he had been definitely insulted and enraged, Beethoven improvised in such a way that Steibelt left the room before he had concluded, refused ever to meet him again, and even made it a condition that Beethoven was not to be invited where his own company was desired.

When Beethoven gave me a lesson he was, I might almost say, unnaturally patient. This, as well as his friendly treatment of me, which very seldom varied, I must ascribe principally to his attachment and love for my father. Thus he often would have me repeat a single number ten or more times. In the Variations in F major, Op. 34, dedicated to Princess Oldescalchi, I was obliged to repeat almost the entire final Adagio variation seventeen times; and even then he was not satisfied with the expression in the small cadenza, though I thought I played it as well as he did. That day I had well-nigh a two hour lesson. When I left out something in a passage, a note or a skip, which in many cases he wished to have specially emphasized, or struck a wrong key, he seldom said anything; yet when I was at fault with regard to the expression, the *crescendi* or matters of that kind, or in the character of the piece, he would grow angry. Mistakes of the other kind, he said, were due to chance; but these last resulted from want of knowledge, feeling or attention. He himself often made mistakes of the first kind, even when playing in public.

Once we were taking a walk and lost our way so completely that we did not get back to Döblingen, where

Beethoven lived, until eight o'clock. Throughout our walk he had hummed and, in part, howled, up and down the scale as we went along, without singing any individual notes. When I asked him what it was he replied: "The theme for the final Allegro of the Sonata (in F major, Op. 57) has occurred to me." When we entered the room he ran to the piano without taking off his hat. I sat down in a corner and soon he had forgotten me. Then he raged on the keys for at least an hour, developing the new Finale of this Sonata (which appeared in 1807) in the beautiful form we know. At last he rose, was surprised to see me still there and said: "I cannot give you a lesson to-day; I still have work to do."

In the year 1802 Beethoven composed his Third Symphony (now known under the title of *Sinfonia eroica*) in Heiligenstadt, a village an hour and a half distant from Vienna. In writing his compositions Beethoven often had some special object in mind, though he often laughed and scolded about musical tone-paintings, especially those of a more trifling nature. In this connection Haydn's "Creation" and his "Seasons" sometimes served him as a text, for all he did not contest the composer's great merits, and gave the most deserved praise to many of his choruses and other compositions. In his Symphony Beethoven had thought of Bonaparte, but Bonaparte when he still was First Consul. At that time Beethoven held him in the highest esteem and compared him to the great consuls of ancient Rome. I myself, as well as other intimate friends of his have seen this Symphony, already scored, lying on his table, with the name "Bonaparte" at the very top of the title-page, and at the very bottom "Luigi van Beethoven," without another word. How and wherewith the gap was to be filled in I do not know. I was the first to announce to him the news that Napoleon had declared himself emperor, whereupon he flew into a rage and cried:

"Then he, too, is nothing but an ordinary mortal! Now he also will tread all human rights underfoot, will gratify only his own ambition, will raise himself up above all others and become a tyrant!" Beethoven went to the table, took hold of the top of the title-page, tore it off and flung it on the ground. This first page was rewritten, and not until then was the Symphony entitled *Sinfonia eroica.* Later Prince Lobkowitz bought the right to use this composition for a few years from Beethoven and it was several times performed in his palace. It was there it chanced that Beethoven, who was himself conducting it, in the second section of the first Allegro where such a long series of half-notes moves against the beat, so completely put out the orchestra that it had to begin again from the beginning.

In the same Allegro Beethoven plays the horn a shabby trick. A few measures before the theme again appears in its complete form in the second section, Beethoven has the horn announce it, while the two violins are still holding a chord on the second. One who does not know the score inevitably feels that the horn-player has miscounted and come in at the wrong time. At the first rehearsal of the Symphony, which was horrible, but in which the horn-player entered at the right time, I was standing beside Beethoven; and thinking he had made a mistake, said: "That damned horn-player! Can't he count! This sounds atrociously false!" I think I came very near getting a box on the ear, and Beethoven did not forgive me for a long time.

Beethoven liked to see women, especially lovely, youthful faces and usually, when he passed some girl who could boast of her share of charm, he would turn around, gaze keenly at her through his glasses, and then laugh or grin when he saw I had noticed him. He was very often in love, but as a rule only for a short time. When I once teased him about his conquest of a certain beautiful lady he admitted that she had captivated him more potently and for a longer period of time—seven whole months—than any other.

One evening I went to him in Baden to continue my lessons. There I found a beautiful young lady sitting on the sofa beside him. Feeling that I had come at an inopportune time, I was about to retire when Beethoven held me back and said:

"First play me something!"

He remained seated behind me with the lady. I already had been playing a long time when Beethoven suddenly cried: "Now play something sentimental," then, not long after, "Something melancholy," then, "Something passionate"; and so on. From what came to my ears I could take for granted that he had in some way offended the lady, and was trying to smooth it over with these whimseys. At last he jumped up and cried: "Why, those are all things I have written!" I had, in fact, played nothing but movements from his own works, connecting one with the other by short modulations, and this seemed to have pleased him. The lady now left, and, to my great surprise, Beethoven did not know who she was. I only heard that she had entered shortly before I came, in order to make Beethoven's acquaintance. We soon followed her to find out where she lived and, later, what her social position might be. We could see her in the distance—it was a clear, moonlit night— but suddenly she disappeared. Talking of one thing and another we walked about for an hour and a half in the adjacent beautiful valley. When I left Beethoven, however, he said: "I must find out who she is and you must help me." A long time afterwards I met her in Vienna and discovered that she was the mistress of a foreign prince. I informed Beethoven of what I had learned; but neither from him nor from any other person did I ever hear anything more about her.

Beethoven never visited me more frequently than when I was lodging in the house of a tailor who had three very beautiful but absolutely reputable daughters. To them he refers in the conclusion of his letter of June 24, 1804, in which he says: "Do not do too much tailoring, remember me to the fairest of the fair, and send me half a dozen needles."

Beethoven suffered repeatedly, and as early as 1802, [indeed, even earlier than 1800, as appears from his first letters to Dr. Wegeler] from defective hearing, but the trouble soon disappeared again. He was so sensitive about his incipient deafness, that one had to be very careful about calling his attention to his deficiency by talking loudly. When he did not understand something he usually blamed the absent-mindedness to which he really was subject in the highest degree. He lived much of the time in the country, where I often went to take a lesson. Sometimes, in the morning, around eight o'clock, after breakfast, he would say to me: "First let us take a little walk." We would start out, but several times we did not return until three or four o'clock, after we had eaten something in a village. On one of these excursions Beethoven gave me the first startling proof of his increasing deafness, which Stephan von Breuning already had mentioned to me. I had called his attention to a shepherd who was blowing his syringa-wood flute very passably in the forest. For a whole half-hour Beethoven heard absolutely nothing at all, and though I repeatedly assured him (which was not the case), that I myself heard nothing either he grew extremely quiet and glum. . . . When, on occasion, he did seem in good spirits, though this was not often the case, he usually went to extremes.

Beethoven was extremely good-natured, but just as easily inclined to anger or suspicion, motived by his deafness, but even more by the conduct of his brothers. Any unknown could easily defame his most proven friends; for he was all too quick and unquestioning in crediting their lies. He would then neither reproach the person suspected nor yet ask him for an explanation, but his manner toward him would immediately show the greatest haughtiness and the most supreme contempt. Since he was extraordinarily violent in all he did, he would also try to find his supposed enemy's most vulnerable spot, in order to indulge his rage. Hence it often was impossible to tell how one stood with him until the matter was cleared up, in most cases by merest chance. Then, however, he would try to atone for the wrong he had done as quickly and effectually as possible.

Etiquette and all that etiquette implies was something Beethoven never knew and never wanted to know. As a result, his behavior when he first began to frequent the palace of the Archduke Rudolph often caused the greatest embarrassment to the latter's entourage. An attempt was made to coerce Beethoven into the deference he was supposed to observe. This, however, Beethoven found unendurable. He promised betterment, it is true, but—that was the end of it. One day, finally, when he was again, as he termed it, being "sermonized on court manners," he very angrily pushed his way up to the Archduke, and said quite frankly that though he had the greatest possible reverence for his person, a strict observance of all the regulations to which his attention was called every day was beyond him. The Archduke laughed good-humoredly over the occurrence, and commanded that in the future Beethoven be allowed to go his way unhindered; he must be taken as he was.

Beethoven attached no importance to his autograph compositions. In most cases, once they had been engraved, they lay about in an adjoining room or in the middle of his work-room scattered over the floor among other music. I often have put his music in order, yet when Beethoven was looking for something, everything was turned upside down again. I could at that time have carried off all those original autograph compositions of his which already had been engraved, and had I asked him for them, I am sure he would have given them to me without a moment's hesitation.

In Vienna Beethoven already had taken violin lessons from Krumpholz and at first, when I was there, we occasionally played his sonatas for violin together. But it really was awful music, for in his enthusiastic zeal his ear did not tell him when he had attacked a passage with the wrong fingering (even then Beethoven did not hear well).

In his manner Beethoven was very awkward and helpless; and his clumsy movements lacked all grace. He seldom picked up anything with his hand without dropping or breaking it. Thus, on several occasions, he upset his ink-well into the piano which stood beside his writing-desk. No furniture was safe from him; least of all a valuable piece; all was over-turned, dirtied and destroyed. How he ever managed to shave himself is hard to understand, even making all allowance for the many cuts on his cheeks. And he never learned to dance in time to the music.

At times Beethoven was extremely violent. One day, at noon, we were eating dinner in the "Swan" tavern when the waiter brought him the wrong dish. No sooner had Beethoven remarked about it and received a somewhat uncivil reply, than he took up the platter——it was calf's lights with an abundance of gravy—and flung it at the waiter's head. The poor fellow was carrying a whole slew of other portions, intended for other guests, on his arm—an art in which Viennese waiters are very adept—and was quite helpless. The gravy ran down his face, and he and Beethoven shouted and abused each other, while all the other guests burst into laughter. Finally Beethoven, looking at the waiter—who, licking up the gravy trickling down his face with his tongue, would attempt to curse, then have to return to his licking while he cut a most comical phiz, worthy of Hogarth—burst out laughing himself.

Beethoven hardly knew what money was, which frequently gave rise to disagreeable incidents; for suspicious by nature, he often thought he was being cheated when this was not the case. Easily excited, he would call people cheats to their faces and, where waiters were concerned, often had to make up for it with a tip. Finally, in the taverns which he was most accustomed to frequent, all came to know his oddities and his absent-mindedness, and let him say and do what he wished, even permitting him to leave without paying his bill.

In many matters Beethoven was very forgetful. Once he had received from Count Browne a handsome saddlehorse, in return for the dedication of the Variations in A major, No. 5, on a Russian song. He rode it a few times, but soon forgot it, and, what was worse, forgot about its feed. His servant, who quickly noticed this, began to hire out the horse for money which he slipped into his own pocket, and, in order not to arouse Beethoven's suspicions, put off handing in the feed bill for a long time. Finally, to Beethoven's great surprise, a very large feed bill was presented to him which suddenly recalled to him his horse, as well as his negligence with regard to it.

Beethoven took great pleasure in recalling his early youth and his Bonn friends, although in reality those had been hard times for him. He frequently spoke of his mother, in particular, with love and emotion, and often called her a fine, kind-hearted woman. Of his father, who was chiefly to blame for their domestic difficulties, he spoke seldom and with reluctance; but any harsh word let fall by a third person made him angry. All in all, he was a dear, good fellow; only his variable humor and his violence where others were concerned, often did him disservice. And no matter what insult or injustice had been done him by any one, Beethoven would have forgiven him on the spot, had he met him when crushed by misfortune.

JOSEF AUGUST RÖCKEL
(1806)

The tenor Josef August Röckel (1783-1870) was entrusted with the *Florestan* rôle in the second version of Beethoven's opera "Fidelio," performed on April 10, 1806. After the *première* of the opera on November 20, 1805, followed by two repetitions, Beethoven's friends saw clearly the necessity for changes and cuts, if "Leonore," as the original version was called, was not to remain a failure. Röckel's vivid narrative of the memorable meeting in December, 1805, at the palace of Prince Lichnowsky, when Beethoven finally agreed to changes in his opera, follows.

It was not until we were on our way to the Prince's palace that Mayer [bass-singer; brother-in-law of Mozart] informed me that we would find Beethoven there among his most intimate friends, and that together with the other opera artists who had taken part in the fiasco of his opera "Leonore," we would once more give a critical performance of the work, in order to convince the Master himself of the necessity of a revision. Since Beethoven held the former tenor uniquely responsible for the failure of the opera, I myself, in whose voice he placed more confidence, was to sing the rôle of Florestan at sight, in this solo performance. At the same time, together with Mayer and the other artists, I was continually to present to the Master, using the most urgent pleas, the need of cuts and changes and, finally, the fusion of the first two acts.

I shuddered at the thought of having to sing the difficult part of Florestan at first sight, for the composer, a composer as hard to satisfy as he was given to outbursts of passion; though I frequently had heard it sung by my former teacher and present rival, and, in part, had studied it with him. I dreaded quite as much the stage intrigues of the offended tenor, whose successor the present step would make me. I should have liked best of all to turn back again, and would have done so had not Mayer clung to my arm and literally dragged

Mähler's First Portrait of Beethoven, 1804

(Courtesy Beethovenhaus, Bonn)

Portrait of Beethoven by Neugass, 1806
(Courtesy Beethovenhaus, Bonn)

me along with him. Thus we entered the Prince's
hôtel and ascended the brilliantly lighted stairs down
which several lackeys in livery, carrying empty tea-
trays, came to meet us. My companion, familiar with
the customs of the house, looked much annoyed and
murmured: "Tea is over. I am afraid your hesitation
has created a very delicate situation for our stomachs."
   We were led into a music-room with silken draperies,
fitted out with chandeliers lavishly supplied with candles.
On its walls rich, splendidly colorful oil paintings by
the greatest masters, in broad, glittering golden frames
bespoke the lofty artistic instincts as well as the wealth
of the princely family owning them. We seemed to
have been expected; for Mayer had told the truth: tea
was over, and all was in readiness for the musical performance to begin. The Princess, an elderly lady of
winning amiability and indescribable gentleness, yet as
a result of great physical suffering (both her breasts had
been removed in former years) pale and fragile, already
was sitting at the piano. Opposite her, carelessly reclining in an arm-chair, the fat Pandora-score of his
unfortunate opera across his knees, sat Beethoven. At
his right we recognized the author of the tragedy "Cori-
olan," Court Secretary Heinrich von Collin, who was
chatting with Court Counsellor Breuning of Bonn, the
most intimate friend of the composer's youth. My
colleagues from the opera, men and women, their parts
in hand, had gathered in a half-circle not far from the
piano. As before, Milder was Fidelio; Mlle. Müller
sang Marzelline; Weinmüller, Rocco; Caché the door-
keeper Jaquino; and Steinkopf the Minister of State.
After I had been presented to the Prince and Princess,
and Beethoven had acknowledged our respectful greetings, he placed his score on the music-desk for the
Princess and—the performance began.
   The two initial acts, in which I played no part, were
sung from the first to the last note. Eyes sought the

clock, and Beethoven was importuned to drop some of the long-drawn sections of secondary importance. Yet he defended every measure, and did so with such nobility and artistic dignity that I was ready to kneel at his feet. But when he came to the chief point at issue itself, the notable cuts in the exposition which would make it possible to fuse the two acts into one, he was beside himself, shouted uninterruptedly "Not a note!" and tried to run off with his score. But the Princess laid her hands, folded as though in prayer, on the sacred score entrusted to her, looked up with indescribable mildness at the angry genius and behold—his rage melted at her glance, and he once more resignedly resumed his place. The noble lady gave the order to continue, and played the prelude to the great aria: *In des Lebens Frühlingstagen.* So I asked Beethoven to hand me the part of Florestan. My unfortunate predecessor, however, in spite of repeated requests had not been induced to yield it up, and hence I was told to sing from the score, from which the Princess was accompanying at the piano. I knew that this great aria meant as much to Beethoven as the entire opera, and handled it from that point of view. Again and again he insisted on hearing it—the exertion well-nigh overtaxed my powers—but I sang it, for I was overjoyed to see that my presentation made it possible for the great Master to reconcile himself to his misunderstood work.

Midnight had passed before the performance—drawn out by reason of many repetitions—at last came to an end. "And the revision, the curtailments?" the Princess asked the Master with a pleading look.

"Do not insist on them," Beethoven answered sombrely, "not a single note must be missing."

"Beethoven," she cried with a deep sigh, "must your great work then continue to be misunderstood and condemned?"

"It is sufficiently rewarded with your approval, your Ladyship," said the Master and his hand trembled slightly as it glided over her own.

Then suddenly it seemed as though a stronger, more potent spirit entered into this delicate woman. Half-kneeling and seizing his knees she cried to him as though inspired: "Beethoven! No—your greatest work, you yourself shall not cease to exist in this way! God who has implanted those tones of purest beauty in your soul forbids it, your mother's spirit, which at this moment pleads and warns you with my voice, forbids it! Beethoven, it must be! Give in! Do so in memory of your mother! Do so for me, who am only your best friend!"

The great man, with his head suggestive of Olympian sublimity, stood for many moments before the worshipper of his Muse, then brushed his long, falling curls from his face, as though an enchanting dream were passing through his soul, and, his glance turned heavenward full of emotion, cried amid sobs: "I will—yes, all— I will do all, for you—for my your—for my mother's sake!" And so saying he reverently raised the Princess and offered the Prince his hand as though to confirm a vow. Deeply moved we surrounded the little group, for even then we all felt the importance of this supreme moment.

From that time onward not another word was said regarding the opera. All were exhausted, and I am free to confess that I exchanged a look of relief not hard to interpret with Mayer when servants flung open the folding-doors of the dining-room, and the company at last sat down to supper at plentiously covered tables. It was probably not altogether due to chance that I was placed opposite Beethoven who, in spirit no doubt still with his opera, ate noticeably little; while I, tormented by the most ravenous hunger, devoured the first course with a speed bordering on the ludicrous. He smiled as he pointed to my empty plate: "You have swallowed your food like a wolf—what have you eaten?" "I was so famished," I replied, "that to tell the truth, I never noticed what it was I ate."

"That is why, before we sat down, you sang the part of Florestan, the man starving in the dungeon, in so masterly and so natural a manner. Neither your voice nor your head deserves credit, but your stomach alone. Well, always see to it that you starve bravely before the performance and then we will be sure of success."

All those at the table laughed, and probably took more pleasure in the thought that Beethoven had at last plucked up heart to joke at all, rather than at his joke itself.

When we left the Prince's palace Beethoven spoke to me again: "I have the fewest changes to make in your part; so come to my house in the course of the next few days to get it; I will write it out for you myself."

A few days later I presented myself in the anteroom, where an elderly servant did not know what to do with me, since his master was bathing at the moment. This I knew because I heard the splashing of the water which the noble eccentric poured out over himself in veritable cascades while giving vent to bellowing groans, which in his case, it seemed, were outbursts of content. On the old servant's unfriendly countenance I read the words: "Announce or dismiss?" in grumpy, wrinkled letters, but suddenly he asked: "Whom have I the honor——?"

I gave my name: "Joseph Röckel."

"Well, that's all right," said the old Viennese, "I was told to let you in."

He went and immediately afterward opened the door. I entered the place consecrate to supreme genius. It was almost frugally simple and a sense of order appeared never to have visited it. In one corner was an open piano, loaded with music in the wildest confusion. Here, on a chair, reposed a fragment of the *Eroica*. The individual parts of the opera with which he was busy lay, some on other chairs, others on and under the table which stood in the middle of the room. And, amid chamber music compositions, piano trios and symphonic sketches, was placed the mighty bathing apparatus in which the Master was laving his powerful chest with the cold flood. He received me without any fuss, and I had an opportunity of admiring his muscular system and his sturdy bodily construction. To judge by the latter the composer might look forward to growing as old as Methusaleh, and it must have taken a most powerful inimical influence to bring this strong column to so untimely a fall.

Beethoven greeted me affably, gave me a contented smile, and while he was dressing told me what pains he had taken to write out my voice part from the illegible score with his own hand, so that I might receive it as soon as possible and in an absolutely correct form.

A few weeks later the other members of the opera cast also had their parts in the new version. We were all astonished at Beethoven's capacity for hard work, and that in so short a time he had completed the reshaping of his genial score, which we once more performed in the *Theater an der Wien,* no later than March 29, 1806, that is to say, hardly more than four months after its first short stage appearance; but this time we had a comfortable "Viennese" audience.

The management had guaranteed the composer a percentage and I, since I had so willingly taken over the great rôle which really lay outside the range of those I habitually sang, had been promised an additional honorarium. Beethoven quarrelled violently with the director before the beginning of the opera because his work, which he had expressly named "Fidelio," was once more, for commercial reasons, presented on the play-bills under its old title of "Leonore," familiar owing to Paër's opera. We spared no possible effort to make the opera triumph, and though we were not completely successful the first time, the theatre was much better filled for the second and third performances, and even the critics did some, if not all justice to the work.

Yes, it pleased more, yet did not please as much as an art-work rising so high above the level of anything before heard should please. This was evident to us when we glanced at the house, still not quite full; and to Beethoven when he got his percentage, regarding the small amount of which he was complaining to Court Banker Braun, when I sought out the latter the day after the third performance (of the new version), to receive my stipend from him. While I accidentally chanced to be waiting in the anteroom to the Baron's business office, I heard a violent altercation which the financier was carrying on with the enraged composer in the adjoining room. Beethoven was suspicious, and thought that his percentage of the net proceeds was greater than the amount which the Court Banker, who was at the same time director of the *Theater an der Wien*, had paid him. The latter remarked that Beethoven was the first composer with whom the management, in view of his extraordinary merits, had been willing to share profits, and explained the paucity of the box-office returns by the fact that the boxes and front row seats all had been taken, but that the seats in which the thickly crowded mass of the people would have yielded a return as when Mozart's operas were given, were empty. And he emphasized that hitherto Beethoven's music had been accepted only by the more cultured classes, while Mozart with his operas invariably had roused enthusiasm in the multitude, the people as a whole. Beethoven hurried up and down the room in agitation, shouting loudly: "I do not write for the multitude—I write for the cultured!"

"But the cultured alone do not fill our theatre," replied the Baron with the greatest calmness, "we need the multitude to bring in money, and since in your music you have refused to make any concessions to it, you yourself are to blame for your diminished percentage of return. If we had given Mozart the same interest in the receipts of his operas he would have grown rich."

This disadvantageous comparison with his famous predecessor seemed to wound Beethoven's tenderest susceptibilities. Without replying to it with a single word, he leaped up and shouted in the greatest rage: "Give me back my score!"

The Baron hesitated and stared as though struck by lightning at the enraged composer's glowing face, while the latter, in an accent of the most strenuous passion repeated: "I want my score—my score, at once!"

The Baron pulled the bell-rope; a servant entered.

"Bring the score of yesterday's opera for this gentleman," said the Baron with an air; and the servant hastened to return with it. "I am sorry," the aristocrat continued, "But I believe that on calmer reflection—." Yet Beethoven no longer heard what he was saying. He had torn the gigantic volume of the score from the servant's hand and, without even seeing me in his eagerness, ran through the anteroom and down the stairs.

When the Baron received me a few minutes later this composed gentleman was unable to conceal a slight apprehension; he appeared to realize the value of the treasure with which he had parted. Out of sorts, he remarked to me: "Beethoven was excited and over-hasty; you have some influence with him; try everything —promise him anything in my name, so that we can save his work for our stage."

I excused myself and hastened to follow the angry Master to his Tusculum. All was in vain, however, he would not allow himself to be soothed. The revision of "Fidelio" already had been put away in the manuscript closet, whence not until seventeen years later did the Sleeping Beauty of the new world of opera, the youthful Schröder-Devrient, conjure it forth from oblivion's spider-webs like a Phœnix newly risen.

The Baron de Trémont
(1809)

Under the title of "The Baron de Trémont. Souvenirs of Beethoven and Other Contemporaries," J. G. Prod'homme contributed a number of the latter to "The Musical Quarterly," July, 1920. They are preserved at the National Library in Paris in six bulky manuscript volumes, apparently compiled by the Baron de Trémont from 1840 to 1850, and containing in a more or less reminiscent form the biographies of 257 of his contemporaries. Louis-Philippe-Joseph-Girod de Vienney (1799-1852) was created a Baron of the Empire in 1810 in recognition of his services as Auditor of the Council of State. He met Beethoven in the previous year, while on a diplomatic mission to Vienna. The Baron de Trémont continued to be a musical enthusiast and *mæcenas* for the remainder of his life. He prided himself on having had for fifty years (1798-1849), except during forced absences from Paris, musical *réunions* at his home "at which all the celebrated musicians, either French or foreign, were pleased to display their talents."

Does not our vanity count for something in all that makes us feel flattered by being well received and giving pleasure to some person of bad character, churlish and eccentric, rather than by one possessing all the qualities that amiability and amenity of manner are capable of suggesting? To carry out the comparison still further, if a dog belonging to some one else is vicious and prone to bite, and yet fawns on us, we think more of him for this than we do of a good beast that rushes eagerly to crouch at our feet.

Such was the impression produced on me by Beethoven. I admired his genius and knew his works by heart when, in 1809, as Auditor to the Council of State while Napoleon was making war on Austria, I was made the bearer of the Council's despatches to him. Although my departure was hurried, I made up my mind that in case the army should take Vienna I must not neglect the opportunity to see Beethoven. I asked Cherubini to give me a letter to him. "I will give you one to Haydn," he replied, "and that excellent man will make you welcome; but I will not write to Beethoven; I should have to reproach myself that he refused to receive some one recommended by me; he is an unlicked bear!"

Thereupon I addressed myself to Reicha. "I imagine," said he, "that my letter will be of no use to you. Since the establishment of the Empire in France, Beethoven has detested the Emperor and the French to such a degree that Rode, the finest violinist in Europe, while passing through Vienna on his way to Russia, remained a week in that city without succeeding in obtaining admission to him. He is morose, ironical, misanthropic; to give you an idea of how careless he is of convention it will suffice to tell you that the Empress [princess of Bavaria, the second wife of Francis II] sent him a request to visit her one morning; he responded that he would be occupied all that day, but would try to come the day after."

This information convinced me that any efforts to approach Beethoven would be vain. I had no reputation, nor any qualification which might impress him; a repulse seemed all the more certain because I entered Vienna after its second bombardment by the French army, and besides, was a member of Napoleon's Council. However, I intended to try.

I wended my way to the inapproachable composer's home, and at the door it struck me that I had chosen the day ill, for, having to make an official visit thereafter, I was wearing the every-day habiliments of the Council of State. To make matters worse, his lodging was next the city wall, and as Napoleon had ordered its destruction, blasts had just been set off under his windows.

The neighbors showed me where he lived: "He is at home (they said), but he has no servant at present, for he is always getting a new one, and it is doubtful whether he will open."

I rang three times, and was about to go away, when a very ugly man of ill-humored mien opened the door and asked what I wanted.

"Have I the honor of addressing M. de Beethoven?" —"Yes, Sir! But I must tell you," he said to me in German, "that I am on very bad terms with French!"— "My acquaintance with German is no better, Sir, but my message is limited to bringing you a letter from M. Reicha in Paris."—He looked me over, took the letter, and let me in. His lodging, I believe, consisted of only two rooms, the first one having an alcove containing the bed, but small and dark, for which reason he made his toilet in the second room, or salon. Picture to yourself the dirtiest, most disorderly place imaginable—blotches of moisture covered the ceiling; an oldish grand piano, on which the dust disputed the place with various pieces of engraved and manuscript music; under the piano (I do not exaggerate) an unemptied *pot de nuit;* beside it, a small walnut table accustomed to the frequent over-turning of the secretary placed upon it; a quantity of pens encrusted with ink, compared wherewith the pro-verbial tavern-pens would shine; then more music. The chairs, mostly cane-seated, were covered with plates bearing the remains of last night's supper, and with wearing apparel, etc. Balzac or Dickens would con-tinue this description for two pages, and then would they as many more with a description of the dress of fill illustrious composer; but, being neither Balzac nor Dickens, I shall merely say, I was in Beethoven's abode.

I spoke German only as a traveller on the highways, but understood it somewhat better. His skill in French was no greater. I expected that, after reading my letter, he would dismiss me, and that our acquaintance would end then and there. I had seen the bear in his cage; that was more than I had dared hope for. So I was greatly surprised when he again inspected me, laid the letter unopened on the table, and offered me a chair; still more surprised, when he started a conversation. He wanted to know what uniform I wore, my age, my office, the aim of my journey; if I were a musician, if I intended to stay in Vienna. I answered, that Reicha's letter would explain all that much better than I could.

"No, no, tell me," he insisted, "only speak slowly, because I am very hard of hearing, and I shall understand you."

I made incredible conversational efforts, which he seconded with good will; it was a most singular medley of bad German on my part and bad French on his. But we managed to understand each other; the visit lasted nearly three-quarters of an hour, and he made me promise to come again. I took my leave, feeling prouder than Napoleon when he entered Vienna. I had made the conquest of Beethoven!

Do not ask how I did it. What could I answer? The reason can be sought only in the *bizarrerie* of his character. I was young, conciliatory and polite, and a stranger to him; I contrasted with him; for some unaccountable reason he took a fancy to me, and, as these sudden likings are seldom passive, he arranged several meetings with me during my stay in Vienna, and would improvise an hour or two for me alone. When he happened to have a servant he told her not to open when the bell rang, or (if the would-be visitor heard the piano) to say that he was composing and could not receive company.

Some musicians with whom I became acquainted were slow to believe it. "Will you believe me," I told them, "if I show you a letter he has written me in French?"— "In French? that's impossible! he hardly knows any, and he doesn't even write German legibly. He is

incapable of such an effort!"—I showed them my proof.
"Well, he must be madly in love with you," they said;
"what an inexplicable man!"

This letter—so precious an object to me—I have had
framed. Call to mind the reflection which heads this
article; my vanity would scarcely have moved me to do
as much for Papa Haydn.

I fancy that to these improvisations of Beethoven's
I owe my most vivid musical impressions. I maintain
that unless one has heard him improvise well and quite
at ease, one can but imperfectly appreciate the vast
scope of his genius. Swayed wholly by the impulse of
the moment, he sometimes said to me, after striking a
few chords: "Nothing comes into my head; let's put it
off till———." Then we would talk philosophy, religion,
politics, and especially of Shakespeare, his idol, and always in a language that would have provoked the
laughter of any hearers.

Beethoven was not a man of *esprit*, if we mean by
that term one who makes keen and witty remarks. He
was by nature too taciturn to be an animated conver-
sationalist. His thoughts were thrown out by fits and
starts, but they were lofty and generous, though often
rather illogical. Between him and Jean-Jacques Rousseau there was a bond of erroneous opinion springing from
the creation, by their common misanthropic disposition,
of a fanciful world bearing no positive relation to human
nature and social conditions. But Beethoven was well-
read. The isolation of celibacy, his deafness, and his
sojournings in the country, had led him to make a study
of the Greek and Latin authors and, enthusiastically, of
Shakespeare. Taking this in conjunction with the kind
of singular, though genuine, interest which results from
wrong notions set forth and maintained in all good faith,
his conversation was, if not specially magnetic, at least
original and curious. And, as he was well affected towards me, by a whimsey of his atrabilious character he

preferred that I should sometimes contradict him rather than agree with him on every point.

When he felt inclined to improvisation on the day appointed, he was sublime. His tempestuous inspiration poured forth lovely melodies, and harmonies unsought because, mastered by musical emotion, he gave no thought to the search after effects that might have occurred to him with pen in hand; they were produced spontaneously without divagation.

As a pianist, his playing was incorrect and his mode of fingering often faulty, whence it came that the quality of tone was neglected. But who could think of the pianist? He was absorbed in his thoughts, and his hands had to express them as best they might.

I asked him if he would not like to become acquainted with France. "I greatly desired to do so," he replied, "before she gave herself a master. Now, my desire has passed. For all that, I should like to hear Mozart's symphonies—(he mentioned neither his own nor those of Haydn)—in Paris; I am told that they are played better at the Conservatoire than anywhere else. Besides, I am too poor to take a journey out of pure curiosity and probably requiring great speed."—"Come with me, I will take you along."—"What an idea! I could not think of allowing you to go to such expense on my account."—"Don't worry about that, there's no expense; all my charges for the post are defrayed, and I am alone in my carriage. If you would be satisfied with a single small room, I have one at your disposal. Only say yes. It's well worth your while to spend a fortnight in Paris; your sole expense will be for the return journey, and less than fifty florins will bring you home again."—"You tempt me; I shall think it over."

Several times I pressed him to make a decision. His hesitation was always a result of his morose humor. "I shall be overrun by visitors!"—"You will not receive them."—"Overwhelmed by invitations!"—"Which you will not accept."—"They will insist that I play, that I compose!"—"You will answer that you have no time." —"Your Parisians will say that I am a bear."—"What does that matter to you? It is evident that you do not know them. Paris is the home of liberty, of freedom from social conventions. Distinguished men are accepted there exactly as they please to show themselves, and should one such, especially a stranger, be a trifle eccentric, that contributes to his success."

Finally, he gave me his hand one day and said that he would come with me. I was delighted—again from vanity, no doubt. To take Beethoven to Paris, to have him in my own lodgings, to introduce him to the musical world, what a triumph was there!—but, to punish me for my pleasurable anticipations, the realization was not to follow them.

The armistice of Znaim caused us to occupy Moravia, whither I was sent as intendant. I remained there four months; the Treaty of Vienna having given this province to Austria, I returned to Vienna, where I found Beethoven still of the same mind; I was expecting to receive the order for my return to Paris, when I received one to betake myself immediately to Croatia as intendant. After spending a year there, I received my appointment to the prefecture of l'Aveyron, together with an order to wind up an affair at Agram with which I had also been charged, and then to travel in all haste to Paris to render an account of my mission before proceeding to my new destination. So I could neither pass through Vienna nor revisit Beethoven.

His mind was much occupied with the greatness of Napoleon, and he often spoke to me about it. Through all his resentment I could see that he admired his rise from such obscure beginnings; his democratic ideas were flattered by it. One day he remarked, "If I go to Paris, shall I be obliged to salute your emperor?" I assured him that he would not, unless commanded for an audience, "And do you think he would command me?"—"I do not doubt that he would, if he appreciated your importance; but you have seen in Cherubini's case that he does not know much about music."—This question made me think that, despite his opinions, he would have felt flattered by any mark of distinction from Napoleon. Thus does human pride bow down before that which flatters it. . . .

When Napoleon took possession of Vienna for the second time, his brother Jerome, then King of Westphalia, proposed to Beethoven that he should become his *maître de chapelle*, at a salary of 7000 francs. As I was then at Vienna, he asked my advice, in confidence. I think I did well in advising him not to accept the offer, but to observe his agreement with regard to the stipulated pension [from Archduke Rudolph and Princes Kinsky and Lobkowitz]; not that I could already foresee the fall of that royalty, but Beethoven would not have stayed six months at Jerome's court. . . .

To show how little thought Beethoven gave to those who were to execute his music, we only need examine the *grande sonate* for piano and violin dedicated to his friend Kreutzer. This dedication might almost be taken for an epigram, for Kreutzer played all his passages *legato*, and always kept his bow on the string; now, this piece is all in *staccato* and *sautillé*—and so Kreutzer never played it.

BETTINA VON ARNIM AND GOETHE
(1810–1812)

One of the most extraordinary books in world-literature is Goethe's "Correspondence with a Child" (Boston, Ticknor, 1868). The child was Bettina Brentano. Born in 1785, she married in 1811 the poet Achim von Arnim. Her genial but rather unnatural precocity fascinated other great men besides Goethe, but her writings are altogether too hyper-romantic for present taste. In 1810 she visited Vienna and made the acquaintance of Beethoven. She promptly informed Goethe of the meeting in her letter of May 28, 1810. It requires little imagination to see that she overdrew the picture. Indeed, Bettina's temperament and imagination were so vivid that Beethoven scholars have come to doubt even the authenticity of one or more Beethoven letters supposedly written to her. The first letter quoted below was not addressed to Goethe but to the Bavarian Apellrat Dr. Anton Bihler. It is followed by Bettina's letter of May 28, 1810 to Goethe; not in its entirety but as Thayer (II, 187-189) has it with certain judicious cuts. One of these cuts occur after the words "He was seated at the pianoforte." The episode there related, apparently belonged to Bettina's hyper-sentimental inventory of reminiscences (whether actual or only imagined), since she repeated it with embellishments in a letter written years later to Prince von Pückler-Muskau in whose correspondence and diaries it was published in 1873. The episode as there remembered precedes in the following her account of the intercourse between Goethe and Beethoven at Teplitz in 1812 in the translation of Thayer (II, 226-227) and it is followed by a significant paragraph which Thayer omitted. Between Bettina's two letters to Goethe the reader will find Goethe's answer to her first letter and after her effusion to Prince von Pückler-Muskau, Goethe's own impressions of Beethoven expressed in saner language—a welcome antidote to the gushing romanticism of the "child" Bettina, whose poetizing, however, cannot obscure the substantially credible reporting of her meetings with Beethoven.

Bettina von Arnim to Anton Bihler.

BUKOWAN, July 9, 1810.

I did not make Beethoven's acquaintance until the last days of my stay there. I very nearly did not see him at all, for no one wished to take me to meet him, not even those who called themselves his best friends, for fear of his melancholia, which so completely obsesses him that he takes no interest in anything and treats his friends with rudeness rather than civility. A Fantasy he had written, which I heard played in admirable fashion, moved my heart, and from that moment on I felt such a longing that I tried by all means to meet him. No one knew where he lived, since often he keeps himself altogether secluded. His dwelling-place is quite remarkable: in the front room there are from two to three pianos, all legless, lying on the floor; trunks containing his belongings; a three-legged chair; in the second room is his bed which—winter and summer—consists of a straw mattress and a thin cover, a wash basin on a pinewood table, his night-clothes lying on the floor. Here we waited a good half-hour, for he was shaving at the moment. At last he came in. In person he was small (for all his soul and heart were so big), brown, and full of pockmarks. He is what one terms repulsive, yet has a divine brow, rounded with such noble harmony that one is tempted to look on it as a magnificent work of art. He had black hair, very long, which he tosses back, and does not know his own age, but thinks he is fifty-three.

I had been told a great deal about how careful one has to be in order not to rouse his ill will; but I had formed quite another estimate of his noble character and had not been mistaken. Within fifteen minutes he felt so kindly toward me that he would not let me go, but kept walking up and down beside me and even accompanied me home and spent the whole day with us, to the great astonishment of his friends. This man takes a veritable pride in the fact that he will neither oblige the Emperor nor the Archdukes, who give him a pension, by playing for them, and in all Vienna it is the rarest thing in the world to hear him. Upon my asking him to play he replied: "Well, why should I play?"

"Because I would like to fill my life with all that is most wonderful, and because your playing will be an epoch in my life," I said.

He assured me that he would try to deserve this praise, seated himself beside the piano, on the edge of a chair, and played softly with one hand, as though trying to overcome his reluctance to let any one hear him. Suddenly his surroundings were completely forgotten, and his soul expanded in a universal sea of harmony. I have become excessively fond of this man. In all that relates to his art he is so dominating and truthful that no other artist can pretend to approach him; with regard to the rest of his life so naïve, however, that one can do with him what one will.   His absent-mindedness in this last connection has made him a veritable object of ridicule; and he is taken advantage of to such an extent that he seldom has enough money to provide the commonest necessities.   His friends and brothers use him; his clothing is torn, he looks quite out at the elbows (something which Nussbaumer should note), and yet his appearance is noble and imposing.   In addition he is quite hard of hearing and can hardly see.   But when he has just composed something he is altogether deaf, and his eyes are confused as they turn toward the outer world: this is because the whole harmony moves on in his brain and his thoughts can busy themselves with nothing else.   Hence he is cut off from all that keeps him in touch with the outer world (vision and hearing), so that he lives in the most profound solitude.   When one speaks with him at length for a time and stops for his reply, he will suddenly burst forth into tone, draw out his music-paper and write. He does not follow conductor Winter's method, who sets down what first occurs to him; but first makes a great plan and arranges his music in a certain form in accordance with which he works.

During these last days I spent in Vienna he came to see me every evening, gave me songs by Goethe which he had set, and begged me to write him at least once a month, since he had no other friend save myself. Why am I writing you all this in such detail?   Because, first of all, I believe that like myself you can understand and esteem such a character; secondly, because I know what injustice is done him, merely because people are too petty to comprehend him.   And so I cannot forbear drawing his picture just as I see him.   In addition to all else, he takes care of all who confide in him with regard to music with the greatest kindness: the veriest beginner may put himself into his hands with all confidence. He never grows weary of advising and helping him, this man who simply cannot bring himself to clip off a single hour of his free time.

Bettina von Arnim to Goethe.

VIENNA, May 28 [1810].

When I saw him of whom I shall now speak to you, I forgot the whole world—as the world still vanishes when memory recalls the scene—yes it vanishes. . . . It is Beethoven of whom I now wish to tell you, and who made me forget the world and you; I am still in my nonage, it is true, but I am not mistaken when I say—what no one, perhaps, now understands and believes—he stalks far ahead of the culture of mankind. Shall we ever overtake him?—I doubt it, but grant that he may live until the mighty and exalted enigma lying in his soul is fully developed, may reach its loftiest goal, then surely he will place the key to his heavenly knowledge in our hands so that we may be advanced another step towards true happiness.

To you, I am sure, I may confess I believe in a divine magic which is the essence of intellectual life. This magic Beethoven practises in his art. Everything that he can tell you about is pure magic, every posture is the organization of a higher existence, and therefore Beethoven feels himself to be the founder of a new sensuous basis in the intellectual life; you will understand what I am trying to say and how much of it is true. Who could replace this mind for us? From whom could we expect so much? All human activities toss around him like mechanism, he alone begets independently in himself the unsuspected, uncreated. What to him is intercourse with the world—to him who is at his sacred daily task before sunrise and who after sunset scarcely looks about him, who forgets sustenance for his body and who is carried in a trice, by the stream of his enthusiasm, past the shores of work-a-day things?

He himself said: "When I open my eyes I must sigh, for what I see is contrary to my religion, and I must despise the world which does not know that music is a higher revelation than all wisdom and philosophy, the wine which inspires one to new generative processes, and I am the Bacchus who presses out this glorious wine for mankind and makes them spiritually drunken. When they are again become sober they have drawn from the sea all that they brought with them, all that they can bring with them to dry land. I have not a single friend; I must live alone. But well I know that God is nearer to me than to other artists; I associate with him without fear; I have always recognized and understood him and have no fear for my music—it can meet no evil fate. Those who understand it must be freed by it from all the miseries which the others drag about with themselves."

All this Beethoven said to me the first time I saw him; a feeling of reverential awe came over me when he expressed himself to me with such friendly frankness, seeing that I must have appeared so utterly insignificant to him. I was surprised, too, for I had been told that he was unsociable and would converse with nobody. They were afraid to take me to him; I had to hunt him up alone. He has three lodgings in which he conceals himself alternately—one in the country, one in the city and the third on the bastion. It was in the last that I found him in the third storey, walked in unannounced. He was seated at the pianoforte. . . .

He accompanied me home and on the way he said many beautiful things about art, speaking so loudly and stopping in the street that it took courage to listen to him. He spoke with great earnestness and much too surprisingly not to make me forget the street. They were much astonished to see him enter a large dinner party at home with me. After dinner, without being asked, he sat down at the instrument and played long and marvellously; there was a simultaneous fermentation of his pride and his genius. When he is in such a state of exaltation his spirit begets the incomprehensible and his fingers accomplish the impossible.

Since then he comes to me every day, or I go to him. For this I neglect social meetings, galleries, the theatre, and even the tower of St. Stephen's. Beethoven says "Ah! What do you want to see there? I will call for you towards evening; we will walk through the alleys of Schönbrunn." Yesterday I went with him to a glorious garden in full bloom, all the hot-beds open—the perfume was bewildering; Beethoven stopped in the oppressive sunshine and said: "Not only because of their contents, but also because of their rhythm, Goethe's poems have great power over me, I am tuned up and stimulated to composition by this language which builds itself into higher orders as if through the work of spirits and already bears in itself the mystery of the harmonies.

"Then from the focus of enthusiasm I must discharge melody in all directions: I pursue it, capture it again passionately; I see it flying away and disappearing in the mass of varied agitations; now I seize upon it again with renewed passion; I cannot tear myself from it; I am impelled with hurried modulations to multiply it, and, at length I conquer it:—behold, a symphony! Music, verily, is the mediator between intellectual and sensuous life. I should like to talk with Goethe about this—would he understand me?" ... "Speak to Goethe about me," he said; "tell him to hear my symphonies and he will say that I am right in saying that music is the one incorporeal entrance into the higher world of knowledge which comprehends mankind but which mankind cannot comprehend. ... We do not know what knowledge brings us. The encased seed needs the moist, electrically warm soil to sprout, to think, to express itself. Music is the electrical soil in which the mind thinks, lives, feels. Philosophy is a precipitate of the mind's electrical essence; its needs which seek a basis in a primeval principle are elevated by it, and although the mind is not supreme over what it generates through it, it is yet happy in the process. Thus every real creation of art is independent, more powerful than the artist himself and returns to the divine through its manifestation. It is one with man only in this, that it bears testimony of the mediation of the divine in him. . . . Everything electrical stimulates the mind to musical, fluent, out-streaming generation.

"I am electrical in my nature. I must interrupt the flow of my undemonstrable wisdom or I might neglect my rehearsal. Write to Goethe if you understand what I have said, but I cannot be answerable for anything and will gladly be instructed by him." I promised to write you everything to the best of my understanding. . . . Last night I wrote down all that he had said; this morning I read it over to him. He remarked: "Did I say that? Well, then I had a raptus!" He read it again attentively and struck out the above and wrote between the lines, for he is greatly desirous that you shall understand him. Rejoice me now with a speedy answer, which shall show Beethoven that you appreciate him. it has always been our purpose to discuss music; it was also my desire but through Beethoven I feel for the first time that I am not fit for the task.

To this letter Goethe answered:

Your letter, heartily beloved child, reached me at a happy time. You have been at great pains to picture for me a great and beautiful nature in its achievements and its strivings, its needs and the superabundance of its gifts. It has given me great pleasure to accept this picture of a truly great spirit. Without desiring at all to classify it, it yet requires a psychological feat to extract the sum of agreement; but I feel no desire to contradict what I can grasp of your hurried explosion; on the contrary, I should prefer for the present to admit an agreement between my nature and that which is recognizable in these manifold utterances. The ordinary human mind might, perhaps, find contradictions in it; but before that which is uttered by one possessed of such a dæmon, an ordinary layman must stand in reverence, and it is immaterial whether he speaks from feeling or knowledge, for here the gods are at work strewing seeds for future discernment and we can only wish that they may proceed undisturbedly to development. But before they can become general, the clouds which veil the human mind must be dispersed. Give Beethoven my heartiest greetings and tell him that I would willingly make sacrifices to have his acquaintance, when an exchange of thoughts and feelings would surely be beautifully profitable; mayhap you may be able to persuade him to make a journey to Karlsbad whither I go nearly every year and would have the greatest leisure to listen to him and learn from him. To think of teaching him would be an insolence even in one with greater insight than mine, since he has the guiding light of his genius which frequently illumines his mind like a stroke of lightning while we sit in darkness and scarcely suspect the direction from which daylight will break upon us.

It would give me great joy if Beethoven were to make me a present of the two songs of mine which he has composed, but neatly and plainly written. I am very eager to hear them. It is one of my greatest enjoyments, for which I am very grateful, to have the old moods of such a poem (as Beethoven very correctly says) newly aroused in me. . . .

Bettina to Goethe.

June 6, 1810.

Dearest friend! I communicated your beautiful letter to Beethoven so far as it concerned him. He was full of joy and cried: "If there is any one who can make him understand music, I am the man!" The idea of hunting you up at Karlsbad filled him with enthusiasm. He struck his forehead a blow and said: "Might I not have done that earlier?—but, in truth, I did think of it but omitted to do it because of timidity which often torments me as if I were not a real man: but I am no longer afraid of Goethe." You may count, therefore, on seeing him next year. . . .

I am enclosing both songs by Beethoven; the other two are by me. Beethoven has seen them and said many pretty things about them, such as that if I had devoted myself to this lovely art I might cherish great hopes; but I merely graze it in flight, for my art is only to laugh and sigh in a little pocket—more than that there is none for me.

BETTINA.

Bettina von Arnim to Prince Pückler-Muskau.

Beethoven? I would have liked to have made his acquaintance during my short stay; but no one cared to take me to him because of his eccentric disposition and unsociability. I had to look him up myself. He had three dwelling-places: in the city, in the suburbs and in the country. I found him on the top story of a lofty house; a fortepiano lay on the floor of the anteroom, beside it a shabby bedstead with a straw mattress and a woolen coverlet. . . . The servant said: "That is the master's bed." I entered; he sat at the piano and I drew near and putting my mouth close to his ear (for he was deaf) shouted: "My name is Brentano." He smiled, gave me his hand without rising and replied:

"I have just written a fine song for you." He sang *Kennst du das Land?* not meltingly, not softly. His voice was harsh, carried far beyond cultivation and the desire to please by the urge of passion. He asked: "Well, and how do you like it?" I nodded, and he sang it once more with a fire stirred by the consciousness that he had communicated his fervor; then looked at me in triumph, saw that my eyes and cheeks were aglow and naïvely cried: "Aha!" Then he sang: *Trocknet nicht, Tränen der ewigen Liebe! Ach, nur dem halbgetrockneten Auge wie öde, wie tod ihm die Welt erscheint!* Then he wrote down the movement with figures in a note-book which he carried in his pocket, permitting me while he did so to stroke his tumbled hair into order. He kissed my hand and when I was about to leave, accompanied me. While we were underway he said: "Music is the climate of my soul; it is there that it blossoms and does not merely run to seed, like the thoughts of others who call themselves composers. For few realize what a throne of passion each single musical movement is—and few know that passion itself is music's throne." And thus he talked, as though I had been his intimate friend for years. . . .

Everyone was surprised to see me enter a company of more than forty persons, sitting at the table, hand in hand with the unsociable Beethoven. He took a seat without any demur, saying little, probably because he was deaf. Twice he drew his note-book from his pocket and jotted down a few figures. After dinner the whole company mounted to the roof tower of the house to enjoy the view of the surroundings. When all had descended again and he and I were alone, he drew out his note-book, glanced over it, wrote and crossed out and said: "My song is completed." He next leaned from the window and sang it lustily out upon the air. Then he said: "Eh? It sounds, does it not? It belongs to you if you want it. I wrote it for you. You incited me to do so, for I read it in your glance." During all the time I was in Vienna, he came to see me every day. A lady of the company, one of the best of pianists, played a sonata by him. After listening for a time he said: "That is nothing." He seated himself at the piano and played the same sonata, and one truly could say it was superhuman. He entrusted me with various commissions for Goethe, whom he esteemed above all others.

They got acquainted with each other in Teplitz. Goethe was with him: he played for him; seeing that Goethe appeared to be greatly moved he said: "O, Sir, I did not expect that from you; I gave a concert in Berlin several years ago, I did my best and thought that I had done really well and was counting on considerable applause, but behold! when I had given expression to my greatest enthusiasm, there was not the slightest applause; that was too much for me. I could not understand it; but the riddle was finally resolved by this; the Berlin public is extremely cultured and waved its thanks to me with handkerchiefs wet with tears of emotion. This was all wasted on a rude enthusiast like myself; I had thought that I had merely a romantic, not an artistic audience before me. But I accept it gladly from you, Goethe; when your poems went through my brain they threw off music and I was proud to think that I could try to swing myself up to the same heights which you had reached, but I never knew it in my life and would least of all have done it in your presence, here enthusiasm would have had to have an entirely different outlet. You must know yourself how good it feels to be applauded by intelligent hands; if you do not recognize me and esteem me as a peer, who shall do so? By which pack of beggars shall I permit myself to be understood?" Thus did he push Goethe into a corner, who at first did not know how he could set matters to rights, for he felt that Beethoven was right. The Empress and the Austrian archdukes were in Teplitz and

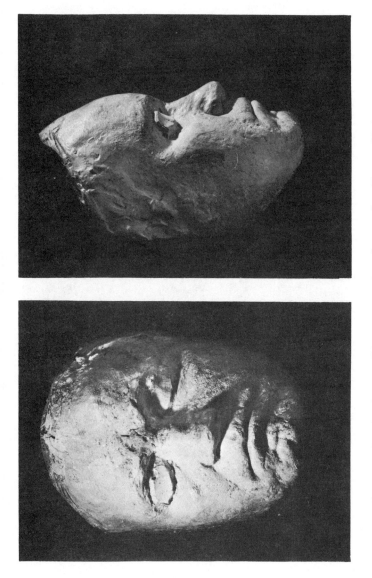

Front and side-view of life-mask of Beethoven by Franz Klein, 1812

(Courtesy Beethovenhaus, Bonn)

Beethoven ·bust by Franz Klein, 1812

(Courtesy Beethovenhaus, Bonn)

Goethe was greatly distinguished by them, and it was by no means a matter of indifference to him to disclose his devotion to the Empress; he intimated as much with much solemn modesty to Beethoven. "Nonsense," said the latter, "that's not the way; you're doing no good by such methods, you must plainly make them understand what they have in having you or they will never find out; there isn't a princess who will appreciate Tasso any longer than the shoe of vanity squeezes her foot—I treated them differently; when I was asked to give lessons to Duke Rainer, he let me wait in the antechamber, and for that I gave his fingers a good twisting; when he asked me why I was so impatient I said that he had wasted my time in the anteroom and I could wait no longer with patience. After that he never let me wait again; yes, I would have showed him that that was a piece of folly which only shows their bestiality. I said to him: "You can hang an order on one, but it would not make him the least bit better; you can make a court councillor or a privy councillor, but not a Goethe or a Beethoven; for that which you cannot make and which you are far from being, therefore, you must learn to have respect, it will do you good." While they were walking there came towards them the whole court, the Empress and the dukes; Beethoven said: "Keep hold of my arm, they must make room for us, not we for them." Goethe was of a different opinion, and the situation became awkward for him; he let go of Beethoven's arm and took a stand at the side with his hat off, while Beethoven with folded arms walked right through the dukes and only tilted his hat slightly while the dukes stepped aside to make room for him, and all greeted him pleasantly; on the other side he stopped and waited for Goethe, who had permitted the company to pass by him where he stood with bowed head. "Well," he said, "I've waited for you because I honor and respect you as you deserve, but you did those yonder too much honor."

Afterwards Beethoven came running to us and told us everything and was glad like a child because he had so teased Goethe.—The talks are all literally true. Nothing essential has been added; Beethoven narrated the episode repeatedly in the same fashion. That was important for me in more than one way; I spoke about it to the Duke of Weimar who was also in Teplitz. He then had a lot of fun about it with him (Goethe) without telling him how he got the story.

Goethe to his wife.

TEPLITZ, July 19, 1812.

. . . ₁More concentrated, more energetic and more intimate [inniger] I have never yet seen an artist. I can very well understand how singular he must stand in his relations with the world.

*Goethe to his friend Zelter, mason, musician and teacher
of Mendelssohn.*

KARLSBAD, September 2, 1812.

I made the acquaintance of Beethoven in Teplitz. His talent amazed me. However, unfortunately, he is an utterly untamed personality, not at all in the wrong, if he finds the world detestable, but he thereby does not make it more enjoyable either for himself or others. He is very much to be excused, on the other hand, and very much to be pitied, as his hearing is leaving him, which, perhaps, injures the musical part of his nature less than his social. He, by nature laconic, becomes doubly so because of this lack.

IGNAZ MOSCHELES
(1810–1814)

If Moscheles (1794-1870) in his reminiscences of Beethoven, as appended by him to his English translation (1841) of Schindler's biography of the master, gives 1809 as the year in which he finished his studies under Weber (Dionys, not Carl Maria von Weber), this was a lapse of memory: actually he had left Weber to study with Albrechtsberger, erstwhile teacher of Beethoven, in the previous year. Moscheles began his long, honorable and fruitful career as pianist and composer in Prague at the age of fourteen, when he performed a pianoforte concerto of his own composition. That Beethoven thought highly of Moscheles is evidenced by the fact that he entrusted in 1814 to his young admirer the task of making the vocal score of "Fidelio."

In the year 1809,[1] my studies with my master, Weber, closed; and being then also fatherless, I chose Vienna for my residence to work out my future musical career. Above all, I longed to see and become acquainted with *that man* who had exercised so powerful an influence over my whole being; whom, though I scarcely understood, I blindly worshipped. I learnt that Beethoven was most difficult of access, and would admit no pupil but Ries; and, for a long time, my anxiety to see him remained ungratified. In the year 1810, however, the longed-for opportunity presented itself. I happened to be one morning in the music-shop of Domenico Artaria, who had just been publishing some of my early attempts at composition, when a man entered with short and hasty steps, and gliding through the circle of ladies and professors assembled on business or talking over musical matters, without looking up, as though he wished to pass unnoticed, made his way direct for Artaria's private office at the bottom of the shop. Presently Artaria called me in, and said, *"This is Beethoven!"* and, to the composer, "This is the youth of whom I have just been speaking to you." Beethoven gave me a friendly nod, and said he had just heard a favorable account of me. To somewhat modest and humble expressions which I stammered forth he made no reply, and seemed to wish to break off the conversation. I stole away with a greater longing for that which I had sought than I had felt before this meeting, thinking to myself—"Am I

[1] It should be 1808.

then indeed such a nobody that he could not put one musical question to me?—nor express one wish to know who had been my master, or whether I had any acquaintance with his works?'' My only satisfactory mode of explaining the matter and comforting myself for this omission was in Beethoven's tendency to deafness, for I had seen Artaria speaking close to his ear.

But I made up my mind that the more I was excluded from the private intercourse which I so earnestly coveted, the closer I would follow Beethoven in all the productions of his mind. I never missed the Schuppanzigh Quartets, at which he was often present, or the delightful Concerts at the Augarten, where he conducted his own Symphonies. I also heard him play several times, which however he did but rarely, either in public or private. The productions which made the most lasting impression upon me, were his Fantasia with orchestral accompaniments and chorus, and his Concerto in C minor. I also used to meet him at the houses of MM. Zmeskall and Zizius, two of his friends, through whose musical meetings Beethoven's works first made their way to public attention: but, in place of better acquaintance with the great man, I had mostly to content myself on his part with a distant salute.

It was in the year 1814, when Artaria undertook to publish a pianoforte arrangement of Beethoven's "Fidelio," that he asked the composer whether I might be permitted to make it: Beethoven assented, upon condition that he should see my arrangement of each of the pieces, before it was given into the engraver's hands. Nothing could be more welcome to me, since I looked upon this as the long wished-for opportunity to approach nearer to the great man, and to profit by his remarks and corrections. During my frequent visits, the number of which I tried to multiply by all possible excuses, he treated me with the kindest indulgence. Although his increasing deafness was a considerable hindrance to our conversation, yet he gave me many instructive hints, and even played to me such parts as he wished to have arranged in a particular manner for the pianoforte. I thought it, however, my duty not to put his kindness to the test by robbing him of his valuable time by any subsequent visits; but I often saw him at Maelzel's, where he used to discuss the different plans and models of a Metronome which the latter was going to manufacture, and to talk over the "Battle of Vittoria," which he wrote at Maelzel's suggestion. Although I knew Mr. Schindler, and was aware that he was much with Beethoven at that time, I did not avail myself of my acquaintance with him for the purpose of intruding myself upon the composer. I mention these circumstances to show how very difficult of access this extraordinary man was, and how he avoided all musical discussion; for even with his only pupil, Ries, it was very seldom that he would enter into any explanations. In my later intercourse with him, he gave me but laconic answers on questions of art; and on the character of his own works, made only such condensed remarks as required all my imagination and fancy to develop what he meant to convey. The impatience naturally accompanying his infirmity of deafness, no doubt greatly increased his constitutional reserve in the latter part of his life.

During one of my visits to Vienna, my brother, who is a resident of Prague, made a journey expressly to see me; and one morning, finding I had an appointment with Beethoven, was exceedingly anxious to get a sight of a man of such celebrity, whom he had never yet had an opportunity of seeing. It was very natural that I should wish to gratify his curiosity, but I told him, that although he was my own brother, yet I knew the peculiarities of the man so well, that nothing could induce me to commit the indiscretion of an introduction. He was, however, too intent upon his wish to let the opportunity escape

without a further endeavour, and said that, surely, I
might allow him to call, as if in furtherance of another
appointment which we had mutually made. To this I
consented, and off we went to Beethoven's, where I left
my brother in the passage below to wait the issue of our
arrangement. I remained with Beethoven about half
an hour, when taking out my watch and looking at it, I
hastily wrote in his conversation-book that I had a
particular appointment at that hour, and that I appre-
hended my brother was still waiting below to accompany
me. Beethoven, who was sitting at the table in his
shirt-sleeves, instantly started from his seat, and quitting
the room with precipitation, left me in no little embarrassment, wondering what was to follow. In a minute afterwards back he came, dragging in my brother by the
arm, and in a hurried manner forced him into a seat.
"And is it possible," said he, "that you, too, could think
me such a bear as not to receive your brother with
kindness?" My brother, who had before received some
vague insinuations that the renowned composer was
not at all times in his sober senses, looked as pale as
ashes, and only began to regain his self-possession on
hearing the question which Beethoven so kindly, yet so
reproachfully, asked me; for it appeared that the latter
had rushed precipitately down the stairs, and, without
saying a word, seized my brother by the arm and dragged
him up-stairs as if he had caught hold of a criminal.
No sooner was my brother fairly seated than he behaved
in the most kind and obliging manner towards him,
pressing him to take wine and other refreshments. This
simple but abrupt act clearly shows, that however strange
his manners were, he had at heart that kindly and good
feeling which ever accompanies genius. If we were to
take the external manner for the internal man, what
egregious mistakes should we often make!

    1808. It goes without saying that Beethoven, that
great man, was the object of my most profound venera-

tion.   In view of my own high opinion of him I could not comprehend where the Vienna society ladies found the courage to invite him to their musical performances and play him his compositions.   He must have liked it, however, for he often was to be met at these evening entertainments.   It is possible that even then his wretched deafness may have made him loathe to play himself, and that hence he entrusted his new compositions to these feminine hands.   Yet what was my surprise when, one day, in the house of Court-conductor Salieri, who was not at home, I saw a card lying on the table, on which might be read, in his laconic style: "Pupil Beethoven called!"   This set me thinking.   A Beethoven still could learn something from a Salieri?   Then with how much more reason could I.   Salieri had been Gluck's pupil and most ardent admirer; though, as was well known, he would not acknowledge the merit of Mozart and his works.

I went to him, nevertheless, became his pupil and also, for three years, was his assistant at the Opera and as such privileged to visit all the theatres free of charge. Life in dear old Vienna was gay and full of variety in those days.

1814.   When I came early in the morning to Beethoven, he was still lying in bed; he happened to be in remarkably good spirits, jumped up immediately, and placed himself, just as he was, at the window looking out on the Schottenbastei, with the view of examining the "Fidelio" numbers which I had arranged.   Naturally, a crowd of street boys collected under the window, when he roared out, "Now what do these confounded boys want?"   I laughed, and pointed to his own figure.   "Yes, yes; you are quite right," he said, and hastily put on a dressing-gown.

When we came to the last grand duet, "Namenlose Freude," and I had written the words of the text— "Ret-terin des Gat-ten," he struck them out and altered

them to "Rett-erin des Gatt-en"; "for no one," said he,
"can sing upon *l.*" Under the last number I had written
"Fine mit Gottes Hülfe" (the end with the help of God).
He was not at home when I brought it to him; and on
returning my manuscript, the words were added, "O,
Mensch, hilf dir selber!" (Oh, man, help thyself!).

Louis Spohr
(1812–1816)

The impressions of Beethoven which Spohr recorded in his autog-
raphy belong to the most vivid we possess. Louis Spohr (1784-
1859) frankly confessed his inability to comprehend Beethoven's
music of the last period. He attributed Beethoven's "esthetic
aberrations" to his deafness, but apparently it never occurred to
Spohr that his own ears might have been at fault. Considered in
his time either the equal of Paganini as a violinist or second only
to him, Louis Spohr laid much greater stress on his importance and
fame as a composer. As such, his popularity generations ago
certainly was not inferior to that of Beethoven. His music was
much more chromatic and much more "romantic" than Beethoven's.
Hence, in a way, more "modern," but such externals of style do not
determine the longevity of music—the music of Beethoven, by far
the greater genius, lives, including the (in Spohr's opinion "monstrous," "tasteless" and "trivial") Ninth Symphony, and that of
Spohr, apart from his ever-valuable violin concertos, is dead. That
this should have been the fate of his remarkably beautiful opera
"Jessonda," too, is a pity.

Upon my arrival in Vienna I immediately paid a visit
to Beethoven; I did not find him at home, and therefore
left my card. I now hoped to meet him at some of the
musical parties, to which he was frequently invited, but
was soon informed that Beethoven, since his deafness
had so much increased that he could no longer hear
music connectedly, had withdrawn himself from all musical parties, and had become very shy of all society.
I made trial therefore of another visit; but again without success. At length I met him quite unexpectedly
at the eating-house where I was in the habit of going
with my wife every day at the dinner hour. I had

already given concerts, and twice performed my oratorio. The Vienna papers had noticed them favourably. Beethoven had therefore heard of me when I introduced myself to him, and he received me with an unusual friendliness of manner. We sat down at the same table, and Beethoven became very chatty, which much surprised the company, as he was generally taciturn, and sat gazing listlessly before him. But it was an unpleasant task to make him hear me, and I was obliged to speak so loud as to be heard in the third room off. Beethoven now came frequently to these dining-rooms, and visited me also at my house. We thus soon became well acquainted: Beethoven was a little blunt, not to say uncouth; but a truthful eye beamed from under his bushy eyebrows. After my return from Gotha I met him now and then at the theatre "an der Wien," close behind the orchestra, where Count Palffy had given him a free seat. After the opera he generally accompanied me to my house, and passed the rest of the evening with me. He could then be very friendly with Dorette and the children. He spoke of music but very seldom. When he did, his opinions were very sternly expressed, and so decided as would admit of no contradiction whatever. In the works of others, he took not the least interest; I therefore had not the courage to show him mine. His favorite topic of conversation at that time was a sharp criticism of the management of both theatres by Prince Lobkowitz and Count Palffy. He frequently abused the latter in so loud a tone of voice, while we were yet even within the walls of his theatre, that not only the public leaving it, but the Count himself could hear it in his office. This used to embarrass me greatly, and I then always endeavoured to turn the conversation upon some other subject.

Beethoven's rough and even repulsive manners at that time, arose partly from his deafness, which he had not learned to bear with resignation, and partly from the dilapidated condition of his pecuniary circumstances. He was a bad housekeeper, and had besides the misfortune to be plundered by those about him. He was thus frequently in want of common necessaries. In the early part of our acquaintance, I once asked, after he had absented himself for several days from the diningrooms: "You were not ill, I hope?"—"My boot was, and as I have only one pair, I had house-arrest," was his reply.

But some time afterwards he was extricated from this depressing position by the exertions of his friends. The proceeding was as follows:

Beethoven's "Fidelio," which in 1804 (or 1805) under very unfavorable circumstances (during the occupation of Vienna by the French), had met with very little success, was now brought forward again by the director of the Kärnthnerthor-Theater and performed for his benefit. Beethoven had allowed himself to be persuaded to write a new overture for it (in E), a song for the jailor, and the grand air for Fidelio (with horns-obbligati) as also to make some alterations. In this new form the Opera had now great success, and kept its place during a long succession of crowded performances. On the first night, the composer was called forward several times, and now became again the object of general attention. His friends availed themselves of this favorable opportunity to make arrangements for a concert in his behalf in the great "Redouten Saal" at which the most recent compositions of Beethoven were to be performed. All who could fiddle, blow, or sing were invited to assist, and not one of the most celebrated artists of Vienna failed to appear. I and my orchestra had of course also joined, and for the first time I saw Beethoven direct. Although I had heard much of his leading, yet it surprised me in a high degree. Beethoven had accustomed himself to give the signs of expression to his orchestra by all manner of extraordinary motions of his body. So often as a *sforzando* occurred, he tore his arms, which he had previously crossed upon his breast, with great vehemence asunder. At a *piano*, he bent himself down, bent the lower the softer he wished to have it. Then when a *crescendo* came, he raised himself again by degrees, and upon the commencement of the *forte*, sprang bolt upright. To increase the *forte* yet more, he would sometimes, also, join in with a shout to the orchestra, without being aware of it.

Upon my expressing my astonishment to Seyfried, at this extraordinary method of directing, he related to me a tragi-comical circumstance that had occurred at Beethoven's last concert at the Theatre "an der Wien."

Beethoven was playing a new Pianoforte-Concerto of his, but forgot at the first *tutti* that he was a solo-player, and springing up, began to direct in his usual way. At the first *sforzando* he threw out his arms so wide asunder that he knocked both the lights off the piano upon the ground. The audience laughed, and Beethoven was so incensed at this disturbance that he made the orchestra cease playing, and begin anew. Seyfried, fearing that a repetition of the accident would occur at the same passage, bade two boys of the chorus place themselves on either side of Beethoven, and hold the lights in their hands. One of the boys innocently approached nearer, and was reading also in the notes of the piano-part. When therefore the fatal *sforzando* came, he received from Beethoven's outthrown right hand so smart a blow on the mouth, that the poor boy let fall the light from terror. The other boy, more cautious, had followed with anxious eyes every motion of Beethoven, and by stooping suddenly at the eventful moment he avoided the slap on the mouth. If the public were unable to restrain their laughter before, they could now much less, and broke out into a regular bacchanalian roar. Beethoven got into such a rage, that at the first chords of the solo, half a dozen strings broke. Every endeavour of the real lovers of music to restore calm and attention were for the moment fruitless. The first *allegro* of the Concerto was therefore lost to the public. From that fatal evening on Beethoven would not give another concert.

But the one got up by his friends was attended with the most brilliant success. The new compositions of Beethoven pleased extremely, particularly the Symphony in A-Major (the seventh); the wonderful second movement was *encored* and also made upon me a deep and lasting impression. The execution was a complete masterpiece, in spite of the uncertain and frequently laughable direction of Beethoven.

It was easy to see that the poor deaf *Maestro* of the piano could no longer hear his own music. This was particularly remarkable in a passage in the second part of the first *allegro* of the symphony. At that part there are two pauses in quick succession, the second of which is *pianissimo*. This Beethoven had probably overlooked, for he again began to give the time before the orchestra had executed this second pause. Without knowing it, therefore, he was already from ten to twelve bars in advance of the orchestra when it began the *pianissimo*. Beethoven, to signify this in his own way, had crept completely under the desk. Upon the now ensuing *crescendo*, he again made his appearance, raised himself continually more and more, and then sprang up high from the ground, when according to his calculation the moment for the *forte* should begin. As this did not take place, he looked around him in affright, stared with astonishment at the orchestra, that it should still be playing *pianissimo*, and only recovered himself when at length the long expected *forte* began, and was audible to himself.

Fortunately this scene did not take place at the public performance, otherwise the audience would certainly have laughed again.

As the salon was crowded to overflowing and the applause enthusiastic, the friends of Beethoven made arrangements for a repetition of the concert, which brought in an almost equally large amount. For some time, therefore, Beethoven was extricated from his pecuniary difficulties; but, arising from the same causes, these reoccurred to him more than once before his death.

Up to this period, there was no visible falling off in Beethoven's creative powers. But as from this time, owing to his constantly increasing deafness, he could no longer hear any music, this of necessity must have had a prejudicial influence upon his fancy. His constant endeavour to be original and to open new paths, could no longer, as formerly, be preserved from error by the guidance of the ear. Was it then to be wondered at that his works became more and more eccentric, unconnected, and incomprehensible? It is true there are people who imagine they can understand them, and in their pleasure at that, rank them far above his earlier masterpieces. But I am not of the number, and freely confess that, I have never been able to relish those last works of Beethoven. Yes! I must even reckon the much admired Ninth Symphony among them, the three first movements of which, in spite of some solitary flashes of genius, are to me worse than all of the eight previous symphonies, the fourth movement of which is in my opinion so monstrous and tasteless, and in its grasp of Schiller's "Ode" so trivial, that I cannot even now understand how a genius like Beethoven's could have written it. I find in it another proof of what I already remarked in Vienna, that Beethoven was wanting in æsthetical feeling and in a sense of the beautiful.

And at the time I made Beethoven's acquaintance, he had already discontinued playing both in public and at private parties; I had therefore but one opportunity to hear him, when I casually came to the rehearsal of a new Trio (D-Major 3-4 time) at Beethoven's house. It was by no means an enjoyment; for in the first place the pianoforte was woefully out of tune which, however, troubled Beethoven little, since he could hear nothing of it and, secondly, of the former so admired excellence of the virtuoso scarcely anything was left, in consequence of his total deafness.   In the *forte*, the poor deaf man hammered in such a way upon the keys that entire groups of notes were inaudible, so that one lost all intelligence of the subject unless the eye followed the score at the same time.   I felt moved with the deepest sorrow at so hard a destiny.   It is a sad misfortune for any one to be deaf; how then should a musician endure it without despair?   Beethoven's almost continual melancholy was no longer a riddle to me now.

Johann Wenzel Tomaschek
(1814)

How different this second meeting of Tomaschek with Beethoven from his first, in 1798, described on page 21! The "young foreign artist" who found much favor neither with Beethoven nor with Tomaschek was none other than Meyerbeer and the opera the two gentlemen "roasted" was his "Die beiden Caliphen", just then performed at Vienna.

On October 10, 1814, in the forenoon, together with my brother, I visited Beethoven.   The unfortunate man was especially hard of hearing this day, so that one had to scream rather than talk in order to be understood. The reception room in which he greeted me was anything but splendidly furnished and, incidentally, was as disordered as was his hair.   Here I found an upright piano and on its music-rack the text of a cantata (*Der glorreiche Augenblick*) by Weissenbach; on the keys lay a lead-pencil, with which he sketched out his work; and beside it on a scribbled sheet of music-paper I found a number of the most divergent ideas, jotted down without any connection, the most heterogeneous individual details elbowing each other, just as they may have come to

Crayon sketch of Beethoven
by Letronne in 1814, engraved by Höfel

(Courtesy Beethovenhaus, Bonn)

Mähler's Second Portrait of Beethoven, 1815

(Courtesy Collection Karajan, Salzburg)

his mind. This was the material for his new cantata. Jumbled up just like these musical fragments was his conversation which, as is usually the case with those who are deaf, he carried on in a very loud voice, at the same time continually moving his hand about his ear as though he were groping for his enfeebled sense of hearing. Various particulars of this conversation, during which he dropped many a verb, I shall here relate; omitting, however, some names which do not seem pertinent:

T. Mr. van Beethoven, you will forgive me if I disturb you. I am Tomaschek of Prague, composer to Count Buquoy, and have taken the liberty of visiting you, together with my brother.

B. It gives me real pleasure to make your acquaintance in person—You do not disturb me in the least.

T. Dr. R—— wishes to be remembered to you.

B. What is he doing? I have not heard from him for a long time.

T. He wishes to know how you are getting on with your lawsuit?

B. There is so much red tape that it seems impossible to make any progress.

T. I hear that you have composed a Requiem.

B. I had intended to write a Requiem as soon as the suit was settled. Why should I write it before I have gained my rights?

Then he began to tell me the whole story. But here, too, he spoke without much interconnection, somewhat rhapsodically; and finally the conversation turned to other things. I said:

T. You seem to be very busy, Mr. van Beethoven?

B. Is it not necessary? What would my fame say?

T. Does my pupil Worzichek often visit you?

B. He came to see me a few times, but I have not heard him play. Recently he brought me something he had written, and for a young fellow of his sort it was well done. (Beethoven was speaking of the twelve rhapsodies for piano which later were published, inscribed to me.)

T. You probably go out but seldom?

B. I go hardly anywhere.

T. A new opera by Seyfried is to be given to-night. I have no mind to listen to music of that sort.

B. My God! There have to be composers of that kind, for otherwise what would the rabble do?

T. I am told that there is a young foreign artist in town, who is said to be an extraordinary pianist.

B. Yes, I also have been told of him, but have not heard him myself. My God! Let him stay here three months and then hear what the Viennese think of his playing! I know how popular anything new is in this place.

T. You probably have not met him yourself?

B. I made his acquaintance at the performance of my "Battle," on which occasion several local composers each played an instrument. That young gentleman had been given the bass drum. Ha ha ha! I was not at all satisfied with him; he did not beat it correctly and always came in too late, so that I had to give him a good dressing-down. Ha ha ha! It probably angered him. There is nothing to him; he lacks the courage to strike at the proper time.

This idea made both my brother and myself laugh heartily. Declining Beethoven's invitation to stay for dinner, we took leave of him with the proviso that we were to visit him again before we left.

On November 24, I visited Beethoven once more, for I had a great desire to see him again before I took my departure. I was announced by his servant and at once admitted. If his home had presented a disorderly appearance when first I called on him, this was now more than ever the case. In the middle room I found two copyists, who were copying his cantata, already mentioned, in the greatest haste; in the second room every chair and table was covered with portions of scores which Umlauf, whom Beethoven presented to me, probably was correcting. This gentleman seemed to have a pleasant disposition, for at this our first meeting he was neither cold nor cordial; the impression we made on each other was reciprocal, yet he went away and I—remained. Beethoven received me very politely, but appeared to be very deaf this day, for I had to exert myself to the utmost to make myself understood. I will set down our dialogue:

T. I have come to see you once more before my departure.

B. I thought you already had left Vienna. Have you been here all this time?

T. The whole time, save for a single excursion I made to the battlefields of Aspern and Wagram. Has your health been good in the meantime?

B. As always, there have been nothing but vexations. It is impossible to keep on living here.

T. I see that you are very busy preparing for your concert, and I do not wish to interfere.

B. Not at all, I am glad to see you. There is so much that is unpleasant in connection with a concert, and the corrections are endless!

T. I have just read an announcement that you have postponed your concert.

B. Everything was incorrectly copied. I must have a rehearsal on the day of the performance and hence postponed the concert.

T. There is probably nothing more aggravating and vexatious than preparing for a concert.

B. You are entirely right. So many blunders are made that one cannot get on with things. And the money one has to spend! The manner in which Art is handled nowadays is inexcusable. I have to pay one-third of my receipts to the management and one-fifth to the prison budget. The devil take it! Before it all is over I shall be asking whether music is a free Art or not. Believe me, Art is in a bad way at the present time. How long are you staying in Vienna?

T. I think of leaving on Monday.

B. Then by all means I must give you a ticket to my concert.

T. I thanked him and begged him not to put himself out to do so; but he went into the anteroom and at once returned to say that his servant, who had taken charge of the tickets, was not at home; but that I need only write down my address so that he might send me the ticket. Since he would have it so I wrote down my address for him, and we continued our conversation as follows:

T. Did you go to N. N.'s [Meyerbeer's] opera?

B. No, I understand that things went very badly. I thought of you; you hit the nail on the head when you said you did not expect much from his compositions. The evening after the production I talked with the opera singers in the wine cellar they usually frequent. I told them right out: "There you have gone and distinguished yourselves again! What an asinine trick you have played! You ought to be ashamed of yourselves to think that you still are knownothings, without judgment, that you have made such a stir about this opera! Is it possible that experienced singers should arrive at such conclusions? I should like to talk to you about it, but you would not understand me."

T. I heard the opera. It began with a hallelujah and ended with a requiem.

B. Ha, ha, ha, ha, ha! It is the same when he plays. I often have been asked whether I have heard him—I say no; yet after the comments of those among my acquaintances who are able to form an estimate with regard to such things, I can take for granted that though he has agility he is otherwise a superficial person.

T. I heard that before he left for Paris he played at Mr. ——'s house and did not please very well.

B. Ha, ha, ha, ha! What did I tell you? I know that type. He should settle down here for no more than six months. Then we will hear what they say of his playing. It always has been acknowledged that the greatest pianists were also the greatest composers, but how did they play? Not like the pianists of to-day, who only run up and down the keyboard with passages they have learned by heart—putch, putch, putch! What does that mean? Nothing! The real piano virtuosos, when they played, gave us something interconnected, a whole. When it was written out it could at once be accepted as a well-composed work. That was piano playing, the rest is nothing!

T. It seems very ridiculous to me that N. N. [J. G. Fuchs], who himself appears to have only a very limited idea of the instrument, should have declared him to be the greatest of pianists.

B. He knows nothing of instrumental music. He is a miserable object, as I shall tell him to his face. Once he praised to the skies an instrumental composition with musical goose-feathers and asses' ears sticking out of every corner. I had to laugh at his ignorance with all my heart. He understands singing and should stick to his last, for he knows next to nothing about composition.

T. I, too, am carrying away with me a very diminished idea of * * * 's knowledge.

B. As I have said, he understands nothing save singing.

T. The N. N. [Moscheles], so they tell me, is causing quite a sensation here.

B. My God! He plays prettily, prettily . . . besides he is a . . . He'll not amount to anything. These people have their accustomed social circle, which they frequent. There they are praised, and praised again and that is the end of their Art! I tell you he will not amount to anything. Formerly I was too forward in expressing my opinions and made enemies for myself—now I judge no one because I do not wish to injure anyone, and, besides, I think to myself: if it be something real, then it will maintain itself in spite of all enmity and envy; but if it be not solid, it will tumble down of its own accord, no matter how they try to prop it up.

T. That is my own philosophy.

Meanwhile Beethoven had dressed and made ready to go out. I took leave of him, and he wished me a prosperous journey and invited me to come to see him in the event of my remaining longer in Vienna.

The 28th, which day, at eleven o'clock in the forenoon, brought me to the great Ballroom Hall, where the rehearsal for Beethoven's concert was to be held, was all the more interesting for me. There I met Spohr and State Counsellor von Sonnleithner, and stayed near them until the rehearsal ended. Sonnleithner's animated spirit and apt wit furnished a very attractive contrast to Spohr's calm and equanimity. The Symphony in A major, to which I found it impossible to take a liking, was rehearsed; and then came the new cantata, which did not deny Beethoven's genius, but its declamation and the organic leading of the voices! . . . The solution of this musical problem, as I have said, lay quite beyond the limits of his inspiration.

Madame Milder's tremendous voice penetrated to every corner of the hall; the violin solo, cleanly and neatly played by Mr. Mayseder, on the other hand, sounded feeble. Beethoven made a serious miscalculation when he assigned a solo to the violin to be played in so gigantic a hall. The cantata did not and could not appeal, for its imperfections are of a kind which cannot be concealed

Crayon drawing of Beethoven
by A. v. Kloeber, 1817 or 1818

(Courtesy Beethovenhaus, Bonn)

Oil-portrait of Beethoven by Schimon, 1818

(Courtesy Beethovenhaus, Bonn)

either by genius or by fame. The concert concluded with "The Battle of Vittoria," which carried away the major portion of the audience with enthusiasm. I myself, on the contrary, was very painfully affected on finding Beethoven, whom Providence has perhaps endowed with the loftiest throne in the realm of tone, among the crassest of materialists. They do tell me that he himself has called the work a stupid thing, and that he likes it only because it was a success that took away the breath of the Viennese. I myself believe that it was not the "Battle," but his other magnificent works with which, little by little, Beethoven gained Vienna's favor. When the orchestra was almost entirely submerged by the godless din of drums, the rattling and slambanging, and I expressed my disapproval of the thundering applause to Mr. von Sonnleithner, the latter mockingly replied that the crowd would have enjoyed it even more if their own empty heads had been thumped in the same way. The concert was held with Umlauft conducting, Beethoven standing beside him and beating time, though usually his beat was wrong because of his deafness. This, however, caused no confusion, since the orchestra followed only Umlauft's beat. Quite deafened by the cataract of noise I was glad to get out into the open again.

CIPRIANI POTTER
(1818)

Born at London in 1792, Philip Cipriani Hambly Potter, to give him his full name, died in 1871, after an honorable career as pianist, conductor, composer and principal of the Royal Academy of Music from 1832 to 1859. The ambition to make the acquaintance of Beethoven and, if possible to become his pupil, was aroused in him by John Baptist Cramer, a staunch admirer of Beethoven and the only pianist of his time whom Beethoven respected as a rival. Potter contributed his "Recollections of Beethoven" to "The Musical World" in 1836, from where they were reprinted by the "Musical Times" in 1861. That he made a good impression on Beethoven is evidenced by the master's letter of March 5, 1818 to Ferdinand Ries in which he wrote: "Botter [*sic*] visited me a few times; he appears to be a good man and has talent for composition."

Beethoven's music is now listened to with an attention and delight that his real friends and admirers could scarcely have anticipated.—Not unfrequently, indeed, these feelings border on prejudice, since it is impossible that amateurs generally can appreciate those portions of his works, which the cultivated Professor is often at a loss to understand, nevertheless, it is gratifying to witness the anxiety with which the uninitiated endeavour to comprehend what is termed classical writing, emanating from so great a man; exerting their auricular and intellectual faculties to admire that which, in all probability, is far from being congenial with their predisposed taste and ideas.   This prostration of the understanding at the shrine of acknowledged genius is encouraging to every labourer in the good cause of sterling music, and is the best assurance of a healthy and rational state being at hand.

Many persons have imbibed the notion that Beethoven was by nature a morose and ill-tempered man.   This opinion is perfectly erroneous.   He *was* irritable, passionate, and of a melancholy turn of mind—all of which affections arose from the deafness which, in his latter days, increased to an alarming extent.   Opposed to these peculiarities in his temperament, he possessed a kind heart, and most acute feelings.   Any disagreeable occurrence, resulting from his betrayal of irritability, he manifested the utmost anxiety to remove, by every possible acknowledgment of his indiscretion.   The least interruption of his studies, particularly when availing himself of a happy vein of ideas, would cause him to expose the peculiarities of his temper; a capriciousness not at variance with, and perfectly excusable in, professors of other arts and sciences, when placed in a similar situation.

Another cause for mistaking Beethoven's disposition, arose from the circumstance of foreigners visiting Vienna, who were ambitious of contemplating the greatest genius in that capital, and of hearing him perform. But when, from their unmusical questions and heterodox remarks, he discovered that a mere travelling curiosity, and not musical feeling, had attracted them, he was not at all disposed to accede to their selfish importunities: he would interpret their visit into an intrusion and an impertinence; and consequently, feeling highly offended, was not scrupulous in exhibiting his displeasure in the most pointed and abrupt manner: a reception which, as it was ill-calculated to leave an agreeable impression with those who were so unlucky as to expose themselves to the rebuke, did not also fail in prompting them to represent his deportment unfavourably to the world. He would frequently revert to these intruders when conversing with a friend, and relate many singular anecdotes, resulting from their annoying visits.

When his mind was perfectly free from his compositions, he particularly delighted in the society of one or two intimates. It sensibly comforted him, and at once dispelled the cloud of melancholy that hung over his spirit. His conversation then became highly animated, and he was extremely loquacious.

It would naturally be concluded, that Beethoven's preëminence as a composer, should have placed him above the envy of the profession; but this was far from being the case. No doubt the feeling died with him although it existed during his life to a very considerable extent—particularly in Vienna. This unworthy conduct on the part of the profession together with his own unhappy malady, doubtless increased his melancholy, and rendered him more recluse in his social habits. In justice, however, it should here be stated, that some of his most ardent admirers, both professors and amateurs, resided in Vienna. Latterly his deafness became so aggravated and confirmed, as to oblige those who wished to communicate with him, to have recourse to writing; but being very excitable and tenacious, upon the subject of his infirmity, if they were not rapid in their communication, he would endeavour to anticipate what was intended, or evade the question altogether, by changing the discourse. Some judges are of opinion, that his misfortune had considerable influence upon his writings, and that it contributed to their complexity, particularly his latter productions; but it would have required a much more extended period than was allotted to him, to have caused him to forget the powers or genius of an orchestra. Indeed, had he been spared twenty or thirty years longer, we may conceive him to have contracted a confused idea of musical sounds and combinations; but his great experience of orchestral effects, so satisfactorily exemplified in all his works; his profound knowledge of harmony, and his inexhaustible fancy, would always have assisted him in the accomplishment of any work.

Beethoven's playing was doubtless much impaired by his cruel malady. Although, from experience and a knowledge of his instrument, a musician may imagine the effect of his performance, yet he cannot himself produce that effect when wholly deprived of the sense of hearing, more especially a sensitive man like Beethoven. His infirmity precluded his ascertaining the quantity or quality of tone produced by a certain pressure of his fingers on the pianoforte; hence his playing, latterly, became very imperfect. He possessed immense powers on the instrument; great velocity of finger, united with extreme delicacy of touch, and intense feeling; but his passages were indistinct and confused. Being painfully conscious, therefore, of his inability to produce any certain effect, he objected to perform before any one, and latterly refused even his most intimate friends. These, however, would at times succeed in their desire to get him to the instrument, by ingeniously starting a question in counterpoint; when he would unconsciously proceed to illustrate his theory; and then branching out into a train of thought (forgetting his affliction), he would frequently pour out an extemporaneous effusion, of marvellous power and brilliancy. It is easy to imagine a purely mechanical performer, void of all feeling, previously to a stroke of deafness, who has conquered every difficulty of the instrument, playing a piece of music correctly, and to the satisfaction of those of a reciprocal feeling; but to a conformation like that of Beethoven, where light and shade, and delicacy of expression, were either all or nothing, the full achievement of his object amounted to an almost impossibility.

Anton Schindler
(1819)

Of Schindler, who proudly printed on his visiting-cards *L'ami de Beethoven*, more will be said under a later year. The following is a snap-shot of Beethoven when he was in travail with his "Missa Solemnis" in 1819. Thayer, when quoting Schindler, says that he "presents us with a pathetic, impressive, almost terrifying picture of the state to which his labor lifted" Beethoven, but it may be said that the pictured state essentially is characteristic of many an artist in the act of creating a complicated work.

Towards the end of August, accompanied by the musician Johann Horsalka, still living in Vienna, I arrived at the master's home in Mödling. It was 4 o'clock in the afternoon. As soon as we entered we learned that in the morning both servants had gone away, and that there had been a quarrel after midnight which had disturbed all the neighbors, because as a consequence of a long vigil both had gone to sleep and the food which had been prepared had become unpalatable. In the living-room, behind a locked door, we heard the master singing parts of the fugue in the *Credo*—singing, howling, stamping. After we had been listening a long time to this almost awful scene, and were about to go away, the door opened and Beethoven stood before us with distorted features, calculated to excite fear. He looked as if he had been in mortal combat with the whole host of contrapuntists, his everlasting enemies. His first utterances were confused, as if he had been disagreeably surprised at our having overheard him. Then he reached the day's happenings and with obvious restraint he remarked: "Pretty doings, these! (*Saubere Wirthschaft*). Everybody has run away and I haven't had anything to eat since yesternoon!" I tried to calm him and helped him to make his toilet. My companion hurried on in advance to the restaurant of the bathing establishment to have something made ready for the famished master. Then he complained about the wretched state of his domestic affairs, but here, for reasons already stated, there was nothing to be done. Never, it may be said, did so great an art work as is the *Missa Solemnis* see its creation under more adverse circumstances.

Maurice Schlesinger
(1819)

Born as Moritz, son of the Berlin music-publisher Adolf Martin Schlesinger, he went into business for himself at Paris in 1821 or 1822 and, as a far-sighted, shrewd and progressive music-publisher, soon helped to make musical history. Of Beethoven's works he acquired principally the Pianoforte Sonatas, Op. 109, 110, 111 and the Quartets, Op. 132 and 135. How he won the good will of Beethoven, he amusingly told A. B. Marx in a letter of February 27, 1859, printed in the latter's Beethoven biography.

I cannot refrain from telling how, in the year 1819, I made Beethoven's acquaintance, and owing to what chance I was lucky enough to have him become fond of me. I was in Steiner & Company's vault when Haslinger, their partner, said: "There comes Beethoven. Do you care to make his acquaintance?" When I said that I did he added: "He is deaf. If you have something to say to him write it down at once. He does not like to reveal his affliction to people." He then introduced me and Beethoven invited me to visit him in Baden. This I did a few days later. Stepping from my carriage I entered the tavern, and there found Beethoven stalking out of the door, which he slammed to after him, in a rage. After I had removed some of my travel stains, I went to the house pointed out as his dwelling. His housekeeper told me that I probably would be unable to speak to him, since he had returned home in a rage. I gave her my visiting-card, which she took to him and, to my great surprise, returned a few minutes later and told me to enter. There I found the great man sitting at his writing-desk. I at once wrote down how happy I was to make his acquaintance. This (what I had written) made a favorable impression. He at once gave free rein to his feelings and told me he was the most wretched man in the world; he had but just returned from the tavern, where he had asked for some veal which he felt like eating—and none had been available! All this he said in a very serious, gloomy way. I consoled him, we talked (I myself writing) about other things, and thus he kept me for nearly two hours; and though, afraid of boring or molesting him, I several times rose to go, on each occasion he prevented me from taking my departure. Leaving him, I hurried back to Vienna in my carriage; and at once asked my inn-keeper's son whether he had some roast veal ready. When he said he had, I made him put it in a dish, carefully cover it and, without a word of explanation, sent it back to Baden by the man, in the carriage I had kept, to be presented to Beethoven with my compliments. I was still lying in bed the following morning when Beethoven came to me, kissed and embraced me, and told me I was the most kind-hearted person he had ever met; never had anything given him such pleasure as the roast veal, coming at the very moment when he so greatly longed for it.

Sir John Russell
(1821)

The following is taken from Sir John's book "A tour in Germany, and some of the southern provinces of the Austrian Empire, in 1820, 1821, 1822." (Edinburgh, 1828.)

Beethoven is the most celebrated of the living composers in Vienna and, in certain departments, the foremost of his day.[1] Though not an old man, he is lost to society in consequence of his extreme deafness, which has rendered him almost unsocial. The neglect of his person which he exhibits gives him a somewhat wild appearance. His features are strong and prominent; his eye is full of rude energy; his hair, which neither comb nor scissors seem to have visited for years, overshadows his broad brow in a quantity and confusion to which only the snakes round a Gorgon's head offer a parallel. His general behaviour does not ill accord with the unpromising exterior. Except when he is among his chosen friends, kindliness or affability are not his characteristics. The total loss of hearing has deprived him of all the pleasure which society can give, and perhaps soured his temper. He used to frequent a particular cellar, where he spent the evening in a corner, beyond the reach of all the chattering and disputation of a public room, drinking wine and beer, eating cheese and red herrings, and studying the newspapers. One evening a person took a seat near him whose countenance did not please him. He looked hard at the stranger, and spat on the floor as if he had seen a toad; then glanced at the newspaper, then again at the intruder, and spat again, his hair bristling gradually into more shaggy ferocity, till he closed the alternation of spitting and staring, by fairly exclaiming "What a scoundrelly phiz!" and rushing out of the room. Even among his oldest friends he must be

[1][Foot-note of Sir John.] Beethoven has died since this was written. He died, moreover, in want, amid a people who pretend to be the most devoted worshippers of music and musicians.

humoured like a wayward child. He has always a small paper book with him, and what conversation takes place is carried on in writing. In this, too, although it is not lined, he instantly jots down any musical idea which strikes him. These notes would be utterly unintelligible even to another musician, for they have thus no comparative value; he alone has in his own mind the thread by which he brings out of this labyrinth of dots and circles the richest and most astounding harmonies. The moment he is seated at the piano, he is evidently unconscious that there is anything in existence but himself and his instrument; and, considering how very deaf he is, it seems impossible that he should hear all he plays. Accordingly, when playing very *piano*, he often does not bring out a single note. He hears it himself in the "mind's ear." While his eye, and the almost imperceptible motion of his fingers, show that he is following out the strain in his own soul through all its dying gradations, the instrument is actually as dumb as the musician is deaf.

I have heard him play; but to bring him so far required some management, so great is his horror of being anything like exhibited. Had he been plainly asked to do the company that favour, he would have flatly refused; he had to be cheated into it. Every person left the room, except Beethoven and the master of the house, one of his most intimate acquaintances. These two carried on a conversation in the paper-book about bank stock. The gentleman, as if by chance, struck the keys of the open piano, beside which they were sitting, gradually began to run over one of Beethoven's own compositions, made a thousand errors, and speedily blundered one passage so thoroughly, that the composer condescended to stretch out his hand and put him right. It was enough; the hand was on the piano; his companion immediately left him, on some pretext, and joined the rest of the company, who in the next room, from which they

could see and hear everything, were patiently waiting
the issue of this tiresome conjuration. Beethoven, left
alone, seated himself at the piano. At first he only
struck now and then a few hurried and interrupted notes,
as if afraid of being detected in a crime; but gradually he
forgot everything else, and ran on during half an hour in
a fantasy, in a style extremely varied, and marked, above
all, by the most abrupt transitions. The amateurs were
enraptured; to the uninitiated it was more interesting
to observe how the music of the man's soul passed over
his countenance. He seems to feel the bold, the com-
manding, and the impetuous, more than what is soothing
or gentle. The muscles of the face swell, and its veins
start out; the wild eye rolls doubly wild, the mouth
quivers, and Beethoven looks like a wizard, overpowered
by the demons whom he himself has called up.

Rossini
(1822)

When Rossini in the spring of 1822 visited Vienna to attend the
première of his opera "Zelmira," he was lionized by high and low.
In terms of popular taste, the average music-lover of those days
probably would have called the indisputable genius of him who
created "Il Barbiere di Seviglia" greater than that of Beethoven.
Indeed, the "Rossini craze," as Thayer rather too harshly calls it,
with the change in public taste implied by it, had attracted many
away from the less bewitching art of Beethoven to that of the "Swan
of Pesaro." Their adulation might have gone to the head of a master
more conceited than Rossini and might conveniently have made
him forget the presence of Beethoven in Vienna. Not so with
Rossini; he was too sincere an admirer of Beethoven's art not to
make it a point to pay his respects to him in person. Strange to say,
Schindler and others dispute that the two ever met, but we have
Rossini's affirmative testimony to the contrary. In its most extensive form in the charming "Souvenirs personels. La Visite de R.
Wagner à Rossini" by E. Michotte, who introduced Wagner to
Rossini and made notes of the visit after it took place at Paris in
1860, but did not publish them until 1906. In the course of conversation, Wagner asked Rossini whether he had known Beethoven

Portrait of Beethoven by Stieler, 1819-1820
(Courtesy Edition Peters, Leipzig)

Two sketches of Beethoven by J. D. Böhm,
between 1820 and 1825

(Courtesy Beethovenhaus, Bonn)

personally. Rossini's reminiscent answer follows, extracted here as a monologue.

Yes, that is the truth; in Vienna, precisely at the time I spoke about, the year 1822, when my opera *Zelmira* was performed. I had heard at Milan quartets by Beethoven; needless to say with what admiration. Also, I knew some of his works for piano. At Vienna, I heard for the first time one of his symphonies, the *Eroica*. This music knocked me over. Henceforth I had but one idea: to make the acquaintance of this great genius, to see him, if only once. I approached Salieri whom I knew to be in touch with Beethoven, in the matter. . . . He thought best, in order to please me, to address himself to the Italian poet Carpani, who was *persona grata* with Beethoven . . . and obtained his consent to receive me.

Shall I confess it? When I mounted the stairs leading to the poor lodgings of the great man, I barely mastered my emotions. When the door opened, I found myself in a sort of attic terribly disordered and dirty. I remember particularly the ceiling. It was under the roof and showed crevices through which the rain could not help pouring down in streams.[1]

The portraits of Beethoven which we know, reproduce fairly well his physiognomy. But what no etcher's needle could express was the indefinable sadness spread over his features—while from under heavy eyebrows his eyes shone as from out of caverns and, though small, seemed to pierce one. The voice was soft and slightly veiled.

When we entered, at first he paid no attention to us but for some moments remained bent over proofs which he had just about finished. Then, raising his head, he said in fairly comprehensible Italian: "Ah! Rossini, you, the composer of the *Barbiere di Seviglia?* My congratulations; that is an excellent opera buffa; I have read it

---

[1]This was Beethoven's workroom; his living-quarters, which Rossini did not see, were on the lower floor and in somewhat better condition.

with pleasure and I enjoyed myself. It will be played so long as Italian opera will exist. Do never try your hand at anything but *opera buffa;* you would be doing violence to your destiny by wanting to succeed in a different *genre.*"

"But," interrupted Carpani who had accompanied me (of course, in German, and writing down his words in pencil because of the impossibility of conducting otherwise a conversation with Beethoven, which Carpani translated for me word for word), saying, "The *maestro* Rossini has composed numerous serious operas, *Tancredi, Otello, Mosè;* not so long ago I sent them to you suggesting that you examine them."

"Indeed, I did go through them," answered Beethoven, "but, you see, serious opera does not lie in the nature of the Italians. For the true drama, they know not enough of the science of music; and how should they acquire that in Italy?". . . . "In *opera buffa,*" he continued, "none can equal Italians. Your language and your temperament predestine you for it. Look at Cimarosa: how much superior the comic parts in his operas are to the rest! The same with Pergolesi. You Italians, I know, boast of his sacred music. I concede that the sentiment of his *Stabat* is very touching, but the form lacks variety, the effect is monotonous. On the other hand the *Serva padrona.* . . .

(Here Wagner interrupted Rossini; changing the subject. Before concluding his story about his visit to Beethoven, Rossini expressed pride in being a subscriber to and student of Bach's Complete Works and recorded his admiration for Bach in these memorable words: "Bach . . . is an overwhelming genius. If Beethoven is a prodigy of humanity, Bach is a miracle of God!").

Oh! The visit was short. That is easily understood because one side of the conversation had to be carried on in writing. I expressed to him all my admiration for his genius, all my gratitude for having given me the opportunity to express it. He answered with a deep sigh and the single word: "Oh! *un infelice.*" After a pause he inquired in some detail about the theatres in Italy, about the singers of reputation, whether one performed there often the operas of Mozart and whether I was satisfied with the Italian company at Vienna. Then, wishing me a good performance and success with *Zelmira*, he rose and conducted us back to the door with the remark: "Above all, do a lot 'of the Barber.'"

When I descended those dilapidated stairs, I retained of my visit to this great man an impression so painful— thinking of this destitution and shabbiness—that I could not repress my tears. "Ah!", said Carpani, "that's what he wants. He is a misanthrope, cranky and can't keep friends."

That very evening I attended a gala dinner at the palace of Prince Metternich. I was still upset by that visit, by that lugubrious *un infelice* which had remained in my ears. I confess, I could not rid myself in my heart of a sentiment of embarrassment when I saw myself, by comparison, treated with such consideration by that brilliant Viennese assembly. This led me to say loudly and without mincing words all I thought of the conduct of the Court and the aristocracy towards the greatest genius of the epoch, about whom one bothered so little and whom one left in such distress. The answer was identical with Carpani's. I asked whether nevertheless Beethoven's condition of deafness was not worthy of the deepest pity. . . . Whether it was really charitable to bring to the fore the weaknesses attributed to him in order to find motives for refusing to help him? I added that this would be very easy by means of subscriptions for a very small amount, if all the rich families pledged themselves, to assure him of an annuity large enough to place him for the rest of his life beyond real want. This proposition obtained support from nobody.

After dinner, the evening ended with a reception which assembled in the Metternich salons the foremost names of Viennese society.   There was also a concert.   On the program figured one of the most recently published Trios of Beethoven . . . always *he,* he everywhere, as one says of Napoleon.   The new masterwork was listened to with religious respect and obtained a resplendent success. Hearing it in the midst of all those mundane magnificences, I said to myself sadly that perhaps at that very moment the great man was creating in the isolation of his attic some work of deep inspiration, destined, like his previous ones, to initiate into sublime beauties this same brilliant aristocracy from which he was excluded and which, given over to its pleasures, did not worry about the misery of him who had furnished the pleasures.

Not having succeeded with my attempt to start an annuity-fund for Beethoven, I did not lose courage.   I tried to collect the necessary funds for buying him a house.   I did obtain a few promises of subscription, but, inclusive of my own, the final result was very meagre. Consequently I had to abandon this second project, too.   The general answer was: "You do not know Beethoven.   On the day after he finds himself the owner of a house, he will sell it.   He will never know how to adjust himself to a permanent home; he feels the need of changing his lodgings every six months and his servant every six weeks. . . .

ROCHLITZ
(1822)

Beethoven realized that sooner or later his importance for musical history would warrant an authoritative biography.   In 1826 he endorsed the irresponsible plan of his "Mephisto," as Karl Holz has been called and not quite unjustly, to become his official biographer, but his final and much more adequate choice was Friedrich Johann Rochlitz (1760-1842) who, however, declined the honor, not considering himself competent enough for such a task.   As editor of the influential "Allgemeine Musikalische Zeitung" Rochlitz had done much to form professional and public opinion in favor of Beethoven, but he was not a blind admirer of Beethoven and precisely this critical, though in the main admiring, attitude towards his works inspired Beethoven with respect for Rochlitz. He made the personal acquaintance of Beethoven in the summer of 1822, recorded his impressions originally in letters and then incorporated them in the fourth volume of his essays "Für Freunde der Tonkunst" (1830-32).

I never had seen Beethoven and hence wished all the more that our meeting might take place as soon as possible. No later than the third day of my arrival I spoke about it to N. N., his intimate friend. "He lives out in the country," said the latter. "Then let us drive out there!" "That we can do, but his unfortunate deafness has little by little made him quite unsociable. He knows that you want to visit him; he wishes to make your personal acquaintance; but at the same time we cannot be sure but that, when he sees us arrive, he will not run away because, just as he is sometimes full of the most spontaneous merriment, so he often is seized by the profoundest melancholy. It strikes him out of the blue, without any cause, and he is unable to make head against it. But he comes to town at least once a week, at which times he always sees us, because we attend to his letters and the like. Then he usually is in good spirits and we have him where he cannot escape. So if you are willing to humor the poor, tortured soul to the extent of letting us inform you at once and then—it is only a matter of a few steps—come in as though by chance. . . ."

Of course, I was more than glad to accede to his proposal. The next Saturday morning the messenger came to me. I went and found Beethoven conducting a lively conversation with N. N. The latter is used to him and understands him fairly well, reading his words from the movements of his face and lips. Beethoven seemed to be pleased, yet he was disturbed. And had I not been prepared in advance, his appearance would have disturbed me as well.   Not his neglected, almost uncivilized outward semblance, not the thick black hair which bristled about his head and the like, but his appearance as a whole.   Picture to yourself a man of approximately fifty years of age, small rather than of medium size, but with a very powerful, stumpy figure, compact and with a notably strong bone structure, about like that of Fichte, but fleshier, and, especially, with a rounder, fuller face; a red, healthy complexion; restless, glowing, and when his gaze is fixed even piercing eyes; not given to movement and when moving, moving hastily; with regard to his facial expression, especially that of the eyes, intelligent and full of life, offering a mingling or an occasional momentary alteration of the heartiest amiability and shyness; in his whole attitude that tension, that uneasy, worried striving to hear peculiar to the deaf who are keenly sensitive; now a merrily and freely spoken word; again, immediately after, a relapse into gloomy silence; and in addition, all that which the thinker and meditator himself contributes and which is continually sounding together with all the rest—such is the man who has given happiness to millions, a purely spiritual happiness.

In broken sentences he made some friendly and amiable remarks to me.   I raised my voice as much as I could, spoke slowly, with sharp accentuation, and thus out of the fulness of my heart conveyed to him my gratitude for his works and all they meant to me and would mean to me while life endured.   I signaled out some of my favorites, and dwelt upon them; told him how his symphonies were performed in model fashion in Leipzig, how all of them were played each recurring winter season, and of the loud delight with which the public received them.   He stood close beside me, now gazing on my face with strained attention, now dropping his head. Then he would smile to himself, nod amiably on occasion, all without saying a word.   Had he understood me?

Had he failed to understand? At last I had to make an end, and he gave my hand a powerful grip and said curtly to N. N.: "I still have a few necessary errands to do." Then, as he left, he said: "Shall we not see each other again?" N. N. now returned. "Did he understand what I said?" I queried. I was deeply moved and affected. N. N. shrugged his shoulders. "Not a word!" For a long time we were silent and I cannot say how affected I was. Finally I asked, "Why did you not at least repeat this or that to him, since he understands you fairly well?" "I did not wish to interrupt you and, besides, he very easily gets sensitive. And I really hoped he would understand much of what you said, but the noise in the street, your speech, to which he is unaccustomed and, perhaps, his own eagerness to understand everything, since it was perfectly clear to him that you were telling him pleasant things. . . . He was so unhappy." I cannot describe the sensations which filled me as I left. The man who solaced the whole world with the voice of his music, heard no other human voice, not even that of one who wished to thank him. Aye, it even became an instrument of torture for him. I had my mind made up not to see him again, and to send Mr. Härtel's proposal to him in writing.

Some two weeks later I was about to go to dinner when I met the young composer Franz Schubert, an enthusiastic admirer of Beethoven. The latter had spoken to Schubert concerning me. "If you wish to see him in a more natural and jovial mood," said Schubert, "then go and eat your dinner this very minute at the inn where he has just gone for the same purpose." He took me with him. Most of the places were taken. Beethoven sat among several acquaintances who were strangers to me. He really seemed to be in good spirits and acknowledged my greeting, but I purposely did not cross over to him. Yet I found a seat from which I could see him and, since he spoke loud enough, also could hear nearly all that he said. It could not actually be called a conversation, for he spoke in monologue, usually at some length, and more as though by hapchance and at random.

Those about him contributed little, merely laughing or nodding their approval. He philosophized, or one might even say politicized, after his own fashion. He spoke of England and the English, and of how both were associated in his thoughts with a splendor incomparable—which, in part, sounded tolerably fantastic. Then he told all sorts of stories of the French, from the days of the second occupation of Vienna. For them he had no kind words. His remarks all were made with the greatest unconcern and without the least reserve, and whatever he said was spiced with highly original, naïve judgments or humorous fancies. He impressed me as being a man with a rich, aggressive intellect, an unlimited, never resting imagination. I saw him as one who, had he been cast away on a desert isle when no more than a growing, capable boy, would have taken all he had lived and learned, all that had stuck to him in the way of knowledge, and there have meditated and brooded over his material until his fragments had become a whole, his imaginings turned to convictions which he would have shouted out into the world in all security and confidence.

When he had finished his meal he rose and came over to me. "And is all well with you in this old Vienna of ours?" he asked amiably. I answered in the affirmative by signs, drank to his health and asked him to pledge me. He accepted, but beckoned me to a little side-room. This suited me to a T. I took the bottle and followed him. Here we were by ourselves, save for an occasional peeper who soon made himself scarce. He offered me a little tablet upon which I was to write down whatever my signs did not make clear. He began by praising Leipzig and its music; that is to say the music chosen for performance in the churches, at concerts and in the theatre.

Otherwise he knew nothing of Leipzig and had only passed through the city when a youth on his way to Vienna. "And even though nothing is printed about the performances but the dry records, still I read them with pleasure," he said. "One cannot help but notice that they are intelligent and well inclined toward all. Here, on the contrary. . . ." Then he started in, rudely enough, nor would he let himself be stopped. He came to speak of himself: "You will hear nothing of me here." "It is summer now," I wrote. "No, nor in winter either!" he cried. "What should you hear? 'Fidelio'? They cannot give it, nor do they want to listen to it. The symphonies? They have no time for them.[1] My concertos? Everyone grinds out only the stuff he himself has made. The solo pieces? They went out of fashion here long ago, and here fashion is everything. At the most Shuppanzigh occasionally digs up a quartet, etc." And despite all the exaggeration in what he said a modicum of reason and truth remains. At last he had relieved himself and harked back to Leipzig. "But," said he, "you really live in Weimar, do you not?" He probably thought so because of my address. I shook my head. "Then it is not likely that you know the great Goethe?" I nodded my head vigorously. "I know him, too," said Beethoven, throwing out his chest, while an expression of the most radiant pleasure overspread his face.

"It was in Karlsbad[2] that I made his acquaintance—God only knows how long ago! At that time I was not yet altogether deaf, as I now am, though I heard with great difficulty. And what patience the great man had with me! What did he not do for me!" He told numerous little anecdotes and gave the most enjoyable details. "How happy it all made me at the time! I would have died for him ten times over. Then, while

---

[1] They were, however, repeatedly performed.
[2] Not at Karlsbad, but at Teplitz in 1812.

I still was head over heels in trouble, I thought out my
music for his 'Egmont'; and I did make a success of it,
did I not?" I was prodigal of each and every movement
which might indicate acquiescence and pleasure. Then
I set down that we gave this music, not only whenever
"Egmont" was performed, but almost every year at
least once in concert, with a kind of explanation, mainly
made up of a summarization of those scenes of the drama
with which the music is most intimately concerned. "I
know! I know!" he cried. "Since that Karlsbad summer I read Goethe every day—that is, when I read at
all. He killed Klopstock for me. You are surprised?
Now you are laughing? Aha, it is because I used to
read Klopstock! For years I put up with him, when I
took my walks and elsewhere. Well, then, it is true that
I did not always know at what he was driving. He hops
about so from pillar to post; and he always begins altogether too much from top to bottom. Always *maestoso*
and in D-flat major! Is it not so? Yet he is lofty and
he uplifts the soul. When I did not understand him,
then I made my guess and comprehended more or less.
If only he did not want to die all the time! Death comes
soon enough to all of us. Well, at any rate, what he
writes always sounds well. But Goethe—he is alive,
and he wants us all to live with him. That is why he
can be set to music. There is no one who lends himself
to musical setting as well as he. I do not like to write
songs. . . ."

Here, dear Härtel, I had the most wonderful opportunity to present your idea and execute your com-
mission. I wrote down your suggestion[1] and your pledge,
looking as serious as possible the while. He read it.
"Ha!" he cried and flung up his hand. "That would
be a man-sized job! That might yield something!" He
went on in this fashion for a time, picturing the thought
to himself in a manner anything but inept, while, with

To compose a setting of "Faust." Beethoven already had this in mind in 1808.

his head thrown back, he stared at the ceiling. "But," he next began, "for some time past I have been carrying about with me the idea of three other great works. Already I have hatched out much in connection with them, that is to say, in my head. These I must first get rid of: two great symphonies (the Ninth and the Tenth, which last never came to be performed) each different from the other, and each also different from all my other ones, and an oratorio. And that will be a long-winded affair; for you see, for some time past I find I no longer settle down to write so easily. I sit and think and think and what I have to say is all there, but it will not get down to paper. I dread beginning works of such magnitude. Once I have begun, then, all goes well...." And in this strain he continued for a long time. I have my doubts anent the success of your idea. Yet let us live in hopes, since the suggestion has caught his fancy, and he assured me again and again that he would not forget it.

Our third meeting was the merriest of all. He came here, to Baden, this time looking quite neat and clean and even elegant. Yet this did not prevent him—it was a warm day—from taking a walk in the Helenental. This means on the road all, even the Emperor and the imperial family, travel, and where everyone crowds past everyone else on the usually narrow path; and there he took off his fine black frockcoat, slung it across his shoulder from a stick, and wandered along in his shirt-sleeves. He stayed from about ten in the forenoon to six o'clock in the evening. His friends Jener and Gebauer kept him company. During the entire visit he was uncommonly gay and at times most amusing, and all that entered his mind had to come out. ("Well, it happens that I am unbuttoned to-day," he said and the remark was decidedly in order.) His talk and his actions all formed a chain of eccentricities, in part most peculiar. Yet they all radiated a truly childlike amiability, carelessness, and confidence in every one who

approached him. Even his barking tirades—like that
against his Viennese contemporaries, which I already
have mentioned—are only explosions of his fanciful
imagination and his momentary excitement. They are
uttered without haughtiness, without any feeling of
bitterness and hatefulness—and are simply blustered out
lightly, good-humoredly, the offsprings of a mad, humorous mood. In his life he often shows—and for the
sake of his own subsistence only too often and too decidedly—that to the very person who has grievously
injured him, whom he has most violently denounced one
moment, he will give his last dollar the next, should
that person need it.

To this we must add the most cheerful recognition of
merit in others, if only it be distinctive and individual.
(How he speaks of Handel, Bach, Mozart!) He does
not, however, where his greater works are concerned,
allow others to find fault (and who would have the
right to do so?) yet he never actually overvalues them;
and with regard to his lesser things is more inclined, perhaps, to abandon them with a laugh than any other
person. He does this the more since once he is in the
vein, rough, striking witticisms, droll conceits, surprising and exciting paradoxes suggest themselves to him in a
continuous flow. Hence in all seriousness I claim that
he even appears to be amiable. Or if you shrink from
this word, I might say that the dark, unlicked bear
seems so ingenuous and confiding, growls and shakes his
shaggy pelt so harmlessly and grotesquely that it is a
pleasure, and one has to be kind to him, even though he
were nothing but a bear in fact and had done no more
than a bear's best.

The tale of this particular day, however, or rather
the sum total of his little original storiettes, I shall have
to reserve to communicate to you verbally, otherwise
how shall I, a guest at this health resort, who is not
supposed to write, ever end my letter. Nevertheless,

when I had thrust our good Beethoven into the carriage and was walking up and down in this charming valley, I once more felt very serious. This time my reflections did not turn only, as on the first time I met him, on the grievous complaint with which fate had afflicted Beethoven. After all, I realized that he also had his hours of great gladness and perfect happiness. In other hours, also good ones, he lived in his art or in his plans and dreams regarding it; the evil hours, however, are thrown into the bargain and he takes them, pours out his soul with regard to them and then forgets them. After all, who may claim to be any better off?

Wilhelmine Schröder-Devrient
(1822)

This great dramatic artist (1804-1860) made her operatic *début* in 1821 as "Pamina" in Mozart's "Magic Flute." The very next year she established herself as one of the consummate artists of her time as "Leonore" in Beethoven's opera "Fidelio." Indeed, this until then ill-fated work owed much of its rise to permanent popularity to her. Richard Wagner's admiration for her is well attested by his treatise "About Actors and Singers" (1872). Two years before her death she received an offer to tour America, but could not accept it. The following reminiscences of Beethoven she contributed in 1846 to Schilling's "Beethoven Album."

It was in the year 1823 [actually November 3, 1822] when for the birthday of the defunct Emperor Francis I, Beethoven's "Fidelio," which had been lying dormant for several years, was put in rehearsal again at the Vienna *Kärnthnertor* theatre. My children's shoes no more than discarded, I already had made my first timid attempts as a budding singer and probably owing more to the lack of some other, more fitting impersonatrix, than because of any conviction that I already was capable of singing the rôle of Leonore, that difficult part was entrusted to me.

With youthful unconcern, and far removed from realizing the magnitude of my task, I undertook the study of the rôle to which, at a later period, I was principally indebted for the fact that my name was mentioned abroad among the names of other German artists with especial recognition. Under the guidance of my intelligent mother many a trait of Leonore's character became clear to me; at the same time I was still too young, too little developed inwardly completely to conceive what was taking place in Leonore's soul; those emotions for which Beethoven had found his immortal harmonies. At the rehearsals, directed by the then conductor Umlauf, the inadequacies of my undeveloped child voice were soon recognized, and many alterations were made in my part so that it would not suffer too greatly in effect. The last rehearsals already had been announced when, before the dress rehearsal, I learned that Beethoven had requested the honor of conducting his work himself on the ceremonial day. At this news I was seized with a nameless dread, and I still recall my illimitable awkwardness at the last rehearsal, which had driven my poor mother and the assisting artists who surrounded me to despair.

But Beethoven sat in the orchestra and waved his baton above the heads of us all, and I never had seen the man before!

At that time the Master's physical ear already was deaf to all tone. With confusion written on his face, with a more than earthly enthusiasm in his eye, swinging his baton too and fro with violent motions, he stood in the midst of the playing musicians and did not hear a single note! When he thought they should play *piano*, he almost crept under the conductor's desk, and when he wanted a *forte*, he leaped high into the air with the strangest gestures, uttering the weirdest sounds. With each succeeding number we grew more intimidated, and I felt as though I were gazing at one of Hoffmann's fantastic figures which had popped up before me.   It was unavoidable that the deaf Master should throw singers and orchestra into the greatest confusion and put them entirely off beat until none knew where they were at. Of all this, however, Beethoven was entirely unconscious, and thus with the utmost difficulty we concluded a rehearsal with which he seemed altogether content, for he laid down his baton with a happy smile.

Yet it was impossible to entrust the performance itself to him, and Conductor Umlauf had to charge himself with the heart-rending business of calling his attention to the fact that the opera could not be given under his direction.   He is said to have resigned himself with a sorrowful heavenward glance; and I found him sitting behind Umlauf in the orchestra the following evening, lost in profound meditation.   You probably know with what enthusiasm the Vienna public greeted "Fidelio" on that occasion, and also that since that performance this immortal work has found a permanent place in the repertoire of the German operatic stage.   Every artist taking part in the performance accomplished his task that evening with enthusiastic devotion; for who would not gladly **have** given his last breath for the wretched Master who heard nothing of all the beauty and glory he had created!   Beethoven followed the entire performance with strained attention, and it seemed as though he were trying to gather from each of our movements whether we had at least half understood his meaning.

In those days they already insisted on calling me a little genius; and that evening it really seemed as though a more matured spirit possessed me, for several genial original traits flashed up in my portrayal which could not have escaped Beethoven's notice, since he himself, the exalted Master, came the following day to express **to** me his thanks and recognition.   I moistened the hand he offered me with hot tears, and in my joy would **have** **exchanged** all the earth's worldly possessions for this

praise from Beethoven's lips. He promised me at the
time to write an opera for me, but unfortunately that
was as far as it went. Soon afterward I left Vienna and
a few years later Beethoven's lofty spirit winged its way
back to that primal bourne from whence it had come.
He did not live to see his "Fidelio" become domiciled
in the capitals of France and Albion, nor to realize that
his childishly timid Leonore of 1823, who later herself
had developed a greater comprehension of his genius,
was able to do her part in securing due and full recognition for so tremendous a work in its German fatherland
as well. The consciousness of having laid down even
one more wreath in Beethoven's spreading hall of fame—
whom would it not fill with joy? And so may these
lines also testify to the gratitude, the veneration I have
vowed and shall continue to vow his lofty spirit as long
as I live.

LOUIS SCHLÖSSER
(1822–1823)

Among the few composers of the nineteenth century who could
truthfully claim to have profited from Beethoven's personal advice
and suggestions was Louis Schlösser (1800-1886), for many years
Court-conductor at Darmstadt. He made Beethoven's acquaintance in 1822 but apparently did not record his impressions in print
until 1885. This interval of more than sixty years may account for
certain obvious embellishments. Also, as so often happens to
autobiographical reminiscences, for an evident conflict between
fact and memory: Schlösser described his leave-taking from Beethoven, on which occasion the master entrusted him with letters to
Cherubini and Schlesinger, as towards the end of May, 1823. This
must have happened early in May for the simple reason that Beethoven's (preserved) letter of credentials and instructions is dated
May 6, 1823.

A journey from my home in Vienna, in the spring of
1822, in the days when carriage-wheels did not yet roar
along iron rails, and the piercing bell-tone and shrilling
whistle of the locomotive did not yet shock auditory

nerves, although the stifling air of the hurrying mail-coach, breathed for several days and nights in succession, on the other hand, which had a dreadful effect on the respiratory organs, was anything but pleasant for a twenty-one-year old disciple of art. Yet the firm conviction that I would extend my fund of knowledge under the auspices of the great local artists of Vienna and the promise, due to the recommendation of my patron Spohr, of receiving lessons from Ignaz von Seyfried, Mayseder and Worzischek, banished all other considerations. Boldly starting out on my pilgrimage, after making a short stop during the Easter holidays in Munich, I made my entry, one fine spring day, into the capital on the blue Danube. And in truth, I could have chosen no more favorable time at which to arrive there. Besides Beethoven, the unattainable, there shone each in his relative, proportionate sphere: Rossini, the Swan of Pesaro, K. M. von Weber, the composer of "Der Freischütz," the older masters Gyrowetz, Kreutzer, Salieri, Weigl, Abbé Stadler, young Franz Schubert, etc. In the theatre at the *Kärnthner* Gate, it was possible to listen to German and Italian opera presented by vocal stars of the very first magnitude in so admirable a fashion that, perhaps, a similar ensemble may not again be heard. On the other hand, church music under Salieri and Eybler, the two Court choir conductors, though not on the same level with the opera; the oratorio societies of Kiesewetter and Mosel; the chamber music concerts of the famous quartet players Schuppanzigh, Mayseder, Holz, Linck, Merk, etc.; and, finally, the literary assemblies in the homes of the poets Castelli, Grillparzer, Auersperg, etc., had an incalculable influence on the music and poesy of this period. If one visualizes this collective achievement, this emulation in productivity, then that epoch of the immediate past may without qualification be described as a brilliant period of æsthetic culture.

Filled with such impressions, in constant touch with the men already named, months had elapsed since my arrival, yet in spite of every effort I had hitherto been unable to see the most sublime of them all, Beethoven, and speak with him.   I had not even been able to find out positively where he lived, since he not only frequently changed his lodging-place, but actually rented various lodgings at the same time, and, in addition, also spent weeks in the outskirts of Baden without any one knowing of it.   Seyfried advised me to inquire after Beethoven between the hours of twelve and one in the Haslinger music house, since there I would be most likely to meet him; and Schuppanzigh accompanied me to a coffee-house where he was wont to read the newspaper. On innumerable occasions I inquired here, there and elsewhere, yet always with the same lack of success. Then, suddenly, as though to put an end to my discouragement, I one day—it was November 4, 1822—to my no little joy, saw the opera "Fidelio" announced on the theatre programme: Wilhelmine Schröder in the title-rôle, Haitzinger as Florestan, Forti as Pizarro and so on, all the other parts taken by artists of the first rank. What a plentitude of enjoyment did not that evening promise me, who never yet had heard this unique dramatic creation by Beethoven!   A whole hour before the opera began I pushed my way up to the box-office, in order to secure a decent seat; for "Fidelio" had not been given for years.   I listened to a performance which was a model in every respect and the impression it made upon me was overpowering.

Napoleon's headquarters had been established at Schönbrunn(1805), and then French soldiers had filled the body of the opera house.   Is it conceivable that the ethic purity and chaste beauty of a work whose very language they did not understand could have aroused a familiar echo in these passing guests used to a more frivolous fare?   Feverishly excited by the wonderful closing hymn, that apotheosis of faithful conjugal devotion, I hardly noticed that the house was gradually growing empty; until my faithful friend Franz Schubert seized my arm to accompany me to the exit. Together with us, three gentlemen, to whom I paid no further attention because their backs were turned to me, stepped out of a lower corridor; yet I was not a little surprised to see all those who were streaming by toward the lobby crowding to one side, in order to give the three plenty of room. Then Schubert very softly plucked my sleeve, pointing with his finger to the gentleman in the middle, who turned his head at that moment so that the bright light of the lamps fell on it and—I saw, familiar to me from engravings and paintings, the features of the creator of the opera I had just heard, Beethoven himself. My heart beat twice as loudly at that moment; all the things I may have said to Schubert I now no longer recall; but I well remember that I followed the Desired One and his companions (Schindler and Breuning, as I later discovered) like a shadow through crooked alleys and past high, gable-roofed houses, followed him until the darkness hid him from sight.

The more strongly the recollection of that evening when I had seen him for the first time increased my longing, the more plans I made regarding the manner in which I might be able to pay my homage to him in person, for I had learned from many sources that he usually declined to receive strangers and, in general, had intercourse with only a few persons, who had long been his intimates. Nor would an epistolary plea have met with better success. What I regarded as impossible of attainment, however, was granted me, like so much in life, through a lucky chance. The ambassador of the Grand-Duke of Hessia, my fellow-countryman Baron von Türckheim, a highly cultured art-lover who seldom missed a musical production, especially an opera, expected me, as a rule, to appear the morning after a performance in his house, where we exchanged our criticisms of what we had heard. Our discussion the day after "Fidelio" was briefer than usual for, interrupting it in the middle, my diplomatic friend began: "You have often stated that you wished you could be introduced to Beethoven. I am so placed that I can gratify your wish at once. Read this letter, it concerns the request sent by Beethoven to the Grand-Duke (to subscribe for a manuscript copy of the *Missa solemnis*) and I have just received the response granting Beethoven's petition in terms of the most appreciative praise for the famous composer. Perhaps you would like to see that it reaches its address, *Kotgasse* No. 60, first flight up, the door to the left? Here is the dispatch, sealed with the Grand-Ducal seal!"

The delight with which I seized the missive mocks all effort at description; and the thought of soon seeing Beethoven thrust every other sensation into the background. I had no more than hastily thanked the good Baron than I hurried down into the street and threw myself into the first carriage which came my way, loudly shouting the address of the house—No. 60, *Wiedener* suburb—as I did so. My fancy had painted the happiest pictures of Beethoven's home, but the nearer I drew to it toward the end of my drive, moving uphill between the steep rows of housefronts in the uncomfortable *Kotgasse* and finally stopping before a low, mean-looking house with a rough stone stairway leading to its entrance, the greater my surprise and an emotion I could not suppress at the thought of hunting up the great tone poet amid such surroundings.

Opposite, in a workshop open to the street, a herculean bell-founder, like Vulcan the Smith, swung a most hefty hammer, so that the strident blows made the air tremble within a wide radius, and drove me as quickly as possible into the interior of the house No. 60, where, without paying any attention to a man, presumably the proprietor, who stepped forward to meet me on the threshold, I at once hurried up the uncomfortable, nearly dark stairs to the first story, door at the left. At times one is overtaken by moods which do not admit of verbal expression and which instinctively, at the thought of soon confronting some extraordinary celebrity, occasion a shyness beyond control. This was my case when, since neither servant nor maid appeared, I carefully opened the outer door and—quite unsuspecting, found myself standing in a kitchen, through which one had to pass to gain the living-rooms. At any rate, I never knew of any other way, for on every subsequent occasion when I came to Beethoven and remained a long time, he himself, at parting, invariably led me through this kitchen anteroom to the stairs. After repeatedly knocking in vain at the real living-room door, I entered and found myself in a rather commodious but entirely undecorated apartment; a large, four-square oak table with various chairs, which presented a somewhat chaotic aspect, stood in the middle of the room. On it lay writing-books and lead-pencils, music-paper and pens, a chronometer, a metronome, an ear-trumpet made of yellow metal and various other things. On the wall at the left of the door was the bed, completely covered with music, scores and manuscripts. I can recall only a framed oil-painting (it was a portrait of Beethoven's grandfather for whom, as is known, he had a child-like reverence) which was the sole ornament I noticed. Two deep window-niches, covered with smooth paneling I mention only because in the first a violin and a bow hung from a nail, and in the other Beethoven himself, his back to me, stood busily writing down figures and the like on the wood, already covered with scribblings.

The deaf Master had not heard me enter, and it was only by stamping vigorously with my feet that I managed to attract his notice and he at once turned around, surprised to see a young stranger standing before him.

Yet before I could address a single word to him, he commenced to excuse himself in the politest manner imaginable because he had not sent out his housekeeper, and
no one had been in attendance to announce me, the while
quickly drawing on his coat; and then first asking me
what I wished. Standing so near this artist, crowned
with glory, I could realize the impression which his distinguished personality, his characteristic head, with its
surrounding mane of heavy hair and the furrowed brow
of a thinker, could not help but make on every one. I
could look into those profoundly serious eyes, note the
amiably smiling expression of his mouth when he spoke,
his words always being received with great interest.

My visit probably occurred shortly after he had eaten
breakfast, for he repeatedly passed the napkin lying beside him across his snow-white teeth, a habit, incidentally,
in which I noticed he often indulged. Steeped in my
contemplation of him I entirely forgot the unfortunate
man's total deafness, and was just about to explain my
reason for being there to him when, fortunately, I recalled the uselessness of speaking at the last moment, and
instead reverentially handed him the letter with its
great seal. After he had carefully opened it and read
its contents his features visibly brightened; he pressed
my hands gratefully, and after I had given him my visiting-card, expressed his pleasure at my visit and added
(I shall use his very language): "These are heartening
words which I have read. Your Grand-Duke expresses
himself not alone like a princely Mæcenas, but like a
thorough musical connoisseur with comprehensive knowledge. It is not only his acceptance of my work which
pleases me, but the value he attaches to art in general,
and the recognition he concedes my activities." He had
seized his ear-trumpet, so I explained the unbounded
veneration accorded his genial works, with what enthusiasm they were heard, and what an influence the
perfection of his intellectual creations had exercised on

the cultural level of the day. Though Beethoven was so impervious to flattery of any kind, my words which came stammering from the depths of my soul, nevertheless seemed to touch him, and this induced me to tell about my nocturnal pursuit of him after the performance of "Fidelio." "But what prevented you from coming to see me in person?" he asked. "I am sure you have been told any amount of contradictory nonsense; that I have been described as being an uncomfortable, capricious and arrogant person, whose music one might indeed enjoy, but who personally was to be avoided. I know these evil, lying tongues, but if the world considers me heartless, because I seldom meet people who understand my thoughts and feelings, and therefore content myself with a few friends, it wrongs me."

He had put down his ear-trumpet, for speaking into it agitated his nerves too greatly; his complaint, so he insisted, did not lie in the weakness of the auditory canals, but was seated in the intestines; his physicians in treating him had made a false diagnosis their point of departure, etc. In fact, our conversation continued as follows: I wrote down briefly the short questions and bits of information which I addressed to him on the sheets of paper lying at hand, and he then answered in the greatest detail, so that not only did no hiatus ever occur but his calmness and patience when I asked him to explain certain passages in his scores actually astonished me. Under these circumstances, in which the sovereignty of his genius breaks through every constricting barrier, whereas a critical pedantry would consider such ventures unsurmountable, he expressed himself with a conviction which carried one away with it. At times, in these conversations, he let fall many sarcastic remarks about the actual art currents of the day in Vienna, which slumbered profoundly under the spell of Italian superficiality, and with no less sharpness did he express himself anent the speechlessness of various princely gentlemen, a matter which was not made clear to me until later, and then in a far more drastic manner.

Greatly pleased with the unanticipated success of this visit, I made no bones of informing him of the purpose my stay in Vienna, and the choice of my teachers, of which he approved. Of his own accord he asked me to show him some of my work in order to be able to judge my capabilities. It happened that I had just completed a cantata for solos, choruses and orchestra, as well as an overture and entr'acte music to the tragedy "Correggio." "You had better send both to me or, still better, bring them to me the day after to-morrow yourself and eat here at noon. It is true that I cannot offer you a splendid dinner, but neither one of us shall rise hungry from the table. *Ça suffit!*" he added, for from time to time he liked to inject a few French words (with Cherubini, so the latter told me personally, when he was in Vienna in 1804, Beethoven had conversed only in French). Then he wrote down his address for me on a square sheet of paper which I have treasured like a relic to this day, and in exchange for which I handed him my own, the Archduke Charles Hotel, in the *Kärnthnergasse* fourth floor, and then took my leave.

Arrived home and walking up and down in my room, the event of the day seemed almost like a beautiful dream. Was this actually the incomparable tonal hero, accorded the most devoted reverence by all classes, whose genius, by striking the shackles from the infinity of the psychic had called into being a new era of culture, the productions of whose intellect had established the superiority of German tonal art in every part of the civilized world? And to-day, in my presence, this depth of sentience, the renunciation of all external glory, and the personal sympathy which he had accorded me and my youthful ambitions, my reaction to which was to represent such a precious gain to me at a future day. "Do not hesitate to avail yourself of me whenever I can be useful to you or be of service to you in any way," had been his parting words.

All my friends assured me that I had been received by Beethoven in an extremely rare and exceptional manner.

Spring had appeared almost overnight, and it was on March 3, a sunny morning that, waiting for the hour of my invitation to strike, I was improving this and that in my cantata, dressed in my best and seated at the piano, when the servant opened the door and—to my anything but small surprise Beethoven stood on the threshold. I could hardly believe my eyes: the famous composer had not balked at the four flights of steps in order to pay me, a neophyte of only twenty years of age, a return visit. What I did and said in my first confusion I do not know; he, on the other hand, well aware of my embarrassment, at once began to speak: he had called, in order since it was such a pleasant day, to take me along for a little walk before dinner, and to improve the occasion by making the acquaintance of my lodgings, instruments, music and pictures of my parents, which I had mentioned to him. And he actually began to turn the pages of my copy-books of contrapuntal exercises, to look over my little hand-library, in which he found his favorites, Homer and Goethe, and I even had to submit to him a drawing of mine, and all of these things he examined attentively and praised. That I was flushed with joy at being permitted to walk through the thronged streets on the way to the *Volksgarten* beside the man I reverenced, and to what degree his intelligent remarks and his comprehensive knowledge allowed me to recognize the lofty flight of his genius in every direction, I need not stress. At such moments when, full of his subject, he spoke, the wealth of ideas which escaped his mouth appeared truly astonishing.

During our absence his housekeeper had made all the necessary preparations. The table and the dinner

were most painstakingly served, so that all ran like
clockwork. Beethoven was a very model of a paternal
Amphytrion in word and in deed. He continually
apologized for his bachelor housekeeping (which on this
day, at all events, called for no apologies), never wearied
of conversing, and also mentioned the time when he, a
youth of no more than twenty-two years of age, after
the death of his father Johann (who died December 18,
1792) had for the second time made a pilgrimage to
Vienna, which since that time he never again had left.
The coffee he himself prepared with a newly-discovered
machine, whose construction he even explained to me
in great detail. We drank it in an adjoining room which,
although the door always stood open, I never yet had
entered. There I also saw the magnificent grand piano
by Broadwood, and on it the *de luxe* edition of Handel's
works: both had been presented to him by London,
and one volume lay open on the piano-rack.

Did he still play on occasion? I never heard him do
so, but seized the opportunity to remark to him how, at
one time, it had been feared he might in the future make
his home in England, abandoning his homeland, friends
and admirers, and what grief the news of this projected
transmigration had called forth in Germany. It may be
that I had roused recollection of many a bitter experience by touching on this theme, that I had unconsciously opened wounds but scarce healed, for his depression unquestionably testified to the fact; although
this innocent confession, which bore witness of my lively
interest, by no possible chance could have hurt him.
Nor did it, for after he had several times passed his hand
across his forehead, he replied: "In former years I did,
to tell the truth, resolve to leave Vienna. Reasons
which had nothing to do with my profession induced me
to make the resolve, and besides I had received offers
from abroad, especially from England and from Cassel,
which guaranteed me a much larger income, and this

weighed heavily with me in view of my circumstances. My imperial patron and pupil, the Archduke Rudolf, was highly dismayed when he heard of my resolve: 'No, no,' he cried, 'that must never happen! Never should you leave the spot which a Mozart and a Haydn have hallowed before you! And where in the world could you find another Vienna? I shall speak to my brother, the Emperor Francis, I shall speak to Esterhazy, Liechtenstein, Palffy, Lobkowitz, Karoly, to all the princes, so that you are guaranteed a regular, adequate salary which will secure you against all worry anent your existence.' " "And what happened then?" I asked? "I remained, kept on composing, giving my concerts and *Akademien* after the gentlemen, headed by Archduke Rudolf, had agreed to pay me a certain amount, and I had no suspicion these legally binding responsibilities ever would be subject to change; yet something happened which I never had suspected, they did not keep their word.[1] After all, of what concern were those ideals which are interwoven in an artist's life to the aristocracy of birth and fortune!" And he added bitterly: "I must work so that I have enough to live."

To hear such words come from his mouth cut me to the soul; I had not expected them. Yet I hesitated to voice my own opinion regarding this breach of faith, since the communication had visibly excited him. Hence I sought to give his thoughts another direction, by again reverting to the enthusiasm which "Fidelio" so recently had aroused, and remarking in that connection that the hitherto existing lack of understanding for the work had at last been broken down, and that German art looked forward with longing to a new dramatic creation of his pen. "Yet where am I to find a good opera-book, one which appeals to me?" he replied. "I have received verses according to agreement from many poets, but they have no idea of the requisites necessary to the mu-

---

[1]This unjust suspicion had become an *idée fixe* with Beethoven.

sician, and I shall never set frivolous subjects to music. Grillparzer promised me a book, 'Melusine,' and I have more confidence in him than in others—well, we shall see what comes of it."

It is a matter of common knowledge that this hope, unfortunately, never was gratified. The Ninth Symphony filled his imagination, dwelling in the loftiest spheres, and the completion of this giant work at the time thrust every other occupation into the background. Yet I could deduce from this reply that several new quartets and sonatas, whose manuscripts he already had sent off, would shortly appear. These were the world-famous last String Quartets, Op. 127, 130, 132 and 135; and the great Sonatas Op. 109, 110 and 111. All of them are incomparable master works.

When the hour of parting neared and I expressed my thanks to him for all that his noble hospitality had granted me physically and spiritually, he called out after me, under the door: "To our next meeting!"

For all that a more rigorous examination cannot free Beethoven from the reproach of momentary loss of temper and disregard for the forms of good society, these lesser shadows, in view of the very limited intercourse with the outside world entailed by his deafness, and his ever-increasing absorption in the inner world of his own thoughts, after all, establish a just claim to consideration where he is concerned. My personal, quite objective recollection preserves only the echo of a high-hearted, sensitive character, whose kindness and patience with regard to what I had written and printed positively shamed me, and even far from home and on alien soil was to be of happy omen for me. And I consider quite as open to question the credibility of a number of anecdotes current about him in Vienna regarding his eccentricities and extravagances, since, in my opinion, they neither reflected his innocent humor nor, with regard to matters artistic, were in accord with the man's clear, unreserved expressions of opinion. It goes without saying that these remarks apply only to the period here considered in particular, since Beethoven, whose earlier days had been overshadowed by many sombre clouds, was fifty-four years old, and, in contrast to the past, had grown much quieter and more composed in manner.

In the meantime he was living alternately in the delightful Helenental near Baden, where in Nature's open, his creative powers drew their richest nourishment among the hills and the heavily-leaved woods, and where ideas, as he expressed himself, flowed to him in quantity. I visited him there, for he felt himself much indisposed: the germ of his future illness was even then present in his body, and yet I could not help but admire the strength of soul with which he fought against it. Nothing about him betrayed his suffering during our excursions in common through the surrounding country; the pictures of the landscapes captured completely his eyes and his feelings, and is it not due to his life in the country that we owe the ideal description in his incomparable Pastoral Symphony?

Only a few weeks later we met in the *Kärnthnerstrasse*. His keen eye discovered me first; and coming up to me he at once seized me by the arm with the words: "If you can spare the time then accompany me to the *Paternostergassel*, to Steiner's (the music shop of Steiner and Haslinger) whom I want to give a good set-down. These publishers always have all sorts of excuses handy. When it comes to bringing out my compositions they would like to put it off until I am dead, because they think they then would do a better business with them; but I shall know how to meet them." (literally). At this encounter I had been surprised at the very onset to find Beethoven, usually so careless about his attire, dressed with unwonten elegance, wearing a blue frock coat with yellow buttons, impeccable white knee-breeches, a vest to match, and a new beaver hat, as usual on the back of his head. I left him at the entrance of the shop, which was crowded with people while, thanking me for escorting him, he entered Mr. Steiner's office with the latter. I could not resist telling my teacher Mayseder, who lived in the neighborhood, about the striking metamorphosis of Beethoven's elegant appearance, an event which, however, caused Mayseder far less surprise that it had caused me, for he said with a smile: "This is not the first time that his friends have taken his old clothes during the night and laid down new ones in their place; he has not the least suspicion of what has happened and puts on what lies before him with entire unconcern." This is the only really striking occurrence I am able to relate concerning him; nor did I investigate further to ascertain whether the matter really happened as said, though I must again remark that I never observed any evidence of absent-mindedness on Beethoven's part.

I shall only add to what has gone before the last conversation I had with this profoundly serious thinker. One day I brought him a new, somewhat complicated composition I had written, and after he had read it he remarked: "You give too much, less would have been better; but that lies in the nature of heaven-scaling youth, which never thinks it possible to do enough. It is a fault maturer years will correct, however, and I still prefer a superfluity to a paucity of ideas." "What shall I do to find the right way and—how did you yourself attain that lofty goal?" I added, timidly. "I carry my thoughts about with me for a long time, sometimes a very long time, before I set them down," he replied. "At the same time my memory is so faithful to me that I am sure not to forget a theme which I have once conceived, even after years have passed. I make many changes, reject and reattempt until I am satisfied. Then the working-out in breadth, length, heighth and depth begins in my head, and since I am conscious of what I want, the basic idea never leaves me. It rises, grows upward, and I hear and see the picture as a whole take shape and stand forth before me as though cast in a single piece, so that all that is left is the work of writing it down. This goes quickly, according as I have the time, for sometimes I have several compositions in labor at once, though I am sure never to confuse one with the other. You will ask me whence I take my ideas? That I cannot say with any degree of certainty: they come to me uninvited, directly or indirectly. I could almost grasp them in my hands, out in Nature's open, in the woods, during my promenades, in the silence of the night, at earliest dawn. They are roused by moods which in the poet's case are transmuted into words, and in mine into tones, that sound, roar and storm until at last they take shape for me as notes.''

I had listened to him with unexpressible sensations; had taken his words deeply to heart. . . .

May was drawing to a close and with it my stay of well-nigh two years in Vienna. I was heavy-hearted to think I had to leave and Beethoven, too, was visibly moved; there was a pathos in his farewell, as though he had a premonition we would not again see each other: I could have sunk down at his feet. And when I seized the pen to thank him for the last time for the infinite kindness which he had shown me, he at once drew back my hand. "No thanks!" he cried, "there is no need of it between us: what I have done came from the heart. And now no more emotion! A man should be firm and brave in all things. Will you come to Vienna again before long? When do you leave?" "On the 26th or 27th," I answered. "Then you will no doubt allow me to molest you with letters and with commissions I would like to have attended to in Paris; and you might tell the music publisher Schlesinger, verbally, that I know the reason why he delays publishing my manuscripts, but

I shall no longer endure it." A gloomy sadness veiled my eyes when a short time after I left the admirable man who has achieved so much for the art of tone.

I was, however, to enjoy a marvelous experience the day before my departure. Early in the morning, while putting my belongings in order, I heard a gentle knocking without and opened the door. What do I see? It is Beethoven who enters the room. My astonishment may be conceived when he discovered me in a hurly-burly of clothes and trunks, music and instruments. He hardly noticed it, however, but at once declared that he had only come in order to wish me a prosperous trip for the last time, and to deliver to me the promised letters to Cherubini and the publisher Schlesinger (unsealed because of the French postal service). Not knowing whether he would find me at home he had, as a precaution, written me a special letter of instruction, which I was to read carefully. This letter, a holy relic in my album, contained, in fact, the most exact instructions about the commissions with which I had been entrusted, and closed with the assurance of his most cordial devotion. When I had read it and had promised him to attend to everything as well as possible, he continued: "I have also brought you a little souvenir: I know that you will attach some value to it. Take it for remembrance's sake and continue to think well of me!" With trembling hands I received the precious sheet of music-paper. It contained a canon for six voices on the words: " 'Man should be noble, helpful and good!' Words by Goethe, tones by Beethoven. Vienna, in May, 1823." On the back was written: "A prosperous journey, my dear Mr. Schlösser! May all things turn out as according to your wish, Your most devoted Beethoven."

I walked down-stairs with him, hand in hand, and when we had reached the bottom stood looking after him for a long time, until he had vanished from my sight.

Edward Schulz
(1823)

Under the title of "A Day with Beethoven, Extract of a Letter from Vienna to a Friend in London" appeared in the musical magazine "The Harmonicon" of 1824 the following vivid narrative. It is by Edward Schulz, not a German, as one might infer from his name, but an Englishman. If September 28, 1823, was for him a *dies faustus*, so it was for Beethoven, since apparently it was one of the comparatively very few days on which Beethoven for some mysterious physical reason could dispense with the use of an ear-trumpet. Had Mr. Schulz, probably in company of the publisher Haslinger, visited Beethoven a day sooner or later, presumably he could not have written that the accounts of the master's deafness were exaggerated.

I now fulfil the promise I made on my departure for Germany last summer, of giving you, from time to time, an account of whatever might appear to me interesting in the fine arts, particularly in music; and as I then told you that I should not confine myself to any order of time and place, I commence at once with Vienna.   This is the city, which, speaking of music, must be called by way of eminence, the capital of Germany.   As to the sciences, it is quite otherwise, it being generally considered as one of the most inferior of the German universities.   The north of Germany has at all times possessed the best theorists: the Bachs, Marpurg, Kirnberger, Schwenke, Türk; but the men most celebrated for composition were always more numerous in the south, above all in Vienna.   Here Mozart, Haydn, Beethoven, Hummel, M. v. Weber, Spohr, etc., not only received their musical education, but most of them produced the works which have acquired them the greatest celebrity; and even at the present period Vienna abounds with eminent musicians: C. Kreutzer, Stadler, Mayseder, C. Czerny, Pixis, and that young prodigy on the pianoforte, Liszt. To give you a succinct account only of the present state of music in Vienna, would exceed the limits of a letter. I, therefore, will rather devote the remainder of this to one

who is still the brightest ornament of that imperial city—
Beethoven. You must not, however, expect from me
now anything like a biography; that I shall reserve for
a future communication. I wish now to give you only a
short account of a single day's visit to that great man,
and, if in my narration, I should appear to dwell on
trifling points, you will be good enough to attribute it to
my veneration for Beethoven, which leads me to consider
everything highly interesting that is in the slightest
degree connected with so distinguished a character.

The 28th of September, 1823, will be ever recollected
by me as a *dies faustus;* in truth, I do not know that I
ever spent a happier day. Early in the morning, I went
in company with two Vienna gentlemen—one of whom,
Mr. H., is known as the very intimate friend of Beethoven—to the beautifully situated village of Baden,
about twelve miles from Vienna, where the latter usually
resides during the summer months. Being with Mr. H.,
I had not to encounter any difficulty in being admitted
into his presence. He looked very sternly at me at first,
but he immediately after shook me heartily by the hand,
as if an old acquaintance; for he then clearly recollected
my first visit to him in 1816, though it had been but of
very short duration. A proof of his excellent memory.
I found, to my sincere regret, a considerable alteration
in his appearance, and it immediately struck me that he
looked very unhappy. The complaints he afterwards
made to Mr. H. confirmed my apprehensions. I feared
that he would not be able to understand one word of
what I said; in this, however, I rejoice to say, I was much
deceived, for he made out very well all that I addressed
to him slowly and in a loud tone. From his answers it
was clear, that not a particle of what Mr. H. uttered
had been lost, though neither the latter, nor myself, used
a machine. From this you will justly conclude, that
the accounts respecting his deafness lately spread in
London, are much exaggerated. I should mention

though, that when he plays on the pianoforte, it is generally at the expense of some twenty or thirty strings, he strikes the keys with so much force. Nothing can possibly be more lively, more animated and—to use an epithet that so well characterizes his own symphonies—more energetic than his conversation, when you have once succeeded in getting him into good humour; but one unlucky question, one ill-judged piece of advice—for instance, concerning the cure of his deafness—is quite sufficient to estrange him from you forever. He was desirous of ascertaining, for a particular composition he was then about, the highest possible note of the trombone, and questioned Mr. H. accordingly, but did not seem satisfied with his answers. He then told me, that he had in general taken care to inform himself through the different artists themselves, concerning the construction, character, and compass of all the principal instruments. He introduced his nephew to me, a fine young man of about eighteen, who is the only relation with whom he lives on terms of friendship, saying: "You may propose to him an enigma in Greek, if you like"; meaning, I was informed, to acquaint me with the young man's knowledge of that language. The history of this relative reflects the highest credit on Beethoven's goodness of heart; the most affectionate father could not have made greater sacrifices on his behalf, than he has made. After we had been more than an hour with him, we agreed to meet at dinner, at one o'clock, in that most romantic and beautiful valley called *das Helenenthal*, about two miles from Baden. After having seen the baths, and other curiosities of the village, we called again at his house about twelve o'clock and, as we found him already waiting for us, we immediately set out on our walk to the valley. B. is a famous pedestrian, and delights in walks of many hours, particularly through wild and romantic scenery. Nay, I was told that he sometimes passes whole nights on such excursions, and is frequently missed at home for several days. On our way to the valley, he often stopped short, and pointed out to me its most beautiful spots, or noticed the defects of the new buildings. At other times he seemed quite lost in himself, and only hummed in an unintelligible manner. I understood, however, that this was the way he composed, and I also learnt, that he never writes one note down till he has formed a clear design for the whole piece. The day being remarkably fine, we dined in the open air, and what seemed to please B. extremely, was, that we were the only visitors in the hotel, and quite by ourselves during the whole day. The Viennese repasts are famous all over Europe, and that ordered for us was so luxurious, that B. could not help making remarks on the profusion which it displayed   "Why such a variety of dishes?" he exclaimed, "man is but little above other animals, if his chief pleasure is confined to a dinner table." This and similar reflections he made during our meal. The only thing he likes in the way of food is fish, of which trout is his favorite. He is a great enemy to all *gêne*, and I believe that there is not another individual in Vienna who speaks with so little restraint on all kinds of subjects, even political ones, as Beethoven. He hears badly, but he speaks remarkably well, and his observations are as characteristic and as original as his compositions. In the whole course of our table-talk, there was nothing so interesting as what he said about Handel. I sat close by him, and heard him assert very distinctly, in German, "Handel is the greatest composer that ever lived."[1] I cannot describe to you with what pathos, and I am inclined to say, with what sublimity of language, he spoke of the "Messiah" of this immortal genius.—Every one of us was moved, when he said, "I would uncover my head, and kneel down on his tomb!" H. and I tried repeatedly, to turn the conversation to

---

[1]Mozart expressed himself in a similar manner; and Haydn, when at a performance in Westminster Abbey, of the "Messiah," was nearly overpowered by its sublime strains, and wept like a child.

Mozart, but without effect; I only heard him say, "in a monarchy we know who is the first"—which might, or might not, apply to the subject.   Mr. C. Czerny—who, by-the-by, knows every note of Beethoven by heart, though he does not play one single composition of his own without the music before him—told me, however, that B. was sometimes inexhaustible in his praise of Mozart.   It is worthy of remark that this great musician cannot bear to hear his own earlier works praised; and I was apprized that a sure way to make him very angry is to say something complimentary of his Septetto, Trios, etc.   His latest productions, which are so little relished in London, but much admired by the young artists of Vienna, are his favorites.   His second Mass he looks upon as his best work, I understood.   He is at present engaged in writing a new opera, called *Melusine*, the words by the famous, but unfortunate poet, Grillparzer. He concerns himself very little about the newest productions of living composers, insomuch, that when asked about the *Freischütz*, he replied, "I believe *one* Weber has written it."   You will be pleased to hear that he is a great admirer of the ancients.   Homer, particularly his Odyssey, and Plutarch he prefers to all the rest; and, of the native poets, he studies Schiller and Goethe in preference to any other; this latter is his personal friend. He appears, uniformly, to entertain the most favourable opinion of the British nation; "I like," said he, "the noble simplicity of English manners," and added other praises.   It seemed to me as if he had yet some hopes of visiting this country together with his nephew.   I should not forget to mention that I heard a MS. trio of his, for the pianoforte, violin, and violoncello, which I thought very beautiful and it is, I understood, to appear shortly in London.   The portrait you see of him in the music shops is not now like him, but may have been so eight or ten years back.   I could tell you many things more of this extraordinary man, who, from what I have

seen and learnt of him, has inspired me with the deepest
veneration; but I fear I have taken up your time already
too much.   The friendly and hearty manner in which he
treated me, and bade me farewell, has left an impression
on my mind which will remain for life.   Adieu.

Franz Grillparzer
(1823)

Possibly the great Austrian poet's reminiscences of Beethoven
would never have been recorded, had he not in 1840 felt compelled
to take issue with statements by Ludwig Rellstab affecting the
miscarriage of the project to write in collaboration with Beethoven
an opera on "Melusine." With all his growing respect and admiration for Beethoven, Franz Grillparzer (1791-1872) never quite
seems to have shared Beethoven's esthetic views. His aphorism
"Beethoven : Chaos", however, quoted by Mr. Philip Gordon in his
able article in *The Musical Quarterly* on "Franz Grillparzer : Critic of
Music" ought not to be taken too literally. Mr. Gordon also quotes
Grillparzer's touching words on how he came to write his famous
funeral oration for Beethoven: "Schindler had come to me with the
news that Beethoven was dying and that his friends wanted me to
write a funeral address to be spoken by the actor Anschütz at his
grave. . . . I had come to the second part of the oration, when
Schindler came again and told me that Beethoven had just died.
Then something snapped inside me; the tears rushed from my eyes,
and I could not finish the speech as elegantly as I had begun. However, the address was made . . . I had really loved Beethoven. . . . "

I first saw Beethoven in my boyhood years—which
may have been in 1804 or 1805—at a musical evening
in the home of my uncle, Joseph Sonnleithner, at that
time an associate partner in an art and music business
in Vienna.   Besides Beethoven, Cherubini and the Abbé
Vogler were among those present.   Beethoven in those
days was still lean, dark, and contrary to his habit in
later years, very elegantly dressed.   He wore glasses,
which I noticed in particular, because at a later period
he ceased to avail himself of this aid to his short-sighted-
ness.   I no longer recall whether he himself or Cherubini
played, and only remember that when the servant already

had announced that supper was served, Abbé Vogler sat down at the piano and commenced to play endless variations on an African theme which he had brought in person from its natal land. During his musical exploitation of it the company gradually drifted into the dining-room. Only Beethoven and Cherubini remained. At last Cherubini also disappeared, and Beethoven alone remained standing beside the industriously working pianist. Finally he, too, lost patience, though Abbé Vogler, now entirely deserted, never ceased caressing his theme in everyway, shape and manner. I myself had stayed in the room in my dazed astonishment at the monstrous nature of the entire proceedings. As to what transpired from that moment on, my memory, as often is the case where the recollections of childhood are concerned, is entirely at fault. Who sat beside Beethoven at the table, whether he conversed with Cherubini, and whether Abbé Vogler joined them later—I feel as though a dark curtain had been dropped over all of it in my mind.

One or two years later I was living with my parents during the summer in the village of Heiligenstadt, near Vienna. Our dwelling fronted on the garden and Beethoven had rented the rooms facing the street. Both set of apartments were connected by a hall in common which led to the stairs. My brothers and I took little heed of the odd man who in the meanwhile had grown more robust, and went about dressed in a most negligent, indeed even slovenly way, when he shot past us with a growl. My mother, however, a passionate lover of music, allowed herself to be carried away, now and again, when she heard him playing the piano, and entering the connecting hall would stand, not beside his door, but immediately beside our own in order to listen with devout attention. This she may have done a couple of times when suddenly Beethoven's door flew open, he himself stepped out, saw my mother, hurried back and at once rushed down the stairs into the open, hat on head. From that moment he never again touched his piano. In vain my mother, since every other opportunity was lacking, had a servant assure him that not alone would she no longer eavesdrop on his playing, but that our door leading to the hall should remain locked, and her household, in place of the stairs in common, would make a broad detour and use only the garden entrance. Beethoven remained inflexible and his piano stood untouched until finally the late autumn brought us back to town again.

During one of the summers which followed I made frequent visits to my grandmother, who had a country house in the adjacent village of Döbling. Beethoven, too, was living in Döbling at the time. Opposite my grandmother's windows stood the dilapidated house of a peasant named Flohberger, notorious for his profligate life. Besides his nasty house, Flohberger also possessed a pretty daughter, Lise, who had none too good a reputation. Beethoven seemed to take a great interest in this girl. I can still see him, striding up the *Hirschgasse*, his white handkerchief dragging along the ground in his right hand, stopping at Flohberger's courtyard gate, within which the giddy fair, standing on a hay- or manure-cart, would lustily wield her fork amid incessant laughter. I never noticed that Beethoven spoke to her. He would merely stand there in silence, looking in, until at last the girl, whose taste ran more to peasant lads, roused his wrath either with some scornful word or by obstinately ignoring him. Then he would whip off with a swift turn yet would not neglect, however, to stop again at the gate of the court the next time. Indeed, his interest was so great that when the girl's father was put in the village lock-up (known as the *Kotter*) for assault and battery while drinking, Beethoven personally interceded for his release before the village elders assembled. But as was his habit, he handled the worthy counsellors in so tempestuous a manner that he came near keeping his captive protégé company against his will.

Later I saw him mostly on the street, and once or twice in a coffee-house, where he spent much time with a poet of the Novalis-Schlegel guild, now long since dead and gone, Ludwig Stoll. It was said that they were projecting an opera together. It is inconceivable how Beethoven could have expected to secure something serviceable from this unstable dangler; in fact, anything but—well versified, it is true—mere fantastic fantasies.

Meanwhile I myself had set my feet in the road of publicity. The *Ahnfrau, Sappho, Medea, Ottokar* already had been published, when suddenly Count Moritz Dietrichstein, then intendant of both the Court theatres, sent me word that Beethoven had applied to him to ask whether he could induce me to write an opera libretto for the composer.

The inquiry, I may as well confess, placed me in a decided quandary. First of all, the idea of writing an opera libretto in itself was far from my thoughts; and then I doubted whether Beethoven—who had become totally deaf in the interim, and whose last compositions, despite their lofty value, had assumed a harshness which to me seemed in contradiction with the treatment of the voice-parts—I doubted, I repeat, whether Beethoven still was able to compose an opera. The thought, however, of supplying a great man with a possible opportunity of writing a work which, in any event, would be highly interesting, overweighed all other considerations, and I gave my consent.

Among the dramatic subjects I had noted down for future development were two which, at any rate, seemed to admit of treatment in operatic style. The one moved in the domain of the most exalted passion. Yet aside from the fact that I knew of no singer who could have undertaken the leading rôle, I did not wish to give Beethoven an opportunity, by spurring him on with a half diabolic subject, of drawing still nearer those extremest boundaries of music which already yawned before his feet like threatening abysses. Hence I chose the legend of Melusine, separated and put aside, so far as was possible, its reflective portions and attempted, by the dominance of the choruses and tremendous finales, and by giving the third act a well-nigh melodramatic shape, to adapt myself as well as might be to the peculiarities of Beethoven's last trends.

In the course of the summer of 1823, I visited Beethoven in Hetzendorf, on his invitation, together with Mr. Schindler. I do not know whether Schindler told me while we were underway, or whether someone else had remarked before that Beethoven hitherto had been prevented by urgent work he had been commissioned to do from undertaking the composition of the opera. Hence I avoided touching on the subject in conversation.

We took a walk and conversed together as well as was possible, half-talking, half-writing, while walking. I still recall with emotion that Beethoven, when we sat down to the table, went into the adjoining room and himself brought in five bottles. One he set down by Schindler's plate, one before his own and the remaining three he stood up in a row before me, probably to tell me, in his naïvely savage, good-natured way that I was at liberty to drink as much as ever I wished. When I drove back to town without Schindler, who remained in Hetzendorf, Beethoven insisted upon accompanying me. He sat down with me in the open carriage, but instead of merely going to the outskirts of the village he drove back all the way to town with me, and getting out at the gates started off on his long hour and a half journey home alone, after heartily pressing my hand. As he got out of the carriage I saw a paper lying on the spot where he had been sitting. I thought he had forgotten it and beck-oned him to return. But he shook his head and laughing loudly, like one who thought he had been successful in playing a trick, ran off all the faster in the opposite direction. I unwrapped the paper, and it contained the exact amount of carriage-hire I had agreed to pay my driver. So thoroughly had Beethoven's manner of life estranged him from all the habits and customs of the world that it never occurred to him how insulting such a procedure would have been under any other circum-stances. I took the thing, however, as it was meant, and laughingly paid the coachman with the gift money.

Later I saw him, I no longer remember where, only once more. At that time he said to me: "Your opera is finished." Whether by this he meant completed in his head, or whether the countless note-books in which he was accustomed to jot down individual thoughts and figures for future development, comprehensible only to him, also may have contained the elements of this opera in fragmentary form, I cannot say.

It is certain that after his death not a single note was discovered which with positively might have had refer-ence to our work of collaboration. I myself, incidentally, remained faithful to my resolve not to recall it to him even in the most indirect manner and, since I found our written conversation very inconvenient, did not come near him again until, clad in black and with a burn-ing torch in my hand, I walked behind his coffin.

WEBER
(1823)

Beethoven's respect for Carl Maria von Weber, as a composer, did not approach that for Cherubini, but the sensational success of "Der Freischütz" led him to a study of the score which considerably influenced and changed his opinion of Weber. When the latter went to Vienna to attend the rehearsals and the first performance there of his opera "Euryanthe" on October 25, 1823, Beethoven tendered through Julius Benedict to Weber an invitation to call on him at Baden, where he was spending the early autumn. Of course, Weber accepted the invitation and on October fifth wrote to his wife about his visit to Beethoven:

I was very tired, but yesterday evening had to go out again at six o'clock because the excursion to Baden had been agreed upon for seven-thirty. It took place, the party incuding Haslinger, Piringer and Benedict; unfortunately, however, it rained vilely. The main thing was to see Beethoven. The latter received me with the most touching affection; he embraced me at least six or seven times in the heartiest fashion and finally, full of enthusiasm, cried: "Yes, you are a devil of a fellow, a fine fellow!" We spent the noon-hour together, very merrily and happily. This rough, repellant man actually paid court to me, served me at table as carefully as though I were his lady, etc. In short, this day always will remain a most remarkable one for me, as for all who shared in it. It gave me quite a special exaltation to see myself overwhelmed with such affectionate attention by this great spirit. How saddening is his deafness, for everything must be written down for him. We saw the baths, drank from the spring and at five o'clock drove back again to Vienna.

Weber's son supplements this after family traditions, in his biography of his father (1864) as follows:

The three men were excited when they entered the bare, almost poverty-stricken room inhabited by the great Ludwig. The chamber was in the greatest disorder. Music, money, articles of clothing lay on the floor; the wash was piled on the uncleanly bed, the grand piano, which was open, was thick with dust, there was a chipped coffee-set on the table.

Beethoven came forward to meet them.

Benedict says that King Lear or the Ossianic bards must have resembled him in appearance. His hair was thick, gray and bristly, here and there altogether white; his forehead and skull had an exceptionally broad curve and were high, like a temple; his nose was four-square, like that of a lion, the mouth nobly shaped and soft, the chin broad, with those wonderful shell-formed grooves in all his portraits, and formed by two jaw-bones which seemed meant to crack the hardest nuts. A dark red overspread his broad, pockmarked face; beneath the bushy, gloomily contracted eyebrows, small radiant eyes beamed mildly upon those entering; his cyclopean, four-cornered figure, which towered but slightly above that of Weber, was covered by a shabby house-robe, with torn sleeves.

Beethoven recognized Weber before he had mentioned his name, clasped him in his arms, and cried: "So there you are, you fellow, you devil of a fellow! God greet you!" And then he at once handed him the famous writing-tablet and a conversation ensued, Beethoven in the meantime first of all throwing the music off the sofa and then, quite unconcernedly, dressing in the presence of his guests to go out.

Beethoven complained bitterly about his situation, scolded the management of the theatre, the concert impresarios, the public, the Italians, the popular taste and, in particular, his nephew's ingratitude. Weber, who was greatly moved, advised him to tear himself away from these repulsive, discouraging conditions, and to make an artistic tour of Germany which would give him a chance to see what the world thought of him. "Too late!" cried Beethoven. He pantomimed playing the piano and shook his head. "Then go to England, where they admire you," wrote Weber. "Too late!" cried Beethoven, caught Weber demonstratively beneath the arm, and drew him along with him to the *Sauerhof*, where he ate. There Beethoven showed himself full of kind-heartedness and warmth toward Weber.

Liszt
(1823)

It is a curious fact that occasionally those who began their career as prodigies, in later years develop an aversion against "Wunderkinder." This was true of Beethoven and it required considerable urging on the part of Schindler, as we know from a conversation of his with Beethoven on April 13, 1823, to persuade the master to attend a concert of Franz Liszt, then eleven years old, on the following day. Apparently there is a chronological conflict between this authentic conversation and Liszt's reminiscences of his only visit to Beethoven, which he communicated in 1875 to his pupil, Ilka Horowitz-Barnay. If Czerny took Liszt to Beethoven on the morning of his concert, the discrepancy would disappear.

I was about eleven years of age when my venerated teacher Czerny took me to Beethoven. He had told the latter about me a long time before, and had begged him to listen to me play sometime. Yet Beethoven had such a repugnance to infant prodigies that he always had violently objected to receiving me. Finally, however, he allowed himself to be persuaded by the indefatigable Czerny, and in the end cried impatiently: "In God's name, then, bring me the young Turk!" It was ten o'clock in the morning when we entered the two small rooms in the *Schwarzspanier* house which Beethoven occupied; I somewhat shyly, Czerny amiably encouraging me. Beethoven was working at a long, narrow table by the window. He looked gloomily at us for a time, said a few brief words to Czerny and remained silent when my kind teacher beckoned me to the piano. I first played a short piece by Ries. When I had finished Beethoven asked me whether I could play a Bach fugue. I chose the C-minor Fugue from the Well-Tempered Clavichord. "And could you also transpose the Fugue at once into another key?" Beethoven asked me. Fortunately I was able to do so. After my closing chord I glanced up. The great Master's darkly glowing gaze lay piercingly upon me. Yet suddenly a gentle smile

Oil-portrait of Beethoven by Waldmüller, 1823
(Courtesy Breitkopf & Härtel, Wiesbaden)

Drawing of Beethoven by Decker, 1824
(Courtesy Historisches Museum der Stadt Wien, Vienna)

passed over his gloomy features, and Beethoven came quite close to me, stooped down, put his hand on my head, and stroked my hair several times. "A devil of a fellow," he whispered, "a regular young Turk!" Suddenly I felt quite brave. "May I play something of yours now?" I boldly asked. Beethoven smiled and nodded. I played the first movement of the C-major Concerto. When I had concluded Beethoven caught hold of me with both hands, kissed me on the forehead and said gently: "Go! You are one of the fortunate ones! For you will give joy and happiness to many other people! There is nothing better or finer!" Liszt told the preceding in a tone of deepest emotion, with tears in his eyes and a warm note of happiness sounded in the simple tale. For a brief space he was silent and then he said: "This event in my life has remained my greatest pride—the palladium of my whole career as an artist. I tell it but very seldom and—only to good friends!"

ANTON SCHINDLER
(1814–1827)

"For all errands and commissions I am a very awkward person," Beethoven once characterized his notorious ineptitude for conducting his affairs in a reasonably ordered manner. It was one of the tragedies of his life that nevertheless circumstances compelled him to devote much attention to matters of business, etc., for which he was by temperament unfit. Fortunately he never lacked friends to whom he could appeal for help from the purchase of spoons to weighty contracts, but between his "terrible stubborness" which, so Schindler tells us, he displayed even on his death-bed and his acceptance of unwise advice, the result was not always for the best.

Among his friends who gladly sacrificed their own interests for his comfort and became indispensable to him, Anton Schindler (1795-1864), violinist and conductor, will always retain an honorable place. By mere accident he made the acquaintance of Beethoven in 1814 and renewed it in 1815. Henceforth, until temporarily in 1825 and 1826 superseded by Karl Holz whose influence on Beethoven in certain respects was regrettable, Schindler assumed the functions of a faithful *fac-totum*. Under the circumstances it was but natural that Schindler set himself the task of writing Beethoven's biography. His work, the first on a scale commensurate with the importance of the subject, was issued in 1840, went through several revised editions (the last one in 1909 prepared by Kalischer) and remains to this day a very valuable book, if one seeks an intimate picture of the man Beethoven.

At the beginning of the year 1823 the Breitkopf and Härtel publishing house wished to acquire a picture of our Master, and Waldmüller, professor at the *Akademie*, was chosen to execute it. Prognostics unfavorable for the accomplishment of his purpose on Beethoven's part were pressing work and continuous eye-trouble, with consequent continuous ill-humor. After repeated putting off, the first sitting was arranged, at which Waldmüller was reverential and all too timid, an attitude which in most cases led to no satisfactory result where Beethoven was concerned. We have explained elsewhere how two other painters, Schimon and Stieler, gained their ends by absolutely opposite tactics. For all Waldmüller hurried to fix the outlines of the head and lay his first coat, the Master, engrossed in thought, found he took too long. Every other moment, therefore, he would leave his seat and walk up and down the room in a disgruntled manner, even straying to the writing-desk in the room adjoining. The canvas had not yet been primed when Beethoven made it all too apparent that he could endure no longer. When the artist had left, the Master's rage burst forth, and Waldmüller was called the most wretched of painters—because he had made him sit facing the window. He obstinately rejected every defence. No other sitting took place. The painter, however, completed his picture from imagination, because, as he replied to my protests, he could not afford to lose the honorarium of twenty ducats accorded him.

Beethoven can scarcely have measured more than five feet, four inches, Vienna measure. His body was thick-set, with a powerful bone structure and strong muscles; his head was unusually large, overgrown with long, stubby, almost entirely grey hair, which not infrequently hung neglected about his head and—when in addition his beard had attained an excessive length, which was very often the case—lent him a somewhat unkempt appearance. His forehead was high and broad; his brown eyes which when he laughed were hidden in his head, were small. On the other hand they would suddenly be projected in unusual size, flashing as they rolled about, the pupils almost always turned upward or, immovable, staring down before them as soon as some idea had seized him. Therewith, however, his whole outward appearance would in the same way suddenly undergo a startling transformation, would assume a visibly inspired and imposing semblance, so that his slight figure, like his soul, would tower before one in gigantic size. These moments of sudden inspiration often would surprise him in the midst of the gayest company or in the street, and usually attracted the liveliest attention of all passers-by.

What was going on within him was reflected only in his radiant eyes and face, for he never gesticulated, either with his head or with his hands, save when he stood before the orchestra. His mouth was well-shaped and his lips symmetrically proportioned (when younger his lips are said to have projected somewhat) and his nose was broad. His smile lent his whole face a something exceptionally kind and amiable which, especially in conversation with strangers, made a very grateful impression, since it encouraged them. His laughter on the other hand, often was excessively reverberant and distorted his intellectual and powerfully marked features; then his great head would swell, his face would grow still broader, until the whole effect was that of a grinning mask. It was well that it always lasted but a moment. His chin had an elongated depression in the middle and on either side, which gave it a shell-like conformation and a special peculiarity. His face had a yellowish tinge which, however, disappeared as a result of his continual wandering in the open, especially during the summer, when his full cheeks would be covered with the freshest varnish of red and brown.

A drive in Beethoven's company, from Hetzendorf to Baden, to find him a summer home there, and the actual business of so doing forms one of my drollest recollections of the great eccentric. He at once began to review from memory the long list of houses he had occupied in Baden, their conveniences and inconveniences. Among them all there remained only a single one which suited him. "But the owners told me last year that they would not take me in again." Like statements often had been made by other house owners. When we reached Baden he begged me to go to the house in question with a flag of truce, as his representative, and to promise a greater degree of orderliness and consideration for other indwellers (a chief cause of complaint) in his name. This promise, however, was not considered; and I was turned away. My expectant friend was deeply grieved thereat. Once more the parliamentary was sent to the master locksmith's fortress with new protestations of good behavior. This time a more willing ear was lent them. The unconditional demand that Beethoven once more, as in the year preceding, have shutters put on the windows of the room facing the street was made. In vain we strove to guess the reason for this curious demand. Since providing these requisites for defending the tone-poet's suffering eyes from the glaring sunlight proved to be an urgent necessity, the demand was cheerfully granted. A few days later he moved in.

Yet why the insistence on the shutters?

Beethoven, during his former stay in the house, had occasionally planted himself by the window-shutters, which were only smooth-planed and, as was his habit, had set down on them in lead-pencil yard-long calculations, hapchance musical ideas, in short a veritable miscellany, so that these thin lindenwood boards formed a sort of diary. During the summer of 1822, a family from North Germany lived opposite him. They had observed him while thus occupied and after his departure had bought one of these window-shutters of the master locksmith. Once he had learned the value of a window-shutter thus decorated, the latter had no difficulty in disposing of all four to other visitors at the health resort. When later the Master learned of this trade from the Baden apothecary T——, he burst into Homeric laughter.

Washing and bathing were among the most indispensable necessities of existence for Beethoven. In this respect he was a thorough Oriental. Mohammed has by no means prescribed too many ablutions to suit him. If, while he was working, he did not go out during the forenoon, in order to compose himself, he would stand at the wash-basin, often in extremest negligée and pour great pitchersfull of water over his hands, at the same time howling or, for a change, growling out the whole gamut of the scale, ascending and descending; then, before long, he would pace the room, his eyes rolling or fixed in a stare, jot down a few notes and again return to his water pouring and howling. These were moments of profoundest meditation, nothing worth making a great fuss about had they not resulted in disagreeable consequences in two directions. In the first place, they often incited his servants to laughter, observing which the Master would fly into a rage, which on occasion led him to yield to ridiculous outbreaks. Or he would get into a fight with the landlord when the water leaked through the floor which, unfortunately, often happened. This was a principal reason why Beethoven was everywhere unwelcome as a lodger.

At breakfast Beethoven drank coffee, which he usually prepared himself in a percolator. Coffee seems to have been the nourishment with which he could least dispense and in his procedure with regard to its preparation he was as careful as the Orientals are known to be. Sixty beans to a cup was the allotment and the beans often were counted out exactly, especially when guests were present. Among his favorite dishes was maccaroni with Parmesan cheese. Furthermore, all fish dishes were his special predilection. Hence guests usually were invited for Friday when a full-weight *Schill* (a Danube fish resembling the haddock) with potatoes could be served. Supper was hardly taken into account. A plate of soup and some remnants of the midday meal was all that he took. His favorite beverage was fresh spring water which, in summer, he drank in well-nigh inordinate quantities. Among wines he preferred the Hungarian, *Ofen* variety. Unfortunately he liked best the adulterated wines which did great damage to his weak intestines. But warnings were of no avail in this case. Our Master also liked to drink a good glass of beer in the evening, with which he smoked a pipeful of tobacco and kept the news-sheets company. Beethoven still often visited taverns and coffee-houses in his last years, but insisted in coming in at a back door and being allowed to sit in a room apart. Strangers who wished to see him were directed thither; for he was not changeable and always chose a coffee-house near his own dwelling. He very seldom allowed himself to be drawn into conversation with strangers presented to him in these places. When he had run through the last news-sheet he would hurriedly depart again through the back door.

Beethoven rose at daybreak, no matter what the season, and went at once to his work-table. There he worked until two or three o'clock, when he took his midday meal. In the interim he usually ran out into the open two or three times, where he also "worked while walking." Such excursions seldom exceeded a full hour's time, and resembled the swarming out of the bee to gather honey. They never varied with the seasons and neither cold nor heat were noticed. The afternoons were dedicated to regular promenades; and at a later hour Beethoven was wont to hunt up some favorite beer-house, in order to read the news of the day, if he had not already satisfied this need at some café. At the time when the English parliament was sitting, however, the *Allgemeine Zeitung* was regularly read at home for the sake of the debates. It will be easily understood that our politico was arrayed on the side of the Opposition. Nor was his great predilection for Lord Brougham, Hume and other Opposition orators necessary to this end. Beethoven always spent his winter evenings at home, and devoted them to serious reading. It was but seldom that one saw him busy with music-paper in the evening, since writing music was too taxing for his eyes. In former years this may not have been the case; yet it is quite certain that at no time did he employ the evening hours for composition (creation). At ten o'clock at the latest he went to bed.

Beethoven was especially fond of seating himself at the piano in the twilight and improvising, and often he also played the violin or viola, which instruments always lay ready to hand for this purpose on the piano-top. How this playing sounded, since his outer senses no longer could participate in it, it is needless to say; particularly in the case of the string instruments, which he was unable to tune. His playing must have been torture to the ears of those who lived in the same house. His extemporization on the piano was only occasionally clear but then, usually, possessed a great charm. As a rule the lack of distinctness was due to his habit of laying his left hand on the keyboard in all its breadth, and noisily covering what the right hand often developed in all too delicate a manner. In the last period the

pianoforte manufacturer Konrad Graf devised a reso-
nance-carrier which, placed on the piano, was supposed
to carry the tones to the ear with greater ease.   In the
case of individual tones it attained its object, but harmonic playing completely overwhelmed the ear, because
the air vibrations, restricted to the least possible space,
could not help but produce a deafening effect.

Beethoven had been brought up in the Catholic faith.
That he was really inwardly religious is witnessed by
his whole manner of life; that he never expressed himself with regard to the religious matters or the dogmas
of the various Christian churches, in order to communicate his opinions concerning them, was one of his peculiarities.   It may be said with some measure of certainty
that his religious beliefs were based less on church
dogmas, and that Deism was their source.   Without
visualizing any artificially made theory, he yet all too
plainly recognized God in the world and the world in
God.   His theory in this connection shaped itself up
for him in nature as a whole, and it seems as though the
book already mentioned on various occasions, Christian
Sturms' "Considerations of the Works of God in Nature,"
together with teachings drawn from the philosophic
systems of the Greek sages were his guides along this
road.   It would have been difficult to have maintained
the contrary, once one had realized how he utilized the
content of the writings in question for the benefit of his
inner life.

Since he also came in touch with members of the
clergy during the stays he made in the country, he did
not neglect to call their attention to the aforementioned
book of instruction and devotion and, indeed, even
recommended it for pulpit use.   But he found only deaf
ears and once, when the parish priest of Mödling replied:
"With regard to the apparitions in the firmament our
people need only know that the sun, moon and stars
rise and set, and so forth," the propagandist's zeal was

soon diminished, so that in his last years, aside from bitter sarcasms, not another word anent popular ignorance in this connection passed his lips.

Beethoven invariably had a very poor memory for what lay in the past. It is not uninteresting to consider this circumstance somewhat more closely in order to discover whether it was confined merely to that which concerned him personally, that which he himself had experienced, or also extended to matters musical. He was forgetful in both directions. Unless one were accustomed to it, one could not help noting with surprise how the Master's last-written creations passed entirely out of his mind, with all their details, and that this was not alone the case with works in score, but also held good for piano solos. When he was busy with a new composition, his whole being was visibly preoccupied by it and by nothing else, and whatever he had just completed already lay so far behind in his consciousness that it might have belonged to an earlier period.

Proof to this effect was furnished only too often in connection with copyists or when inquiries were made. He was annoyed unless questioners asked for instructions with the music in hand. With works other than his own it was the same; all had to be shown him if his memory was to recall it. It was noticeable that only works by Mozart and Haydn were exceptions to this rule. Yet his seemingly weak memory was in contradiction to his recollection of the content of the Greek classics. How are we to explain the fact that he could quote long passages from them? When it was a question of discovering where one or the other quote was given, it was as easy for Beethoven to find as a passage in one of his own works. Perhaps it may be explained by the custom, prevalent in his day, of presenting all tonal compositions before a circle of listeners from the written or printed music, and that in consequence the mechanism of memory was not practised in learning by heart.   In a previous epoch the composer himself never played his works from memory.   Coquetting with the mechanical, either in the head or with the hands, was not in accordance with the spirit of the age.

This great child was fond of having a fancy-table covered with all sorts of knickknacks for his amusement but also, perhaps, to serve loftier purposes.   His writing-desk, in earlier years of great circumference, was at one and the same time a fancy-table of the kind mentioned. On it, in the guise of paperweights, were to be seen Cossacks and Hungarian hussars, some candlesticks of varied shapes, several bells, ranging from silver to sheep-bell clay, statuettes of ancient Greeks and Romans, of which only that of Brutus, whom he so much admired, has been preserved, and writing materials of the most recent invention.   In addition were to be seen bell-pulls, in one room with a thick, valuable silk rope, in another with a hempen one, etc.   For furniture of all kinds the Master spent no more than the poorest artisan.   He always bought it of a second-hand dealer.   During his walks about the town he would stop before one or another shop and peer at the window display through his lorgnette until he fell in love with something he saw and bought it.   Many of these articles were intended for his nephew.   His life of continual wandering, the packing and unpacking, however, again and again, soon caused these toys, which at times were more than toys, to disappear from view.   Only a few among them could be preserved.

His musical library was very scantily furnished, and included only a small quantity of his own works.   Among the old Italians Beethoven—like those of his day in general—knew only what was contained in the collection of short pieces by Palestrina, Nanini, Vittoria and others, which Freiherr von Tucher had printed by Artaria in 1824.   This collection he possessed.   Of Josef Haydn and Cherubini there was not a single note; of Mozart part of the score of "Don Giovanni" and a number of sonatas. Nearly all of Clementi's sonatas were represented. These he cherished above all others, and placed them in the first rank of works adapted for beautiful piano playing; this as much because of their lovely, fresh and attractive melodies as in view of the definite, therefore easily understandable form, in which all the movements progressed. Beethoven was not much drawn to Mozart's piano music. Hence for several years in succession the Master had the musical education of the nephew he loved carried on almost exclusively through the medium of the Clementi sonatas. This was something which by no means pleased Karl Czerny, who was teaching his nephew at the time, and was far less prepossessed in favor of Clementi than Beethoven.

In addition Beethoven possessed the two books of Études by John Cramer which thus far had been published. These Études, our Master declared, were the chief basis of worth-while playing. Had he ever realized his own intention of writing a piano method, these Études would have supplied the most important portion of the practical examples in it, for he regarded them as the preparatory school best suited for the study of his own works because of the polyphony which so largely dominated in them.

Of the archsire, Johann Sebastian Bach, but very little was available. With the exception of a few motets, in most cases sung in the family circle at Van Swieten's, however, the choice probably represented most of what the epoch in question knew by Sebastian, namely: the Well-Tempered Clavichord, offering visible signs of intensive study, three books of the *Exercises*, fifteen inventions, fifteen symphonies, and also part of the Toccata in D-minor.

Beethoven's praiseworthy custom of writing down notes regarding himself, his thoughts and his feelings, was also extended to include the details of his housekeeping.   For this purpose he usually employed the blank pages of the calendar, which in this way took shape as a diary.   Diaries of this kind have been found completely covering the years 1819, 1820 and 1823. The first (1819) contains only the following notations:

> On January 31 gave the housekeeper notice.
> February 15 the kitchen-maid entered upon her duties.
> March 8 the kitchen-maid gave two weeks' notice.
> March 22 the new housekeeper entered upon her duties.
> May 12 arrived in Mödling.
> *Miser et pauper sum* (I am poor and wretched).
> May 14 the waitress entered service at 6 *Gulden* monthly.
> July 20 gave the housekeeper notice.

The year 1820, however, already is richer in notices regarding household affairs, for example:

> On April 17 the kitchen-maid entered upon her duties.
> April 19 a poor day (i.e., nothing palatable appeared on the Master's table because owing to his protracted sitting over his work the food already had been over-cooked or altogether spoiled).
> May 16 gave notice to the kitchen-maid.
> May 19 the kitchen-maid left.
> May 30 the woman entered upon her duties.
> July 1 the kitchen-maid entered upon her duties.
> July 28 the kitchen-maid ran away in the evening.
> July 30 the woman from Lower Döbling entered service. During the four evil days, August 10, 11, 12 and 13, I ate in Lerchenfeld (a suburb outside the city limits).
> August 28 the woman's month up (i.e., she had only agreed to stay a month).
> September 9 the girl entered service.
> October 22 the girl left.
> December 12 the kitchen-maid entered service.
> December 18 the kitchen-maid gave notice.
> December the new chamber-maid entered service.

Since the illness of which Beethoven finally died, after four months of suffering, made his usual mental activity impossible for him, from its very inception, it was necessary to think of things which might distract him, and which were in harmony with his intellect and his preferences. Thus it happened that I submitted to him a collection of Schubert's songs and melodies, some sixty in all, and among them many still in manuscript. This was done not alone with the intention of providing him with agreeable entertainment; but also to give him an opportunity of becoming acquainted with Schubert's nature and being, so that he might gain a favorable impression of talents which exaggerators, who no doubt took the same stand with regard to others among Schubert's contemporaries, had made objects of suspicion. The great Master, who formerly had not known even five Schubert songs, was astonished at their number, and refused to believe that Schubert up to that time (February, 1827), already had written five hundred melodies. Yet if the number of songs surprised him, his astonishment passed all bounds when he became acquainted with their content. For several days in succession he could not part with them and spent hours, every day, over *Iphigenias Monolog*, the *Grenzen der Allmacht*, the *Junge Nonne*, the *Viola*, the *Müllerlieder* and others more. With joyous enthusiasm he cried again and again: "In truth, a divine spark lives in Schubert! Had I known of this poem I, too, would have set it to music!" This he said of most of the poems whose subjects, contents and original working-out on Schubert's part he could not sufficiently praise. In the same way he found it almost impossible to understand how Schubert found the leisure "to attack such long poems, many among then comprising ten others," as he expressed it. What he wanted to say was, poems, as long as ten others put together; and of these songs in the grand style alone Schubert has supplied no less than a hundred, songs that are by no means only lyric in character, but which contain the most extended ballads and dialogue scenes and which, since they have been treated dramatically, would be in place even in opera and there, too, would not fail of effect. What

would the great Master have said, in fact, had he seen
the Ossianic songs, *Die Bürgschaft, Elysium, Der Taucher*
and other great songs which have appeared only recently?
In short, the respect Beethoven conceived for Schubert's
talents was so great, that he now insisted upon also
seeing his operas and his piano compositions; but his
illness already had made such headway that it no longer
was possible for him to gratify this desire.　Yet he often
spoke of Schubert and prophesied "that he would yet
attract much attention in the world," while he regretted
that he had not made his acquaintance at an earlier date.

LUDWIG RELLSTAB
(1825)

Artillery officer, professor of history and mathematics, essayist,
novelist, editor, critic, biographer and autobiographer, Ludwig
Rellstab (1799-1860) must also have been quite an actor, if he could
simulate successfully in the presence of Beethoven an impression of
the String-quartet in E flat major, Op. 127, which was not sincere.
It is not difficult to read between the lines of his narrative in his
autobiography "Aus meinem Leben" (1861) that the last quartets
of Beethoven remained quite beyond the comprehension of Rellstab
whose writings are shallow, too florid and verbose.　However, his
description of his visit in 1825 to Beethoven is recognized, except for
trivial errors of detail, as fairly reliable.　Here it is quoted in a condensed version.

With regard to all I expected in and of the imperial
city one thing my enthusiastic youthful soul visioned as
the greatest of all: the hope of seeing Beethoven.　In
truth, the mere sight of this man, so profoundly worshipped, would have satisfied the infinite desire of my
heart, yet in secret I dreamt of even still more wonderful
things, which imaginings, however, somewhat resembled
the airy palaces of faerie.　I nourished the hope—in
reality it was but a feebly dawning one—of inducing
him to take an interest in an opera which I wished to
versify for him.　And no matter how unattainable, how
improbable this goal appeared when I attempted to

regard it as something real and tangible, I still wished to keep the *magna voluisse* on my side. Hence I had taken every possible step which seemed advisable in my case and which seemed likely to pave the way for my project.

Although after we had reached Vienna nothing lay nearer my heart than to pay Beethoven a visit, I thought it first might be well to make some inquiries with regard to the way and manner in which this could be done. In view of the incalculable value a visit of this kind had for me, it is conceivable that I took for granted a similar attitude of mind on the part of many thousands in Vienna, and on this had based my opinion that access to the great man, as in Goethe's case, would be surrounded by difficulties of every kind. Hence I first hunted up several persons whom I knew maintained or had maintained relations with him, such as Grillparzer. Yet wherever I might inquire I was advised to go directly to him: "If you just happen to visit him on one of his bad days," a friend of his told me, "he would not receive you though you were the Emperor himself. Preparations are useless. Honesty, directness and freedom are the best recommendations where he is concerned. Do not allow yourself to be rebuffed by a surly reception; visit him a second time, and he may repay you doubly for any discourtesy he might have shown you the first time." So one morning with a beating heart I resolved to set out for No. 767 *Krugerstrasse*, fourth floor, where Beethoven was living at the time.

When I had ascended the quite considerable number of steps I found at my left a bell-pull with a name half-erased, yet which I thought I could decipher as that of Beethoven. I rang; steps drew near; the door opened; and my pulse raced. Actually I am no longer able to say whether a maid or a young man, Beethoven's nephew, who then was living with him, and whom later I met once or twice, opened the door for me. My high inner tension had robbed me of all consciousness of external happenings. I only recollect that I could not manage to get out the question: "Does Mr. Beethoven live here?" How the gigantic weight of a great name demolishes the pigmy rules and barriers of convention, behind which the immeasurable pettiness of the every-day safeguards its vain rights.

These forms, however, in this case also refused to relinquish their petty claims. I was announced, handing over my letter from Zelter, as a card of admission, and stood waiting in the anteroom. I could still paint it from memory in its half-void, half-disordered confusion. On the floor stood a number of emptied bottles; on a plain table a few plates and two glasses, one of them half-filled. "Could Beethoven have left this half-emptied glass?" I wondered. And the desire seized me to drink what was left, as a secret theft of brotherhood in common, that brotherhood by which German custom binds two hearts.

The door of the adjoining room opened; I was asked to enter. As I stepped timidly over the sacred threshold, I could hear my heart beat. I had already stood in the presence of various great men whom I, the youthful poet, saw tower above me at the same immeasurable heighth; I will mention only Goethe and Jean Paul.

Yet this sensation which now filled me I had not experienced when confronted with the two I have mentioned. I will not arrogantly say that it was an *anch' io sono pittore*[1] which had made access to them free from constraint, and which made it easier to set up the bridge of intellectual communication; yet for all that I belonged to the same artistic realm over which they ruled, we spoke the same language. I had a more valid right to be answered; I could more securely ground that right and, finally, in the field of poetic thought a

---

[1] "I, too, am a painter," the remark attributed to Coreggio when first he saw Raffaele's painting of St. Cecilia.

greater number of connecting threads spun themselves out between us, from one to the other. And this to say nothing of the well-nigh impassible barrier which Beethoven's deaf ear opposed to every more intimate sympathetic approach. And yet, that which in the first moments seemed to separate us, the difference in our creative fields, later approached us one to the other. A mediocre musician, perhaps, would have struck Beethoven as the most negligible, the most tiresome person in the world; a passably talented poet, at least, still gave him something which he himself did not possess yet valued and loved.

As I entered, my very first glance was for him. He was carelessly seated on a disordered bed against the rear wall of the room, one on which he appeared to have been resting only the moment before. In his one hand he held Zelter's letter, the other he stretched amiably out to me with a look of such kindness and at the same time of such suffering that suddenly every separating wall of unease fell, and I advanced toward him whom I so profoundly reverenced glowing with the fullest warmth of affection. He rose, gave me his hand, pressed my own heartily, in true German fashion, and said: "You have brought me a fine letter from Zelter! He is a real protector of true art!" Accustomed to defray the larger part of the burden of conversation, since he could only with difficulty gather what was said in reply, he continued: "I am not quite well, I have been ill. You will not find me very entertaining, for I am very deaf."

What I replied, whether I replied—really, I am unable to say! My looks, my repeated pressures of the hand, will best have expressed that for which, perhaps, words would have failed me, even if, in this instance, I could have spoken as I did to others.

Beethoven invited me to take a seat; and he himself sat down on a chair in front of the bed, moving it over to a table which, two paces away, was completely covered with treasures, with notes in Beethoven's own hand, and with the work with which he was busy at the moment. I took a chair next to his. Then I surveyed the room with a rapid glance. It was as large as the anteroom and had two windows. Beneath the windows stood the grand piano. Otherwise nothing which in any way betrayed comfort or convenience, to say nothing of splendor or luxury, was visible. A writing cabinet, some chairs and tables, white walls with old, dusty hangings—such was Beethoven's room. What cared he for bronzes, mirrored walls, divans, gold and silver! He, to whom all the glory of this world was but vanity, dust and ashes compared with that divine spark which, outshining all else, flames up from his soul!

Thus I sat beside the sick, melancholy sufferer. His hair, almost totally gray, rose bushily and in disorder from his head; not soft, not curly, not stiff, a mixture of all three. His features at first glance seemed lacking in significance: his face was much smaller than I had pictured it in accordance with the likeness which has forcibly constrained it to an appearance of powerful, genial savagery. There was nothing which expressed that brusqueness, that tempestuous, unshackled quality which has been lent his physiognomy in order to bring it into conformity with his works. Yet why should Beethoven's features look like his scores? His complexion was brownish, yet not the strong, healthy tan which the huntsman acquires, but rather one transposed into a sickly, yellowish tone. His nose was narrow and sharp, his mouth benevolent, his eye small, light-gray, yet eloquent. I read sadness, suffering and kindness in his face; yet I repeat, not a trace of the harshness, not a trace of the tremendous boldness which characterizes the impetus of his genius was even evanescently noticeable. I do not wish to deceive the reader with poetic inventions, but to tell him the truth, give a true reflection of a treasured likeness. And in spite of all that just has been said, he lost nothing of that mysterious magnetic power, which so irresistibly enchains us in the external semblance of great men. For the suffering, the mute, silent anguish therein expressed, was not the consequence of a momentary indisposition, since a number of weeks later, when Beethoven felt much better, I recognized it again and again—but was the outcome of the whole unique fatality of his life, which welded the loftiest awards of substantiation with the most cruel renunciatory tests.

It was for this reason that the sight of the deep, silent grief which weighed upon his sadly melancholy brow and lay in his weary eyes filled me with unspeakable emotion. It called for great powers of self-control to sit opposite him and hold back the tear which would out.

After we had seated ourselves Beethoven handed me a slate and a pencil, saying:

"You must write down only what is most important and then I will be able to see my way clear; I have been used to it now for a year." Since he looked at me questioningly, I took up the slate and was about to set down the words: "I had asked Zelter to write you that I wished to do an opera poem for you." Beethoven was watching my hand and with his quick gift of divination fell in before I had finished with: "So Zelter writes me!" And with that he handed me the letter. Then I read it for the first time, and its lofty, dignified language, its profound veneration, its tense laconism of expression impressed me with double power in the sacred presence of the man to whom it was addressed. Beethoven seemed to guess what I felt, for upon him too, the letter could not have failed to have made a deep impression, as I might have gathered from his reception. Hence he repeated what he had said when first he had greeted me: "It is a fine letter! Zelter is a real protector of true art! Greet him heartily from me when you return! You

want to write an opera book for me," he continued,
"and that would give me much pleasure! It is so hard
to find a good poem! Grillparzer has promised me one;
he already has done one; yet we cannot quite comprehend one another. He wants the opposite to what I
want. You will have your troubles with me!"

I tried by pantomime to make him understand that I
would consider no labor too difficult in order to satisfy
him. Taking up the slate again I was about to write
"What type of poem would you like best?" Yet no
sooner had I written "type" than Beethoven resumed
the conversation: "As to the type I am not so much
concerned if only the subject-matter attracts me. Yet
I must be able to take up my task with love and fervor.
I could not compose operas like 'Don Giovanni' and
'Figaro.' I hold them both in aversion. I could not
have chosen such subjects," he continued; "they are too
frivolous for me." As he spoke he looked as though he
meant to say: "I am too profoundly unhappy, my life
is too deeply veiled in gloom, for me to give myself up to
so vain an amusement."

Within me a newly opened world of thought began
to stir too mightily to make it possible for me to reply
at once. Then, too, I listened in the hope of hearing
him say more about Mozart. What jewels Beethoven's
words regarding him would have been if he had expressed
himself spontaneously, yielding to his mood, the inner
urge of truth! An opinion extorted by question would
have been nothing compared to it. He kept silence,
however, and appeared to be waiting for me to speak in
turn.

It was difficult for me to express my most intimate
opinions with regard to a theme which even when two
persons discuss it verbally is hard to make mutually
clear without misunderstandings, and to express a most
intimate opinion by means of mere written aphorisms.
An expedient occurred to me, however, which appeared

decidedly practical with regard to the case in point. I wrote down the line: "I will name the subjects to you."

Beethoven nodded amiably. I took the pencil and wrote: "I shall give you samples in order to win your confidence!"

A gleam of joy crossed his face. He nodded to me, held out his hand and we rose. I saw that he was exhausted and hence seized my hat. And he, encouraging me in my intention of taking leave, yet in a friendly, open way said: "I am so tired and languid to-day! But you must return again very soon!" And then he gave me his hand in farewell, returning my warm pressure most heartily and I went! With what emotions! With what inward jubilation at the radiance of my lucky star and at the same time how stirred with sadness beyond any I had ever experienced! I felt an onrush of power, an urgent vocation to do, to accomplish, a sense of creative might to which nothing appeared impossible, nothing beyond reach; and yet, on the other hand, the actual realization of this hope seemed an impossible dream, one quite unattainable—as, in fact, it never was attained! Such was my first visit to Beethoven.

It seemed best to allow a few days go by before allowing myself to call on Beethoven a second time! And no matter how much I yearned to do so, it will be easy to realize that the magnificent, unfamiliar city might offer a young man full of the joy of life a sufficient quota of pleasures and enjoyments to make the days fly by quickly. At last I once more stood before the sacred portal, but this time my query was answered by the words: "The master is so ill that he can speak to no one!" This was a situation I had not foreseen. I was very much taken back, and must admit that the human egotism with which, unfortunately, we are born had played me a very shabby trick. For my natural reaction, of course, should have been concern and sympathy for so invaluable a life; and yet, when I honestly questioned myself, the only sensation experienced was one of preoccupation with my own disappointed expectations.

Sadly and slowly I descended the eighty or ninety stone steps again.   In the street I met an acquaintance who had seen me coming from Beethoven's door.   From a distance he called out to me: "You have been to see Beethoven?   Have you spoken to him?"   Naturally I told him what had happened.   He replied: "I can give you a little comfort.   This evening—an admission price is charged, it is true, yet the affair is given only for a small, intimate circle of music-lovers—one of Beethoven's latest quartets, still in manuscript, but which has been bought by Steiner (the owner of the present Haslinger music-publishing house) will be played.   I will call for you and take you there."   I accepted his offer with joy.

Toward seven o'clock we found ourselves in a small pub on the *Graben* [the dry fosse or moat surrounding the old, inner city of Vienna] which could not even be called a private *salon*, but at the most a large room; yet in which quite a respectable number of listeners already had gathered, among whom I met, insofar as I had made their acquaintance, the first musicians of Vienna.   There was not space enough to sit, either in the large room or in the small adjoining anteroom; and only a few chairs had been set out.   The four quartet players had barely enough room for their stands and places, and were thickly surrounded.   There were some of the most admirable younger Vienna virtuosos, who had dedicated themselves to their important task with all the enthusiasm of youth, and had held seventeen (or even more) rehearsals before daring to give the enigmatic new composition even a semi-public performance before a number of connoisseurs.   And so impossible of conquest and so insoluable, at that time, did the difficulties and secrets of Beethoven's last quartets still seem to be, that only these enthusiastic young men had been willing to foregather to dare an attempt, while older and more famous players declared that the work could not be performed. It was the Quartet in E-flat major, Op. 127, which they played. And just as the players had been obliged to study, moil and toil until they had clambered up its precipitous heights, so did the listeners find that it was not to be taken too lightly—and with this presumption in mind, it had at once been settled in advance that the work should be played twice in succession.

Beethoven's indisposition did not yield, for April was raw and cheerless. The time for my departure from Vienna drew nearer and nearer, and the apprehension that perhaps I was not destined to see him again began to alarm me.

At last, after an interval of more than two weeks, I determined to attempt another visit. With my heart beating in the old familiar way I rang at the well-known door; it opened—and Beethoven himself confronted me, a surprise which found me so totally unprepared that, in fact, no turn of phrase with which I might skillfully meet the situation presented itself to me. But then who would have thought that Beethoven might open his door himself, like any other simple Vienna burgher, when a stranger rang the bell or knocked. His amiable, friendly nature, however, guided me over all the rocks of embarrassment. For, though at first the unwelcome disturber had made him look out of sorts, he said in a very friendly manner: "Ah, it is you! You have not visited me for a good long while. I even thought you already had left the city!" His words were calculated to surprise me, yet since one could only answer him in writing, I contented myself with accompanying a negative shake of my head with a movement of one hand intended to convey that it would have been impossible for me to depart without having taken leave of him.

Nothing in the world would have prevented me from doing so in writing, at the very least!

Beethoven led me into his room and, as he handed me the writing-slate which lay ever at hand, invited me to sit down. I wrote: "Your illness prevented me from coming to you!" "Ah," he cried, "that should not have kept you! In winter I always am in the same state in which I recently have been. I do not feel well until I move out into the country in summer. Who told you that I had been ill?" I explained briefly in writing what happened to me. He once more shook his head. "I often have my hours of gloom," he went on, "when I tell those about me to admit no one! But they do not know how to make distinctions. I have so many wearisome, irksome visitors! Aristocratic folk! I am useless for that sort of thing!"

"Have you received my poems?" I wrote, seeing that he had paused.

He nodded and pointed to the table where some sheets of my verse lay scattered about among many other papers: "I like them very much," he said, "and when I am well I expect to set some of them to music." I seized his hand and pressed it with all heartiness. This, I thought, spoke more clearly than if I had taken the pencil and set down in formal words: That would be my greatest joy. And Beethoven understood how I meant it; as his glance and answering pressure of the hand informed me.

"In the winter," he began after a few moments, "I do but little. I only elaborate and score what I have written during the summer. Yet even that consumes a great deal of time. At present I still have to work on a Mass. When I once get out into the country again then I shall be in the right mood for everything."

Since he fell silent and seemed to be waiting for me to resume, I wrote down: "I made the acquaintance of your brother last week." These words did not make a favorable impression. A half-annoyed, half-melancholy expression passed over Beethoven's features. "Ah, my brother," he finally said, "he chatters a great deal. He must have bored you greatly."

In order to erase the disagreeable impression my remark had made I wrote down that I had heard his Quartet in E-flat major played at the affair described. A happy smile vivified his languid glance when he read the words; yet it was but momentary; then he spoke, as though in self-reproof: "It is so difficult that they probably played it badly! Did it go at all?"

My written answer, expressed with greatest brevity was: "It had been carefully practised and was played twice in immediate succession." "That is well. It must be heard several times. How did you like it?" To reply to this question caused me no little embarrassment. How was I to explain to him the impression the work had made on me? To this day I have my own scruples anent expressing my conviction that in this last, enigmatic work by Beethoven are to be found only the ruins of the erstwhile youthful and virile exaltation of his genius; that it often is buried beneath the most disordered rubble and wreckage. Yet I still have my compunctions, and often doubts overtake me as to whether, perhaps, it is not my own lack of comprehension which calls forth my impression. What was I to say at that time? Yet I still might express without qualification one truth which, if it did not glorify the work, at least would reveal to the Master the mood into which the composition as a whole had transported me. So I wrote: "I was devoutly and profoundly moved to the depths of my soul!"

And at that very moment such was again the case. Beethoven read and kept silence; we looked at each other and said not a word, yet a world of sensations flooded my breast. Beethoven, too, was unmistakably touched. He rose and went to the window, where he remained standing beside the piano. To see him so near the instrument called up a thought in me which I never before had dared entertain. If he—ah! He would but need to make a half-turn to bring him directly before the keys —if he would only seat himself, pour out his emotions in tone! Filled with a timidly blissful hope I followed him, stepped up to him, and laid my hand on the instrument, an English grand of Broadwood's make. With my left hand I softly sounded a chord, in order to induce Beethoven to turn around; yet he did not seem to have heard it. A few moments later, however, he did turn to me since he saw that my eyes were fixed on the instrument and said: "It is a fine piano! I received it from London as a gift. There are the names of the donors!"

He pointed with his finger to the crossbeam over the keyboard. And there, in fact, I saw the names: Moscheles, Kalkbrenner, Cramer, Clementi and Broadwood himself [actually the names read: Kalkbrenner, Ries, Ferrari, Cramer, Knyvett]. The incident was touching. The wealthy, artistic builder had been able to find no better destination for his instrument, which seems to have been an exceptionally successful example of his skill, than to present it to Beethoven as a gift. The great artists named, as godfathers of this thought, so to say, had reverently signed their names, and thus the curious albumleaf had crossed the sea, in order to lay at the feet of the most exalted, the most celebrated of all the homages of the famous. "It is a handsome gift," he continued, stretching his hands out toward the keys, yet without ceasing to hold my eye. He gently struck a chord. Never again will one penetrate my soul with such a wealth of woe, with so heart-rending an accent! He had struck the C-major chord with his right hand, and played a B to it in the bass, his eyes never leaving mine; and, in order that it might make the soft tone of the instrument sound at its best, he repeated the false chord several times and—the greatest musician on earth did not hear its dissonance!

Whether Beethoven had noticed his error I do not know. Yet when he turned his head from me and toward the instrument, he struck several chord sequences with absolute correctness, as they might lie convenient to an accustomed hand, but then at once ceased playing. That was all I heard him play himself.

My stay in Vienna was nearing its end, at least for the time being. I had difficulty in securing a free hour in which to bid Beethoven adieu, against the chance that I would not see him again when I returned. As to the details of this last visit of mine I can report but little. Beethoven spoke freely, with much animation. I expressed my regrets that during the entire period of my stay in Vienna I had heard but one symphony of his, no quartet (save the one mentioned), that I had not had a chance of listening to a single composition of his in concert and that "Fidelio" had not been given.

This gave him an opportunity of freeing his mind with regard to the taste of the Vienna public. "Since the Italians (Barbaja) have so firmly established themselves here, the best has been crowded out. For the aristocracy the ballet is the main thing about the opera stage. Artistic appreciation is out of the question; they think only of the ballet-dancers. Our good times in this city lie in the past. But that I do not care about: I now wish only to write that which gives me pleasure. If I were well I would be indifferent to it all." Thus he relieved himself in these and similar remarks.

I then wrote down on the tablet: "To-morrow I am travelling to Pressburg and Eisenstadt for a few days; yet we will return by the first of May and, perhaps, will once more spend a few days in Vienna."

Our pleasant excursion into Hungarian territory had been accomplished under the serenest skies of the awakening spring. We still had two days left for Vienna, days into which, it is true, a great deal had to be crowded together. Yet I did manage to snatch an hour in order to hunt up Beethoven once more; for since our last moment of parting I felt that we were more closely connected; that, perhaps, we might approach each other even more intimately; and with this feeling confidence in my undertaking once more grew strong within me.

Hastily I had hurried up the long flight of stairs—but in vain. For the first time I was told that Beethoven was not at home. The first moment I was painfully moved; yet soon reflected that, after all, it probably was best so. My unforgettable moment of farewell could not be repeated; instead of that most glowing recollection I might have carried away a chiller one. Hence I made up my mind to leave behind only my name, with a word of adieu beneath it, that Beethoven might see no heedless negligence on my part had prevented my revisiting him. Once more I cast a glance at the anteroom, at the door before which I had experienced such strangely tense and oppressive moments, then turned quickly away, in an unclear mingling of emotions, which every one who understands such matters will comprehend without description, and which nothing in the world would make comprehensible to one untouched by the fact itself.

I now regarded all these matters as settled, so far as I was concerned, and attended with a greater feeling of ease to what I still had to do in the beautiful, radiant imperial city.

Our departure for Gratz had been fixed for the following afternoon, at six o'clock. Chance rather than a little business errand led me once more to the Steinert music-house, which lay opposite my dwelling.

"It is well that you have come," the proprietor called out to me, "a letter has been left here for you from Beethoven."

"From Beethoven!" I cried joyfully startled, and trembled with impatience until it had been put in my hands. It was, with a mistake in the initial letter of my name, addressed to Mr. L. Nellstab; yet it was truly meant for me! One of Beethoven's letters—for me!

About to go to the country I had to attend to some arrangements, yesterday in person and hence, unfortunately, you made your visit to me in vain. Pardon the state of my health, which is still very poor and since, perhaps, I shall not see you again, I wish you every conceivable benefit and advantage. Think of me when you write your poems!

Your friend,
Beethoven.

For Zelter, the brave maintainer
of true art, all my love and esteem.

May 23, 1825.

I turned over the page and found still more: a reiterated salute and a little canon. Beethoven had written:

"While convalescing, I still find that I am extremely weak; content yourself with this trifling token of remembrance from your friend Beethoven":

Das Schö-ne zu dem Gu-ten. Das

The following year I did not return to Vienna. On March 26, 1827, he yielded up his noble, heavily-burdened, weary soul.

SIR GEORGE SMART
(1825)

In his two volumes of Beethoven-reminiscences of contemporaries, Kerst begins his note on Sir George Smart (1776-1867) with the words "George Smart, an English music-publisher, visited Vienna in 1825." The date is correct, but this could have been a visit in spirit only, since George Smart, the father of Sir George (knighted in 1811) had died long ago. However, in a sense Sir George was a "publisher" of music, too, for he conducted with eminent skill many concerts of the Philharmonic Society of London and numerous music-festivals. Among many other noteworthy events he had to his credit the first performance of the Ninth Symphony at London on March 21, 1825. Indeed, it was because of his ardent championship of Beethoven's symphonies that he visited Vienna and called on Beethoven with whom he thus far had formed an acquaintance by correspondence only. He went to Germany in company with Charles Kemble whose object it was to engage Weber to compose an opera for Covent Garden and it was at Sir George's house that the composer of "Oberon" lived as a guest and died on June 5, 1826.

Sir George kept a diary of his experiences. They were published as "Leaves from the Journal of Sir George Smart" by Longmans, Green & Co., in 1907, and the following narrative is quoted from that delightful book.

Friday, September 9th. . . . We then went to Mecchetti's music shop, they too are publishers, and bought three pieces for Birchall. . . . Mr. Holz, an amateur in some public office and a good violin player, came in and said Beethoven had come from Baden this morning and would be at his nephew's—Carl Beethoven, a young man aged twenty—No. 72 Alleegasse. . . . At twelve I took Ries to the Hotel Wildemann, the lodgings of Mr. Schlesinger, the music-seller of Paris, as I understood from Mr. Holz that Beethoven would be there and there I found him. He received me in the most flattering manner. There was a numerous assembly of professors to hear Beethoven's second new manuscript quartette, bought by Mr. Schlesinger. This quartette is three-quarters of an hour long. They played it twice. The four performers were Schuppanzigh, Holz, Weiss, and Lincke. It is most chromatic and there is a slow movement entitled "Praise for the recovery of an invalid." Beethoven intended to allude to himself, I suppose, for he was very ill during the early part of this year. He directed the performers, and took off his coat, the room being warm and crowded. A staccato passage not being expressed to the satisfaction of his eye, for alas, he could not hear, he seized Holz's violin and played the passage a quarter of a tone too flat. I looked over the score during the performance. All paid him the greatest attention. About fourteen were present, those I knew were Boehm (violin), Marx ('cello), Carl Czerny, also Beethoven's nephew, who is like Count St. Antonio, so is Boehm, the violin player. The partner of Steiner, the music-seller, was also there. I fixed to go to Beethoven at Baden on Sunday and left at twenty-five minutes past two. . . .

Saturday, September 10th. . . . Previous to this sightseeing I called for the music at Artaria's for Birchall, for which I paid, and on our return found a visiting-card from Earl Stanhope and also from Schlesinger of Paris with a message that Beethoven would be at his hotel to-morrow at twelve, therefore, of course, I gave up going to Baden to visit Beethoven, which he had arranged for me to do. . . .

Sunday, September 11th. . . . From hence I went alone to Schlesinger's at the "Wildemann," where was a larger party than the previous one. Among them was L'Abbé Stadler, a fine old man and a good composer of the old school, to whom I was introduced. There was also present a pupil of Moscheles, a Mademoiselle Eskeles and a Mademoiselle Cimia, whom I understood to be a professional player. When I entered Messrs. C. Czerny, Schuppanzigh and Lincke had just begun the trio, Op. 70 of Beethoven, after this the same performers played Beethoven's trio, Op. 79—both printed singly by Steiner. Then followed Beethoven's quartette, the same that I heard on September the 9th, and it was played by the same performers. Beethoven was seated near the pianoforte, beating time during the performance of these pieces. This ended, most of the company departed, but Schlesinger invited me to stop and dine with the following party of ten. Beethoven, his nephew, Holz, Weiss, C. Czerny, who sat at the bottom of the table, Lincke, Jean Sedlatzek—a flute player who is coming to England next year and has letters to the Duke of Devonshire, Count St. Antonio, etc.—he has been to

Italy—Schlesinger, Schuppanzigh, who sat at the top, and myself. Beethoven calls Schuppanzigh Sir John Falstaff, not a bad name considering the figure of this excellent violin player.

We had a most pleasant dinner, healths were given in the English style. Beethoven was delightfully gay but hurt that, in the letter Moscheles gave me, his name should be mixed up with the other professors. However, he soon got over it. He was much pleased and rather surprised at seeing in the oratorio bill I gave him that the "Mount of Olives" and his "Battle Symphony" were both performed the same evening. He believes—I do not—that the high notes Handel wrote for trumpets were played formerly by one particular man. I gave him the oratorio book and bill. He invited me, by his nephew, to Baden next Friday. After dinner he was coaxed to play extempore, observing in French to me, "Upon what subject shall I play?" Meanwhile he was touching the instrument thus:

to which I answered, "Upon that." On which theme he played for about twenty minutes in a most extraordinary manner, sometimes very fortissimo, but full of genius. When he rose at the conclusion of his playing he appeared greatly agitated. No one could be more agreeable than he was—plenty of jokes. He was in the highest of spirits. We all wrote to him by turns, but he can hear a little if you halloo quite close to his left ear. He was very severe in his observations about the Prince Regent never having noticed his present of the score of his "Battle Symphony." His nephew regretted that his uncle had no one to explain to him the profitable engagement offered by the Philharmonic Society last year. I have had a most delightful day. Schlesinger is very agreeable, he knows Weber and Franz Cramer's family. About seven I took a little walk with Carl Czerny— whom Neate taught, he says, to speak English. I then went to his house and played four or five duets with him, they are clever compositions but not easy. He taught young Liszt. About nine I went home by myself, having promised to go to C. Czerny's on Wednesday evening.

On Friday, September 16th, at half-past eight in the morning young Ries came and we went in a hired carriage from Mödling to Baden. The distance is about six miles south of Mödling and sixteen miles southwest of Vienna. The journey cost five florins in paper money and took us about an hour. After walking in the little park and looking at the baths we went to Beethoven's lodgings according to his invitation. These are curiously situated, a wooden circus for horsemanship has been erected in a large court before his house. He has four large-sized rooms opening into each other, furnished *à la genius*, in one is the grand pianoforte, much out of tune, given him by Broadwood, in which is written, besides the Latin line, the names of J. Cramer, Ferrari, and C. Knyvett. Beethoven gave me the time, by playing the subjects on the pianoforte, of many movements of his symphonies, including the Choral Symphony, which according to his account took three-quarters of an hour only in performance. The party present, namely Holz, the amateur violin; Carl Beethoven, the nephew; besides young Ries, agreed that the performance at Vienna only took that time; this I deem to be totally impossible. It seems at Vienna the Recit. was played only with four 'celli and two contra bassi which certainly is better than having the tutti bassi. Beethoven and we deservedly abused Reicha's printed specimen of fugueing. He told me of a Mass, not yet published, which he had composed. We had a long conversation on musical subjects conducted on my part in writing. He is very desirous to come to England. After ordering his dinner with his

funny old cook and telling his nephew to see to the wine,
we all five took a walk. Beethoven was generally in
advance humming some passage. . . . On our return we
had dinner at two o'clock. It was a most curious one
and so plentiful that dishes came in as we came out, for,
unfortunately, we were rather in a hurry to get to the
stage-coach by four, it being the only one going to Vienna
that evening. I overheard Beethoven say, "We will see
how much the Englishman can drink." *He* had the
worst of the trial. I gave him my diamond pin as a
remembrance of the high gratification I received by the
honour of his invitation and kind reception and he wrote
me the following droll canon as fast as his pen would
write in about two minutes of time as I stood at the door
ready to depart.

 He was very gay but I need not write down more, for
memory will ever retain the events of this pleasurable
day with Beethoven.

The canon Sir George mentions reads, with the dedication
translated into English, as follows:

Ars lon - ga   vi - ta bre - vis

Written on the 16th of September, 1825, in Baden, when my
dear talented musical artist and friend Smart (from England)
visited me here.

LUDWIG VAN BEETHOVEN.

GERHARD VON BREUNING
(1825–1827)

Moritz *Gerhard* von Breuning (1813-1892) was the son of Court-
Councilor of War Stephan von Breuning, the friend of Beethoven
since youth and whom by a strange coincidence of Fate he survived
by only two months: he died at Vienna on June 4, 1827. Late in
life, in 1874, Gerhard von Breuning gave to the musical world his

delightfully reminiscent book "Aus dem Schwarzspanierhause" which was to be the great composer's last lodging. Beethoven took a fancy to the bright boy, calling him his "Trousers-button" and his "Ariel." He also interested himself in his musical education. On one occasion, for instance, he had Gerhard play for him, listened critically and recommended Clementi's method instead of Czerny's. The lad's droll remarks often cheered Beethoven but his great friend's misery also weighed heavily at times on the kind-hearted boy. Of this we possess a pathetic proof in one of the *Conversations Hefte* shortly before Beethoven's death: having heard that the sick master's nights were made sleepless by vermin, the solicitous Gerhard brought with him a disinfectant to relieve the dying Beethoven from such torture.

In August, 1825, while taking an afternoon walk with my parents, I was fortunate enough to make Beethoven's acquaintance. We were walking along the promenade which runs around the city of Vienna and cuts its Escarpment (*glacis*) and at the moment we were between the *Kärnthnerthor* and the *Karolinentor*, into which latter gate my father meant to turn to take his way to his office, when we saw a man walking alone making directly for us. Our meeting, no sooner had we sighted one another, was followed on both sides by an unusually friendly exchange of greetings. He was powerful looking, of medium heighth; his walk as well as his very lively movements were energetic; his dress was not elegant but rather that of a plain townsman; and yet there was something about his appearance as a whole which escaped all classifications of caste.

He spoke almost uninterruptedly, asking how we were, questioning us about our present mode of life, our relatives on the Rhein and many other things and—hardly waiting for an answer to his query why my father had not visited him for so long a time, etc.—told us that some time ago he had been living in the *Kothgasse* and of late in *Krugerstrasse*, but that he was spending the summer in Baden. It was with quite special and joyous haste, however, that he informed us that soon—toward

the end of September—he would move into our immediate vicinity, into the *Schwarzspanierhaus* (we were
living in the so-called "Red" house belonging to Prince
Esterhazy, lying opposite to it at right angles) and this
information called forth increased interest on our part.
He added that he expected to see us much and often;
and at once begged my mother at last to put his poorly
managed housekeeping arrangements into order, to keep
eye on them, etc.

My father, though he said less when he did speak,
spoke in a manner noticeably loud and distinct and with
lively gesticulations; and amid hearty and repeated
assurances of both the wish and the will to see much of
him in the near future we parted from him for that day.

The wish I often had expressed to my parents: that
I might meet Beethoven, had at last been granted, and
with youthful impatience I counted the days which
would bring me into that long-yearned for closer touch
with the friend of my father's youth, whose name had
so often been mentioned to me. . . .

On various occasions the flames of love leaped high in
Beethoven's heart, yet ever at bottom with the honest
fundamental thought: "Not until I have the right to
call you mine!"

Once my father told my mother, when she had incidentally said to him that she could not quite understand how Beethoven, since he was neither handsome nor
elegant, but looked positively unkept and unkempt,
could have been such a favorite with the ladies: "And
yet he always has been fortunate with women." Beethoven always, where women were concerned, showed
himself possessed of noble, elevated sentiments, whether
in his friendships or in his love affairs.

On one occasion I visited Beethoven in his house in
the *Ungargasse*, near the Escarpment. He happened to
be standing at the piano with his hands on the keyboard.
When he saw me he brought down both hands on the keys

with a crash, laughed and walked away from the piano. With this he probably meant to say to me: "You thought I was going to play something for you, but that is just what I am not going to do!" Nor did I ask him.

Though all his household affairs were now in such good order [Frau von Breuning had put Beethoven's house-keeping arrangements into shape], the way in which he kept his room continued to be just as disorderly. His papers and possessions were dusty and lay about higgledy-piggledy; and in spite of the dazzling whiteness and cleanliness of his linen and his repeated bodily ablutions, his clothes remained unbrushed. This inordinate bathing may, perhaps, in some past time have been the primary incidental cause and origin of his deafness—perhaps owing to a rheumatic inflammation—rather than his "predisposition for intestinal complaints," as so often has been taken for granted. He always had been in the habit, after he had sat for a long time at the table composing and this had heated his head, of rushing to the wash-stand, pouring pitchersful of water over his overheated head and, after having thus cooled himself off and only slightly dried himself, of returning to his work or, even, in the meanwhile, hastening out into the open for a brief walk. All this was done in the greatest hurry, so that he might not be snatched out of his imaginative flight. How little he thought at the time of the need of drying his thick hair, sopping wet, is proven by the fact that, without his noticing it, the water he had poured over his head would flood the floor in quantities, leak through it, and appear on the room-ceiling of the lodgers living beneath him. This, on occasion, led to annoyances on the part of his fellow-lodgers, the janitor and, finally, the owner of the house, and even was responsible for his being given notice.

He liked to have us invite him to dinner, and would often send us a portion of fish, if he had ordered some bought for himself in the market; for fish was one of his favorite dishes and when he himself liked something he liked so share it with his friends.

Beethoven's outward appearance, owing to that indifference to dress peculiar to him, made him uncommonly noticeable on the street. Usually lost in thought and grumbling to himself, he not infrequently gesticulated with his arms as well when walking alone. When he was in company, he spoke very loudly and with great animation and, since whoever accompanied him was obliged to write down his answers in the conversation note-book, the promenade was interrupted by frequent stops, something which in itself attracted attention and was made more conspicuous by the replies he made in pantomime.

Hence the majority of those whom he met turned around to look when he had passed, and the street boys even poked fun at him and called after him. For this reason nephew Karl disdained to go out with Beethoven and once told him plainly that he was ashamed to accompany him in the street because he looked such a fool, a remark anent which Beethoven expressed himself to us in a deeply hurt and wounded manner. For my own part, I was proud to be allowed to show myself in the company of this great man.

The felt hat then worn, upon Beethoven's homecoming, though it might be dripping wet with rain, after merely giving it a slight shake (a habit he always observed in our house, without concern for what was in the room) he would clap on the very top of the hat-rack. In consequence it had lost its even top and was vaulted in an upward bulge. Brushed infrequently or not at all, before and after it had rained, and then again allowed to grow dusty, the hat acquired a permanently matted appearance. In addition he wore it, so far as possible, back from his face in order to leave his forehead free; while on either side his gray, disordered hair, as Rellstab so characteristically says, "neither curly nor stiff, but a mixture of all," stood out. Owing to his putting on and wearing his hat away from his face and back on his head, which he held high, the hat's hinder brim came into collision with his coat-collar, which at that time shot up high against the back of the head; and gave the brim in question a cocked-up shape; while the coat-collar itself, from its continual contact with the hat brim, seemed to have been worn away. The two unbuttoned coat-fronts, especially those of the blue frock coat with brass buttons, turned outward and flapped about his arms, especially when he was walking against the wind. In the same manner the two long ends of the white neckerchief knotted about his broad, turned-down shirt-collar streamed out. The double lorgnette which he wore because of his near-sightedness, hung loosely down. His coat-tails, however, were rather heavily burdened; for in addition to his watch, which often hung out on the one side, in the pocket of the other he had a folded quarto note-book, anything but thin, besides a conversation note-book in octavo format and a thick carpenter's pencil, for communication with friends and acquaintances whom he might meet; and also, in earlier days, while it still aided him, his ear-trumpet. The weight of the note-books considerably extended the length of the coat-tail containing them and, in addition, the pocket itself because of its own frequent pulling out and that of the note-books, hung down visibly on the same side, turned outward.

The well-known pen and ink drawing [Böhm's drawing, since Lyser's apparently first came into being after Beethoven's death] gives a fair idea of Beethoven's figure, even though he never wore his hat pressed sideways, as the drawing—with its usual exaggeration—presents it. The above sketch of Beethoven's outward appearance had been inextinguishably impressed upon my memory. It was thus that I so often saw him from our windows, toward two o'clock—his dinner-hour—

coming from the direction of the *Schottentor* across the Escarpment where the Votive Church now stands, his body and head, as usual, projecting (not stooping) forward, and bearing down alone upon his own house; or I myself might be walking with him.

In the street, where there was not always sufficient time to write, conversation with him was most difficult, and, that he was absolutely deaf was attested to me by the following striking proof, had proof been needed. Once we expected him for dinner, and it already was almost two o'clock, our dinner-hour. My parents, always suspecting that, lost in composition, he might not remember the appointed time, sent me out to fetch him over. I found him at his work-table, his face turned toward the open door of the room in which stood the piano, working at one of the last (Galitzin) quartets. With a brief upward glance, he bade me wait awhile, until he had set down on paper the thought which preoccupied him at the moment. For a short time I remained quiet, then I moved over to the piano standing nearest at hand, the one by Graff (with the attached resonance-gatherer) and, not convinced of Beethoven's tone-deafness, began to strum softly on the keys. Meanwhile I looked over at him again and again, to see whether this disturbed him. But when I saw that he was quite unconscious of it I played more loudly; then, purposely, very loudly —and my doubts were resolved. He did not hear me at all, and kept on writing with entire unconcern until, having at last finished, he summoned me to go. In the street he asked me something: I screamed the answer directly into his ear; but he understood my gestures rather than my words. Only once, when we were sitting at table, one of my sisters uttered a high, piercing shriek; and to know that he still had been able to hear it made Beethoven so happy that he laughed clearly and gleefully, his dazzlingly white and unbroken rows of teeth fully visible.

Characteristic, too, was the liveliness with which he discussed circumstances that interested him, and at such times it might even chance that walking up and down the room with my father, he would spit into the mirror instead of out of the window, without knowing it.

On September 24, 1826—it was my birthday—Beethoven was again our dinner guest in honor of the occasion. While we were eating, he told us that the Vienna city council had made him a Vienna citizen, and in this connection had informed him that he had become, not an ordinary but an honorary citizen, whereupon he had replied: "I did not know that there were also scandalary citizens in Vienna." [A pun on "Ehrenbürger" and "Schandbürger"].

In the afternoon we all went out to Schönbrunn together, on foot. My mother had a visit to make in Meidling (bordering on Schönbrunn) and I accompanied her. My father, Beethoven and my teacher waited for us on one of the benches in the parterre of the Schönbrunn Garden. When we then went walking in the garden, Beethoven, pointing to the leafy alleys trimmed in wall-pattern according to the French style, said: "Nothing but artifice, shaped up like the old hoop-petticoats! I feel benefited only when I am out where nature is free!" An infantryman passed us. At once he was ready with a sarcastic remark: "A slave, who has sold his independence for five *Kreuzer* a day!"

When we were going home, several boys in the middle of the right-hand park alley in front of the Schönbrunn bridge were playing bowls with a small ball, and the latter accidentally struck Beethoven's foot. Thinking it had been done with malicious intent, to plague him, he at once turned violently on them, calling out: "Who gave you permission to play here? Why do you have to pick out this particular spot for your carrying on?" And he was on the point of rushing on them to drive them away. My father, who feared the brutality of the

street arabs, however, soon calmed him, and, besides, the
ball which had grazed him had caused him no more than
a passing pain.

It was already dark when, returning over the
"Schmelz," we lost our way and were compelled to
walk straight across the ploughed fields. Beethoven
growled melodies to himself, as he swayed rather help-
lessly from one hummock to the next, and, in view of his
near-sightedness, was glad to have a guide for the time
being.

When his nephew Karl was about to take his examination in technics and, in addition, loaded with debts,
felt himself as unprepared in purse as he was in knowledge; besides, furthermore, dreading his uncle's re-
proaches, of which "he had already long since tired and
which he found silly"—he resolved to kill himself. He
bought two pistols, drove out to Baden, climbed the
tower of the ruinous Castle Rauenstein, and high up in
the air, putting both pistols to his temples, pressed the
triggers—and merely superficially injured the periosteum,
yet so that he had to be taken to the General Hospital
in Vienna.

The news was a terrible blow to Beethoven. The
sorrow which the occurrence caused him was indescribable; he was as downcast as a father who has lost his
well-beloved son. My mother met him, seemingly
quite deranged, on the Escarpment. "Do you know
what has happened to me? My Karl has shot himself!"
"And—is he dead?" "No, he only grazed himself; he
is still alive and they hope to be able to save him. But
how he has disgraced me, and I love him so very dearly!"

I must preface what comes next by telling how now
that my ardent desire to enter into close daily communion
with Beethoven had been most fully gratified, I nourished
the further wish to be able, like my father, to call him
"du" [in German the "you" of intimate friendship and
affection]. Had I not long since attached myself to

him with all my soul, and taken no little pride in knowing he loved me and that I, too, was one among the few chosen ones in this connection? I asked my father how I might introduce the subject and whether he would act for me in the matter. My father replied offhand: "If it will give you pleasure all these circumlocutions are unnecessary; simply address him as 'du,' and he will in nowise be offended, but more apt to be pleased. In any event it will not even seem strange to him." Relying on this encouragement, since I was well aware of how entirely at home my father was where Beethoven's mental processes were concerned, I at once made the venture on the occasion of my next visit, when I was alone with Beethoven (this was during the first earlier period of his illness). With a beating heart, it is true, and yet with venturesome boldness I made my attempt and in the first sentence I wrote down of our conversation, I used this form of address. I watched his features with tension when I held up the slate to him. And—it was as my father had foretold—Beethoven never even noticed it, and thus I henceforth continued to address him.

During his illness (toward the end of February, 1827) one forenoon, Handel's complete works—in a handsome bound quarto volume edition—arrived as a present, sent by the harp virtuoso Stumpff. Beethoven had long cherished the wish to own them, and it was in accordance with this very wish, which he had once expressed, that the gift had been made. When at noon I entered his room, as was my daily custom when the clock struck twelve, he at once pointed to the volumes heaped up on the piano, his eyes radiant with pleasure: "See, this is what I have received as a present to-day; they have made me very happy with these works! I have wished to own them for a long time because Handel is the greatest, the most solid of composers; from him I still can learn something. Fetch the books over to me!"

These and other things he said in connection with them, speaking with joyous excitement. And then I began to hand one after another volume to him in his bed. He turned the pages of one volume after the other, as I gave them to him, at times dwelling a while on certain passages, and then at once laying down one after another book to the right, on his bed, against the wall; until at last all were piled up there, where they remained for several hours, for I found them still there that afternoon. Then once more he began to deliver the liveliest eulogies on Handel's greatness, calling him the most classic and thorough of the tone poęts.

Once, as often was the case when I arrived, I found him asleep. I sat down beside his bed, keeping quiet—for I hoped the rest might be strengthening—in order not to awaken him. Meanwhile I turned the pages and read one of the conversation note-books which was still lying ready for use on the little table next the bed, to find out who had lately visited him, and what had been said. And there, among other things, I found in one place: "Your quartet which Schuppanzigh performed yesterday did not appeal to me." When he awoke a short time after I held the sentence up to him and asked him what he had to say to it: "Some day it will suit them," was his laconic reply. He at once added with legitimate self-confidence some brief remarks to the effect that he wrote as seemed well to him, and did not allow himself to be led astray by contemporary opinion: "I know that I am an artist!"

I improved an opportunity to ask him why he had written no second opera. He answered: "I wished to write another opera but I found no suitable text-book for it. I must have a text which stimulates me; it must be something moral, elevating. Texts which Mozart could compose I would never have been able to set to music. I never have been able to get into the mood for setting lewd texts. I have received many text-books,

but as I have said, none which I would wish to have."
And furthermore he said to me: "It was my wish to
write many another thing. I wanted to compose the
Tenth Symphony, and then a Requiem as well, and
the music to 'Faust,' and even a piano method. This
last I would have done in a way different from that
in which others have written them. Well, I shall no
longer get around to that, and, anyhow, so long as I
am sick, I will do no work, no matter how much Diabelli
and Haslinger may urge me; for I have to be in the mood
for it. Often I have been unable to compose for a long
time and then all at once the desire returned to me."

Another time I found a sketch-book lying on a piece of
furniture in the room. I held it up to him, asking
whether he really found it necessary to note down his
inspirations. He replied: "I always carry a note-book
of the kind about me, and when an idea occurs to me, at
once note it down. I even rise at night when something
happens to occur to me, since otherwise I might forget
the idea."

FRIEDRICH WIECK
(1824 or 1826)

Among Beethoven's most distinguished visitors during the last
years of his life was Friedrich Wieck (1785-1873), the teacher principally of Clara Schumann, whose marriage to Robert Schumann he
so strenuously opposed. Wieck, writing from memory for the "Dres-
dener Nachrichten," placed his visit in May, 1826, but Riemann in
the fifth volume of the German edition of Thayer's Beethoven biography argues that the visit probably took place in 1824 in Penzing.

It was in 1826, in May, that I was introduced to Beethoven by his and my own genial friend, the famous
instrument-maker Andreas Stein, as a tone-poet and
writer who had devoted much attention to improving
deafness and to ear-trumpets, and spent several hours
with him. Otherwise, according to Stein's experiences,
he would not have received me. Under the ruddy
grapes the conversation turned on musical conditions

in Leipzig—Rochlitz—Schicht—the *Gewandhaus*—his own housekeeper—his many lodgings, none of which really suited him—his promenades—Hietzing—Schön-brunn—his brother—various silly asses in Vienna— aristocracy—democracy—revolution—Napoleon—Mara, Catalani, Malibran, Fodor—and the gifted singers La-blache, Donzelli, Rubini, etc.—the perfected Italian opera (German opera never could attain perfection ow-ing to the language, and because the Germans could not sing as well as the Italians) and my opinion anent piano playing—the Archduke Rudolph—Fuchs, then a famous musical personage in Vienna—my improved method of piano instruction, etc.—all with the most rapid, continuous writing on my part (for he asked frequent and hasty questions) and with continual stoppages. For he grasped the whole when I had only completed my answer in part; yet all was done with a certain heartfelt sincerity, even in his utterances of despair, and with a deep inward rolling of his eyes and clutchings at his head and hair. All was rough, at times, perhaps, a little rude, yet noble, elegiac, soulful, well-principled, enthusiastic, anticipatory of political mishap. And then?

Then he improvised for me during an hour, after he had mounted his ear-trumpet and placed it on the reso-nance-plate on which already stood the pretty well battered, large grand piano, with its very powerful, rough tone, which had been presented to him by the city of London. He played in a flowing, genial manner, for the most part orchestrally, and was still quite adept in the passing over of the right and left hands (a few times he missed the mark), weaving in the clearest and most charming melodies, which seemed to stream to him unsought, most of the time keeping his eyes turned upward, and with close-gathered fingers. After three hours of the greatest tension, with a beating heart, after the most laborious and rapid writing, and the utmost exertions to return brief and appropriate replies, which he constantly interrupted with new queries, my whole being was filled with profoundest respect, as well as the sincerest joy that such good luck had been my portion. Then, too, there was the wine-drinking, to which I was unaccustomed! After a hearty farewell—and the prospect held out to him that he still would find the right ear-trumpet in the end because science now was making great discoveries in acoustics—I crept away with Andreas Stein quite exhausted and dissolved in the strangest sensations and excited by the whole unprecedented affair, and drove rapidly from Hietzing back home again.

DR. SPIKER
(1826)

Beethoven dedicated the Ninth Symphony to King Frederick William III of Prussia. First performed at Vienna on May 7, 1824, the symphony was published by Schott in Mayence in 1826. In September of this year the Royal Librarian Dr. Spiker visited Beethoven in order to discuss with him certain formalities for conveying the symphony to the King. His reminiscences of the master he published on April 25, 1827, in the "Berlinische Nachrichten." Hence, they possess, in distinction from so many other reminiscences, the value of a record practicably simultaneous with the event.

The manuscript collection mentioned by him at the end of his narrative was bequeathed by Archduke Rudolph to the *Gesellschaft der Musikfreunde* in Vienna which still cherishes it as one of its greatest among its many treasures.

It was not easy to see Beethoven himself in Vienna. His almost total loss of hearing had for result that only a few persons, to whose voices he was accustomed, were able to make him understand them. The inconvenience resulting from the fact that all others who wished to converse with him were obliged to have recourse to writing, possibly may have made it embarrassing for him to see friends in his home. But very little hope of seeing him had been held out to the writer of these lines himself, who most ardently wished to make Beethoven's

personal acquaintance. A certain circumstance, however, facilitated a meeting. Beethoven, as is well known,
after having secured permission from H. M. the King,
had dedicated his last symphony with choruses to the
All-highest and wished to have a perfect copy of the
original score, with all the improvements and interpola-
tions in his own hand reach H. M. as quickly and safely
as possible. We had to come to some understanding in
this connection, which motived an announcement of a
visit on my part, and Beethoven consented to see me.

Beethoven lived in the suburb on the *glacis*, before the
Schottentor, in a section not built up, where one had a
fine view of the capital, with all its magnificent buildings
and their background of landscape, in cheerful, sunny
rooms. Owing to his weak state of health, he made
frequent use of baths in his last years, and hence we (a
close friend of the late composer, Mr. Tobias Haslinger
and I) saw his bathing apparatus in the anteroom.
Opening on it was Beethoven's living-room, in which, in
rather genial disorder, scores, books, etc., were piled
helter-skelter, and in the middle of which stood a grand
fortepiano made by the admirable artist Konrad Graf.
The furniture was plain and the whole appearance of the
room was probably like that of many another person who
pays more attention to inward than to outward order.
Beethoven received us very amiably. He was dressed
in a plain gray morning suit which went very well with
his cheerful, jovial face and his artlessly ordered hair.
After we had enjoyed the lovely view from the windows
of his living-room, he invited us to sit down at a table
with him, and then our conversation began, conducted
on my part in writing, while Mr. Haslinger, to whose
voice Beethoven already was accustomed, shouted into
his ear what he wished to say.

Beethoven, first of all, spoke with great enthusiasm of
our king (King Frederick William IV of Prussia) doing
full justice to his love for the arts and for music in

particular; and expressed his great pleasure at the permission granted him (it had been made known to him by the deceased Prince Hatzfeld) to dedicate his last symphony to the monarch. Thus he also recalled with much emotion a friendly letter from H. M. the regnant Russian Empress Alexandra, in which she had requested him to select a Vienna grand fortepiano for her, and which expressed much enthusiasm with regard to the love for music shown by the royal family. His own circumstances in Vienna, Beethoven only touched upon fleetingly, and seemed to take pains to avoid recalling them. In general, however, he was exceptionally merry and laughed at every jest with the good-humored readiness of a man without guile who believed in all, something not to have been expected in view of the generally current rumor that Beethoven was very gloomy and shy. It was very interesting to see his musical sketch-book which, as he told us, he always carried with him on his walks in order to jot down with his lead-pencil any musical idea which might occur to him. It was full of individual measures of music, suggested figures, etc. Several large books of this kind, in which longer fragments of music had been written down in ink, lay on a desk beside his pianoforte.

Unfortunately his deafness—which also explained a peculiar mechanism fastened to his grand piano, a kind of resonance-holder, beneath which he sat when he played, and which was meant to catch up and concentrate the sound about him—made conversation with him a very wearisome matter which, however, in view of his uncommon liveliness, one seemed to feel but little. Paper and pencil were immediately at hand when we entered, and a page was soon covered with writing, answers to his queries and new questions asked him.

Among the many pictures of Beethoven extant I consider the one drawn of him in his younger years by Louis Letronne and Riedel's engraving those which most

resemble him. There was something unusually alive
and radiant in his eyes, and the mobility of his whole
being undoubtedly prevented anyone from regarding his
death in the near future as probable.

Of the princes of the imperial family none took a more
lively interest in his fate than his protector and patron,
the Archduke-Cardinal Rudolph. He now owns the
most complete collection of Beethoven's works in score,
comprising a long row of volumes in folio, in which all
the most delicate and graceful things we have by Beethoven also may be found. In the case of many works a
portion of the original manuscript has been added as
well, each individual one provided with an artistic
calligraphic title. This collection formerly was in the
possession of Mr. Tobias Haslinger (successor to the
well-known music dealer Steiner) who did so much for
music and its advancement in Vienna. Himself a composer, Haslinger began the collection as a friend of
Beethoven of years' standing, and then handed it over to
the Archduke.

THE END

Schindler to Moscheles.

February 22, 1827.

When you last were here, I already had described to
you Beethoven's financial circumstances without suspecting that the time was so near at hand when we would see
this estimable man approach the end of all in so wretched
a manner. Yes, one may well say "the end of all," for
with regard to his present illness his recovery is out of
the question, though this is something he is not allowed
to know, for all he himself suspects it.

Not until December 3d did he arrive here with his
worthless nephew. While on his journey hither, bad
weather compelled him to stay overnight at a wretched

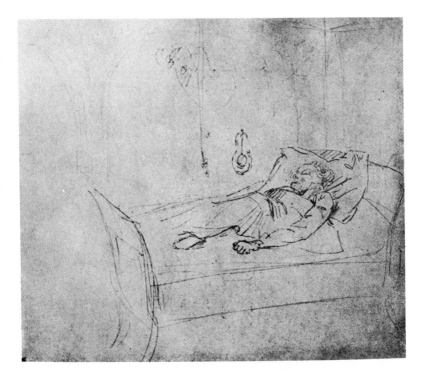

Sketch of the dying Beethoven by Teltscher, 1827
(Courtesy Beethovenhaus, Bonn)

inn, where he contracted such a cold that an immediate inflammation of the lungs resulted and it was in this condition that he arrived. No sooner had this been removed, than he developed all the symptoms of a dropsy which made such rapid headway that he already had to be tapped for the first time on December 18th, since otherwise he would have burst. On January 8th the second operation followed, and on January 20th the third. After the second and third tappings the water was allowed to flow from the wound for eleven days; but no sooner did the wound heal than the rush of water was so tremendously swift that I often feared he would choke before we could get to the operation. Only now do I observe that the rush of water is not so swift as before, since now, if matters continue as at present, some eight or ten days may easily pass before the fourth puncture is made.

Well, my friend, think of Beethoven with such a terrible disease, given his impatience and, above all, with his temperament. Think of his having been brought to this pass owing to that despicable creature, his nephew, and also in part by his brother; for both physicians, Messrs. Malfatti and Professor Wawruch, declare his illness due to the terrible mental disturbances to which this good man was for so long a time subjected by his nephew, as well as to his long stay in the country during the rainy season of the year; something which could not easily be altered because the young gentleman could not remain in Vienna owing to a police order and an opening in a regiment could not at once be found for him. Now he is a cadet with the Archduke Ludwig and treats his uncle just as he did before, though now as then, he depends on him absolutely. The letter to Sir Smart already had been sent him by Beethoven fourteen days ago, for translation into English, yet up to this day no answer has been returned, though he is but a few steps from this place, in Iglau.

Should you, my dear, splendid Moscheles, in connection with Sir Smart, be able so to arrange that the Philharmonic Society accedes to his wish you doubtlessly will be doing him the greatest of benefits; the expenses of this tedious illness are extraordinary, and hence the supposition that as a consequence he will have to suffer privations, torments him day and night; for to be obliged to accept anything from his horrible brother would certainly kill him.

As it is now evident his dropsy is turning into a wasting away, for now he is no more than skin and bones; yet his constitution bids fair to withstand this terrible end for a very long period of time.

What hurts him greatly is the fact that no one here takes any notice of him; and in truth this lack of interest is most striking. Formerly people drove up in their carriages if he were no more than indisposed; now he is totally forgotten, as though he had never lived in Vienna. I myself suffer the greatest annoyance, and earnestly wish that matters may soon take a turn with him, in one or another way, for I am losing all my time since I devote it altogether to him, because he will suffer none other about him, and to abandon him in his absolutely helpless condition would be inhuman.

He now often speaks of a journey to London when he is well again, and already is calculating how both of us may live most cheaply during the trip. But, good God in heaven! Let us hope the journey will take him further than England. He distracts himself, when alone, reading the ancient Greeks, and he also has read with pleasure several of the Walter Scott novels.

Ferdinand Hiller, the composer, in Landau's Beethoven Album, 1877.

Though at that time one heard less about the greatest men than we now do every week about the least noteworthy, the news of Beethoven's illness, nevertheless, had reached Weimar. He was suffering from dropsy. In Vienna, the artists who had visited Hummel reported the worst with regard to his condition. On the one hand it was hopeless; on the other unspeakably sad. Absolute deafness, a continually increasing distrust of everyone on earth, and now, added to this, bodily sufferings—unsuccessful operations—discontent and loneliness—and an appearance which almost excited horror. Thus forewarned we drove out to the suburb. Through a commodious anteroom in which tall closets held thick, corded masses of music, we came (how my heart beat!) into Beethoven's living-room, and were not a little surprised to see the Master to all appearances quite comfortably seated at the window. He wore a long, gray dressing-gown, completely open at the moment, and high boots which reached to his knees. Emaciated by his evil malady he seemed to me, as he rose, to be tall in statue. He was unshaven, his heavy, partly gray hair hung in disorder over his temples, the expression of his features grew very mild and gentle when he caught sight of Hummel, and he seemed to be extraordinarily glad to see him. The two men embraced with the utmost heartiness; Hummel presented me; Beethoven was entirely gracious and I was allowed to sit down opposite him at the window.

As is known, verbal conversation with Beethoven was in part carried on in writing. He spoke, but those with whom he spoke were obliged to write out their questions and answers. For this purpose thick note-books of ordinary writing-paper in quarto format and lead-pencils always lay near him. How annoying must it not have been to this lively man, who so easily became impatient, to have to wait for every reply, to have to endure a pause at every moment of conversation, during which his own mental activity, so to say, was condemned to inaction. Then, too, he followed the writer's hand with greedy eye and seized what had been written with a glance rather than read it.

The continuous manual labor of writing on the part of his visitors naturally greatly hampered liveliness of conversation. I can hardly blame myself, no matter how greatly I regret it, that I did not write out in greater detail all that Beethoven said at the time; in fact, I must even rejoice that the fifteen-year-old boy, who had come to a great city for the first time in his life, had enough self-control to note down any details at all. I can vouch for the absolute exactness of all that I am able to reproduce, however, with a clear conscience. The conversation at first, as was customary, turned on house and Court, our journey and visit, my relations to Hummel and other matters of the sort. Beethoven asked after Goethe with quite special sympathy, and we were able to give him the best of news. Had not the great poet, only a few days before, written some verses alluding to our trip in my album. Poor Beethoven complained greatly about his condition. "Here I have been lying all of four months," he cried, "one loses patience in the end." And much else in Vienna did not seem to suit him and he expressed himself in the most cutting manner with regard to "the present taste in art," and anent "the amateurishness which ruins everything here." Nor was the government, up to its highest heads, spared. "Write a book of penitential psalms and dedicate it to the Empress!" he said laughing morosely, to Hummel who, however, did not follow this well-meant advice.

Hummel, who was a practical person, took advantage of Beethoven's momentarily favorable condition to communicate to him something which cost considerable time to tell. Reprinting was then in fullest blossom. In publishing one of the Master's concertos (I think it was the one in E-flat major) it had chanced that the composition, of which a copy had been purloined from the office of the rightful publisher, had not only been *re*printed, but *pre*printed as well, for the thief, in fact, issued it before the date on which the owner was permitted to print it.

And now Hummel wished to address himself to the illustrious Diet with a petition so that this might be done away with, for which purpose he laid great weight on Beethoven's signature. He sat down in order to explain the matter on paper and in the meantime I had the honor of carrying on the conversation with Beethoven. I did my best and the Master continued to give rein to his part melancholy, part passionate outpourings in the most confidential way. The greater part of them had reference to his nephew, whom he greatly loved, and who—as is known—caused him much unhappiness, and at the time owing to some trifles (for thus Beethoven seemed to regard them) had gotten into difficulties with the authorities. "They hang the little thieves and let the big ones escape!" he cried out peevishly. Asking about my studies and encouraging me he said: "One must always transmit art"; and when I spoke about the exclusive interest which Italian opera then commanded in Vienna he burst out into the remarkable words: "They say, *vox populi, vox Dei*—I never have believed it."

On March 13th Hummel took me to Beethoven the second time. We found that his condition had changed decidedly for the worse. He lay in bed, seemed to be suffering violent pain and occasionally gave a deep groan, although he talked a good deal and with animation. He now appeared to take it to heart that he never had married. Already, on our first visit, he had joked about the matter with Hummel, whose wife he had known as a young, beautiful girl. "You," he said to him on this occasion, with a smile, "you are a lucky man. You have a wife who takes care of you, who is in love with you, while I, poor unfortunate!——" and he sighed heavily. He also begged Hummel to fetch his wife to visit him, though the latter had not been able to bring herself to see in his present state the man whom she had known when he was at the heighth of his powers. A short time before Beethoven had been presented with a picture of the house in which Haydn had been born: he had it near his bed and showed it to us: "I was as pleased as any child," said he—"the cradle of a great man!"

Not long after our second visit the news spread through Vienna that the London Philharmonic Society had sent Beethoven one hundred pounds sterling, in order to ameliorate his sufferings. It was added that the surprise had made so deep an impression on the poor great man that he even felt himself bodily much relieved. When we once more stood by his bedside on the 20th, his remarks, it is true, showed how much the attention had rejoiced him, but he was very weak and spoke only in a low voice and in broken sentences. "I shall probably soon make my way up above," he whispered after we had greeted him.

Similar exclamations he uttered frequently, yet together with them he voiced hopes and projects which, unfortunately, were not to be realized. Speaking of the noble action of the Philharmonic Society and praising the English, he opined that as soon as his condition had improved he would undertake the journey to London. "I shall compose a great overture and a great symphony for them." And then he also wished to visit Madame Hummel (she had come with us) and stop, I no longer recall just where, at all sorts of places. It did not even occur to us to write down anything for him. His eyes, which when last we had seen them, still had shown considerable life, had collapsed, and he found it hard, from time to time, to sit up. It was impossible longer to deceive one's self—the worst was to be anticipated.

Altogether hopeless was the appearance of this extraordinary man when we once more visited him on March 23d, for the last time. He lay there faint and wretched, at times sighing gently. No further word passed his lips;

the perspiration stood out on his brow. Seeing that by some chance he did not have his handkerchief at hand, Hummel's wife took her dainty wisp of battiste and at different times dried his face. Never shall I forget the grateful glance which his broken eyes sent up to her when she did this. While we were spending March 26th in the home of the art-loving Mr. von Liebenberg (who formerly had been Hummel's pupil) in merry company, we were surprised between five and six o'clock by a heavy thunderstorm. A dense fall of snow was accompanied by violent thunder and lightnings which illuminated the whole chamber.

A few hours later guests arrived with the news that Ludwig van Beethoven was no more; that he had died at quarter to five.

Schindler to Moscheles.

March 24, 1827.

My dear Moscheles, when you read these lines, our friend will no longer be among the living. His dissolution advances with giant strides, and we all have but the single wish that we soon may see him relieved of his terrible sufferings. Nothing else remains for us to do. For the past eight days he has been lying like one wellnigh dead, save that there are frequent moments when he gathers his last energies to ask about something or for something. His condition is terrible and exactly like that (as we have recently read) of the Duke of York. He is continually plunged in dull brooding, hangs his head on his breast, and stares for hours at a time at one spot. He seldom recognizes those whom he knows best save when he is told who is standing before him. In short, it is horrifying to see all this: and it is a condition which can endure only a few days longer, for since yesterday all his bodily functions have ceased. So if it be God's will he, and we with him, will soon be relieved.

People now come in crowds to see him once more, although absolutely none are admitted save those bold enough to annoy the dying man in his last hour.

The letter to you, with the exception of a few words at the start, was dictated by him word for word, and probably is his last, although even to-day, quite brokenly, he whispered to me: "Smart—Stumpff—write them!" If it still be possible for him to put his name down on the paper it shall be done. He senses his end, for yesterday he said to me and to Mr. von Breuning: *Plaudite, amici, comœdia finita est.* Then, too, we were lucky enough yesterday to get the testament in shape, though there is nothing to dispose of except some old furniture and manuscripts. He had in hand a quintet for string instruments and the Tenth Symphony, which he mentioned in your letter. Of the quintet two movements are completed. It was intended for Diabelli. The day after he received your letter he was greatly excited and told me much of his plans for the Symphony, which would now be all the more grandiose since he would write it for the Philharmonic Society.

I could only have wished, most earnestly, that you had definitely said in your letter he could only touch this sum of 1,000 florins (as a Corresponding Member) in part; and this is what I had agreed upon with Mr. Rau; but Beethoven stuck to the end of the sentence in your letter. In short, his worries and cares suddenly disappeared when the money arrived and he said happily: "Now we can again treat ourselves to a good day once in a while." There were no more than 340 florins, V. C. [paper-florins] in the cash box and hence for some time we had been restricting ourselves to beef and vegetables, which caused him more grief than anything else. The other day—it was a Friday—he at once had his favorite fish dishes prepared, merely in order to be able to taste them. To be brief, his joy over the noble conduct of the Philharmonic Society at times degenerated into childishness.

A large so-called "grandfather's chair," which cost 50 florins, Viennese, also had to be bought for him, and in it he rests every day for at least half-an-hour, so that his bed can be properly made. . . .

Beethoven's physician, Dr. Wawruch, in retrospect.

May 20, 1827.

Ludwig van Beethoven declared that from earliest youth he had possessed a rugged, permanently good constitution, hardened by many privations, which even the most strenuous toil at his favorite occupation and continual profound study had been unable in the slightest degree to impair. The lonely nocturnal quiet always had shown itself most friendly to his glowing imagination. Hence he usually wrote after midnight until about three o'clock. A short sleep of from four to five hours was all he needed to refresh him. His breakfast eaten, he sat down at his writing-desk again until two o'clock in the afternoon.

When he entered his thirtieth year, however, he began to suffer from hæmorrhoidal complaints and an annoying roaring and buzzing in both ears. Soon his hearing began to fail and, for all he often would enjoy untroubled intervals lasting for months at a time, his disability finally ended in complete deafness. All the resources of the physician's art were useless. At about the same time Beethoven noticed that his digestion began to suffer; loss of appetite was followed by indigestion, an annoying belching, and alternate obstinate constipation and frequent diarrhœa.

At no time accustomed to taking medical advice seriously, he began to develop a liking for spirituous beverages,[1] in order to stimulate his decreasing loss of appetite and to aid his stomachic weakness by excessive use of strong punch and iced drinks and long, tiring

[1]This medical statement, of course, in no way implies that Beethoven was a heavy drinker. On the contrary, he was temperate in his habits.

excursions on foot. It was this very alteration of his
mode of life which, some seven years earlier, had led
him to the brink of the grave. He contracted a
severe inflammation of the intestines which, though it
yielded to treatment, later on often gave rise to intestinal
pains and aching colics and which, in part, must have
favored the eventual development of his mortal illness.

In the late fall of the year just passed (1826) Beethoven
felt an irresistible urge, in view of the uncertain state
of his health, to go to the country to recuperate. Since
owing to his incurable deafness he sedulously avoided
all society, he was thrown entirely upon his own resources under the most unfavorable circumstances for
days and even weeks at a time. Often, with rare endurance, he worked at his compositions on a wooded
hillside and his work done, still aglow with reflection, he
would not infrequently run about for hours in the most
inhospitable surroundings, defying every change of
temperature, and often daring the heaviest snowfalls.
His feet, always from time to time œdematous, would
begin to swell and since (as he insisted) he had to do
without every comfort of life, every solacing refresh-
ment, his illness soon got the upper hand of him.

Intimidated by the sad prospect, in the gloomy future,
of finding himself helpless in the country should he fall
sick, he longed to be back in Vienna, and, as he himself
jovially said, used the devil's own most wretched con-
veyance, a milk-wagon, to carry him home.

December was raw, wet, cold and frosty. Beethoven's
clothing was anything but suited to the unkind season
of the year, and yet he was driven on and away by an
inner restlessness, a sinister presentiment of misfortune.
He was obliged to stop overnight in a village inn, where
in addition to the shelter afforded by its wretched roof
he found only an unheated room without winter windows.
Toward midnight he was seized with his first convulsive
chills and fever, accompanied by violent thirst and pains

in the side. When the fever heat began to break, he drank a couple of quarts of ice-cold water, and, in his helpless state, yearned for the first ray of dawn. Weak and ill, he had himself loaded on the open van and, finally, arrived in Vienna enervated and exhausted.

I was not sent for until the third day. I found Beethoven with grave symptoms of inflammation of the lungs; his face glowed, he spit blood, when he breathed he threatened to choke, and the shooting pain in his side only allowed him to lie in a tormenting posture flat on his back. A strict anti-inflammatory mode of treatment soon brought the desired amelioration; nature conquered and a happy crisis freed him of the seemingly imminent danger of death, so that on the fifth day he was able to sit up and relate to me with deep emotion the story of the adversities he had suffered. On the seventh day he felt so passably well that he could rise, move about, read and write.

Yet on the eighth day I was not a little alarmed. On my morning visit I found him quite upset; his entire body jaundiced; while a terrible fit of vomiting and diarrhœa during the preceding night had threatened to kill him. Violent anger, profound suffering because of ingratitude and an undeserved insult had motived the tremendous explosion. Shaking and trembling, he writhed with the pain which raged in his liver and intestines; and his feet, hitherto only moderately puffed up, were now greatly swollen.

From this time on his dropsy developed; his secretions decreased in quantity, his liver gave convincing evidence of the presence of hard knots, his jaundice grew worse. The affectionate remonstrances of his friends soon appeased the threatening excitement and Beethoven, easily conciliated, soon forgot every insult offered him. His illness, however, progressed with giant strides. Already, during the third week, nocturnal choking attacks set in; the tremendous volume of the water accumulated called for immediate relief; and I found myself compelled to advocate the abdominal puncture in order to preclude the danger of sudden bursting. After a few moments of serious reflection Beethoven agreed to submit to the operation, the more so since the Ritter von Staudenheim, who had been called in as consulting physician, urgently recommended it as being imperatively necessary. The premier chirurgeon of the General Hospital, the Mag. Chir. Hr. Seibert, made the puncture with his habitual skill, so that Beethoven when he saw the stream of water cried out happily that the operation made him think of Moses, who struck the rock with his staff and made the water gush forth. The relief was almost immediate. The liquid amounted to 25 pounds in weight, yet the afterflow must have been five times that.

Carelessness in undoing the bandage of the wound at night, probably in order quickly to remove all the water which had gathered, well-nigh put an end to all rejoicing anent the improvement in Beethoven's condition. A violent erysipelatic inflammation set in and showed incipient signs of gangrene, but the greatest care exercised in keeping the inflamed surfaces dry soon checked the evil. Fortunately the three succeeding operations were carried out without the slightest difficulty.

Beethoven knew but too well that the tappings were only palliatives and hence resigned himself to a further accumulation of water, the more so since the cold, rainy winter season favored the return of his dropsy, and could not help but strengthen the original cause of his ill, which had its existence in his chronic liver trouble as well as in organic deficiencies of the abdominal intestines.

It is a curious fact that Beethoven, even after operations successfully performed, could not stand taking any medicine, if we except gentle laxatives. His appetite diminished from day to day, and his strength could not help but decrease noticeably in consequence of the repeated large loss of vital juices. Dr. Malfatti, who henceforth aided me with his advice, a friend of Beethoven's for many years and aware of the latter's inclination for spirituous beverages, therefore hit upon the idea of recommending iced punch. I must admit that this recipe worked admirably, for a few days at any rate. Beethoven felt so greatly refreshed by the iced spirits of wine that he slept through the whole of the first night, and began to sweat tremendously. He grew lively; often all sorts of witty ideas occurred to him; and he even dreamt of being able to complete the oratorio "Saul and David" which he had commenced.

Yet, as was to have been foreseen, his joy was of short duration. He began to abuse his prescription, and partook freely of the punch. Soon the alcoholic beverage called forth a powerful rush of blood to the head; he grew soporose and there was a rattle when he breathed like that of a person deeply intoxicated; he wandered in his talk and to this, at various times, was added an inflammatory pain in the neck with consequent hoarseness and even total speechlessness. He grew more violent and now, since colic and diarrhœa had resulted from the chilling of the intestines, it was high time to deprive him of this valuable stimulant.

It was under such conditions, together with a rapidly increasing loss of flesh and a noticeable falling off of his vital powers that January, February and March went by. Beethoven in gloomy hours of presentiment, foretold his approaching dissolution after his fourth tapping, nor was he mistaken. No consolation was able longer to revive him; and when I promised him that with the approaching spring weather his sufferings would decrease, he answered with a smile: "My day's work is done; if a physician still can be of use in my case (and then he lapsed into English) his name shall be called wonderful." This saddening reference to Handel's "Messiah" so profoundly moved me that in my inmost soul and with the deepest emotion I was obliged to confirm the truth of what he had said.

And now the ill-fated day drew ever nearer. My noble and often burdensome professional duty as a physician bade me call my suffering friend's attention to the momentuous day, so that he might comply with his civic and religious duties. With the most delicate consideration I set down the admonitory lines on a sheet of paper (for it was thus that we always had made ourselves mutually understood). Beethoven, slowly, meditatively and with incomparable self-control read what I had written, his face like that of one transfigured. Next he gave me his hand in a hearty, serious manner and said: "Have them send for his reverence the pastor." Then he grew quiet and reflective, and nodded me his: "I shall soon see you again," in friendly wise. Soon after Beethoven attended to his devotions with the pious resignation which looks forward with confidence to eternity.

When a few hours had passed, he lost consciousness, began to grow comatose, and breathed with a rattle. The following morning all symptoms pointed to the approaching end. The 26th of March was stormy, and clouded. Toward six in the afternoon came a flurry of snow, with thunder and lightning.—Beethoven died.— Would not a Roman augur, in view of the accidental commotion of the elements, have taken his apotheosis for granted?

THE FUNERAL

VIENNA, March 29, 1827.[1]

No sooner had his friends, with bleeding hearts, done him love's last services, than they came together to determine the solemn details of his funeral, which, owing to the preparations necessary, was set for the afternoon

[1] Contemporary report, reprinted by Kerst from Landau's "Beethoven-Album," 1877.

of March 29th.   Cards of invitation were at once printed and distributed in lavish quantity.   The mild, beautiful spring day lured a countless number of the curious into the open, to the Escarpment of the Alser suburb before the *Schottentor,* at the so-called *Schwarzspanierhaus* in which Beethoven had lived.   The crowding incident to a gathering of some 20,000 persons of every class finally became so great that the gates of the house of mourning had to be locked, since its spacious court, in which Beethoven's corpse had been biered, no longer could accommodate the densely packed multitude.   At four-thirty the clerical dignitaries appeared, and the procession set out and, for all the distance to the church, in a straight line, amounts to no more than 500 feet, yet it took more than an hour and a half to traverse because of its extremely slow progress made through the swaying crowds, which could not have been kept in order without using violence. Eight singers of the Royal and Imperial Court Opera carried the coffin.   Before they raised it to their shoulders, however, they intoned the chorale from B. A. Weber's opera "Wilhelm Tell."   Then all the mourners—artistic colleagues of the deceased, friends and admirers of his exalted genius, poets, actors, tone-poets, etc., all in deepest mourning, with black gloves, fluttering crape, bouquets of white lilies fastened to their left arms and torches with crape ribands—formed in order.   After the crucifer who led the procession, came four trombone-players and sixteen of the best singers in Vienna, who alternately blew and sang the *Miserere mei Deus*, whose melody had been composed by the deceased Master himself.

It was, in fact, in the late autumn of the year 1812, when he was staying with his brother in Linz, that choirmaster Glöggl of the local cathedral had asked him for some short trombone pieces for his "Turners" (city musicians) to be used on All Saints' Day.   Beethoven wrote a so-called *Equale a quatro tromboni*, true to the venerable ancient style, but stamped with the originality of his own bold harmonic structure. Out of this four-part composition for the brasses, choirmaster von Seyfried, quite in the spirit of the creator of these serious devotional mortuary hymns, then shaped a four-part vocal chorus to the words of the psalms mentioned which, thus admirably sung and alternating with the hollowly reverberating chords of the trombones, made a tremendously moving impression. After the band of priests, including all those in the funeral procession, followed the splendidly ornamented bier, surrounded by the conductors and choirmasters Eybler, Hummel, Seyfried and Kreutzer, on the right, and Weigl, Gyrowetz, Gänsbacher and Würfel on the left, holding the long white ribbon-ends which hung down from above. They were accompanied on each side by the torch-bearers, among them Castelli, Grillparzer, Bernard, Anschütz, Böhm, Czerny, Lablache, David, Pacini, Rodichi, Meric, Mayseder, Merk, Lannoy, Linke, Riotto, Schubert, Weidmann, Weiss, Schuppanzigh, etc., etc.

The pupils of the Vienna Konservatorium and Saint-Anna Music School, as well as the most distinguished notabilities, such as Count Moritz von Dietrichstein, Court Counsellors von Mosel and Breuning (the latter the friend of Beethoven's youth and executor of his testament) brought up the rear of the ceremonially inclusive processional.

Upon reaching the church the corpse received the blessing before the high-altar, during which ceremony the sixteen-voice male chorus sang the hymn *Libera me, Domine, de morte æterna*, which Seyfried had set in the "lofty style." When the splendid hearse, drawn by four horses, drove off with the lifeless clay past the aligned crowd, it was escorted by more than two hundred equipages. At the cemetery-gates Master Anschütz with the most solemn pathos and emotion spoke the incomparably beautiful funeral oration written by

Grillparzer, whose profound feeling and masterly presentation moved every heart, so that many a burning tear flowed from generous eyes in memory of the departed prince of tone. Many hundreds of copies of the two poems by Castelli and Schlechta, respectively, were distributed among those present who, after the coffin together with its three laurel wreaths had been lowered into the grave, departed the sacred resting-place, profoundly touched, as the twilight shadows began to fall.

Franz Grillparzer's Funeral Oration.

Standing by the grave of him who has passed away, we are in a manner the representatives of an entire nation, of the whole German people, mourning the loss of the one highly acclaimed half of that which was left us of the departed splendor of our native art, of the fatherland's full spiritual bloom. There yet lives—and may his life be long!—the hero of verse in German speech and tongue; but the last master of tuneful song, the organ of soulful concord, the heir and amplifier of Händel and Bach's, of Haydn and Mozart's immortal fame is now no more, and we stand weeping over the riven strings of the harp that is hushed.

The harp that is hushed! Let me call him so! For he was an artist, and all that was his, was his through art alone. The thorns of life had wounded him deeply, and as the cast-away clings to the shore, so did he seek refuge in thine arms, O thou glorious sister and peer of the Good and the True, thou balm of wounded hearts, heaven-born Art! To thee he clung fast, and even when the portal was closed wherethrough thou hadst entered in and spoken to him, when his deaf ear had blinded his vision for thy features, still did he ever carry thine image within his heart, and when he died it still reposed on his breast.

He was an artist—and who shall arise to stand beside him?

As the rushing behemoth spurns the waves, so did he rove to the uttermost bounds of his art. From the cooing of doves to the rolling of thunder, from the craftiest interweaving of well-weighed expedients of art up to that awful pitch where planful design disappears in the lawless whirl of contending natural forces, he had traversed and grasped it all. He who comes after him will not continue him; he must begin anew, for he who went before left off only where art leaves off. Adelaide— and Leonora! Triumph of the heroes of Vittoria—and the humble sacrificial song of the Mass!—Ye children of the twice and thrice divided voices! heaven-soaring harmony: "Freude, schöner Götterfunken," thou swan-song! Muse of song and the seven-stringed lyre! Approach his grave and bestrew it with laurel!

He was an artist, but a man as well. A man in every sense—in the highest. Because he withdrew from the world, they called him a man-hater, and because he held aloof from sentimentality, unfeeling. Ah, one who knows himself hard of heart, does not shrink! The finest points are those most easily blunted and bent or broken! An excess of sensitiveness avoids a show of feeling! He fled the world because, in the whole range of his loving nature, he found no weapon to oppose it. He withdrew from mankind after he had given them his all and received nothing in return. He dwelt alone, because he found no second Self. But to the end his heart beat warm for all men, in fatherly affection for his kindred, for the world his all and his heart's blood.

Thus he was, thus he died, thus he will live to the end of time.

You, however, who have followed after us hitherward, let not your hearts be troubled! You have not lost him, you have won him. No living man enters the halls of the immortals. Not until the body has perished, do their portals unclose. He whom you mourn stands from now onward among the great of all ages, inviolate forever. Return homeward therefore, in sorrow, yet resigned! And should you ever in times to come feel the overpowering might of his creations like an onrushing storm, when your mounting ecstasy overflows in the midst of a generation yet unborn, then remember this hour, and think, We were there, when they buried him, and when he died, we wept.

A CATALOG OF SELECTED
DOVER BOOKS
IN ALL FIELDS OF INTEREST

A CATALOG OF SELECTED DOVER
BOOKS IN ALL FIELDS OF INTEREST

CONCERNING THE SPIRITUAL IN ART, Wassily Kandinsky. Pioneering work by father of abstract art. Thoughts on color theory, nature of art. Analysis of earlier masters. 12 illustrations. 80pp. of text. 5⅜ x 8½. 23411-8 Pa. $4.95

ANIMALS: 1,419 Copyright-Free Illustrations of Mammals, Birds, Fish, Insects, etc., Jim Harter (ed.). Clear wood engravings present, in extremely lifelike poses, over 1,000 species of animals. One of the most extensive pictorial sourcebooks of its kind. Captions. Index. 284pp. 9 x 12. 23766-4 Pa. $14.95

CELTIC ART: The Methods of Construction, George Bain. Simple geometric techniques for making Celtic interlacements, spirals, Kells-type initials, animals, humans, etc. Over 500 illustrations. 160pp. 9 x 12. (USO) 22923-8 Pa. $9.95

AN ATLAS OF ANATOMY FOR ARTISTS, Fritz Schider. Most thorough reference work on art anatomy in the world. Hundreds of illustrations, including selections from works by Vesalius, Leonardo, Goya, Ingres, Michelangelo, others. 593 illustrations. 192pp. 7⅛ x 10¼. 20241-0 Pa. $9.95

CELTIC HAND STROKE-BY-STROKE (Irish Half-Uncial from "The Book of Kells"): An Arthur Baker Calligraphy Manual, Arthur Baker. Complete guide to creating each letter of the alphabet in distinctive Celtic manner. Covers hand position, strokes, pens, inks, paper, more. Illustrated. 48pp. 8¼ x 11. 24336-2 Pa. $3.95

EASY ORIGAMI, John Montroll. Charming collection of 32 projects (hat, cup, pelican, piano, swan, many more) specially designed for the novice origami hobbyist. Clearly illustrated easy-to-follow instructions insure that even beginning papercrafters will achieve successful results. 48pp. 8¼ x 11. 27298-2 Pa. $3.50

THE COMPLETE BOOK OF BIRDHOUSE CONSTRUCTION FOR WOOD-WORKERS, Scott D. Campbell. Detailed instructions, illustrations, tables. Also data on bird habitat and instinct patterns. Bibliography. 3 tables. 63 illustrations in 15 figures. 48pp. 5¼ x 8½. 24407-5 Pa. $2.50

BLOOMINGDALE'S ILLUSTRATED 1886 CATALOG: Fashions, Dry Goods and Housewares, Bloomingdale Brothers. Famed merchants' extremely rare catalog depicting about 1,700 products: clothing, housewares, firearms, dry goods, jewelry, more. Invaluable for dating, identifying vintage items. Also, copyright-free graphics for artists, designers. Co-published with Henry Ford Museum & Greenfield Village. 160pp. 8¼ x 11. 25780-0 Pa. $10.95

HISTORIC COSTUME IN PICTURES, Braun & Schneider. Over 1,450 costumed figures in clearly detailed engravings–from dawn of civilization to end of 19th century. Captions. Many folk costumes. 256pp. 8⅜ x 11¾. 23150-X Pa. $12.95

CATALOG OF DOVER BOOKS

STICKLEY CRAFTSMAN FURNITURE CATALOGS, Gustav Stickley and L. & J. G. Stickley. Beautiful, functional furniture in two authentic catalogs from 1910. 594 illustrations, including 277 photos, show settles, rockers, armchairs, reclining chairs, bookcases, desks, tables. 183pp. 6½ x 9¼.   23838-5 Pa. $11.95

AMERICAN LOCOMOTIVES IN HISTORIC PHOTOGRAPHS: 1858 to 1949, Ron Ziel (ed.). A rare collection of 126 meticulously detailed official photographs, called "builder portraits," of American locomotives that majestically chronicle the rise of steam locomotive power in America. Introduction. Detailed captions. xi + 129pp. 9 x 12.   27393-8 Pa. $13.95

AMERICA'S LIGHTHOUSES: An Illustrated History, Francis Ross Holland, Jr. Delightfully written, profusely illustrated fact-filled survey of over 200 American lighthouses since 1716. History, anecdotes, technological advances, more. 240pp. 8 x 10¾.
25576-X Pa. $12.95

TOWARDS A NEW ARCHITECTURE, Le Corbusier. Pioneering manifesto by founder of "International School." Technical and aesthetic theories, views of industry, economics, relation of form to function, "mass-production split" and much more. Profusely illustrated. 320pp. 6⅛ x 9¼. (USO)   25023-7 Pa. $9.95

HOW THE OTHER HALF LIVES, Jacob Riis. Famous journalistic record, exposing poverty and degradation of New York slums around 1900, by major social reformer. 100 striking and influential photographs. 233pp. 10 x 7⅞.
22012-5 Pa. $11.95

FRUIT KEY AND TWIG KEY TO TREES AND SHRUBS, William M. Harlow. One of the handiest and most widely used identification aids. Fruit key covers 120 deciduous and evergreen species; twig key 160 deciduous species. Easily used. Over 300 photographs. 126pp. 5⅜ x 8½.   20511-8 Pa. $3.95

COMMON BIRD SONGS, Dr. Donald J. Borror. Songs of 60 most common U.S. birds: robins, sparrows, cardinals, bluejays, finches, more—arranged in order of increasing complexity. Up to 9 variations of songs of each species.
Cassette and manual 99911-4 $8.95

ORCHIDS AS HOUSE PLANTS, Rebecca Tyson Northen. Grow cattleyas and many other kinds of orchids—in a window, in a case, or under artificial light. 63 illustrations. 148pp. 5¼ x 8½.   23261-1 Pa. $5.95

MONSTER MAZES, Dave Phillips. Masterful mazes at four levels of difficulty. Avoid deadly perils and evil creatures to find magical treasures. Solutions for all 32 exciting illustrated puzzles. 48pp. 8¼ x 11.   26005-4 Pa. $2.95

MOZART'S DON GIOVANNI (DOVER OPERA LIBRETTO SERIES), Wolfgang Amadeus Mozart. Introduced and translated by Ellen H. Bleiler. Standard Italian libretto, with complete English translation. Convenient and thoroughly portable—an ideal companion for reading along with a recording or the performance itself. Introduction. List of characters. Plot summary. 121pp. 5¼ x 8½.
24944-1 Pa. $3.95

TECHNICAL MANUAL AND DICTIONARY OF CLASSICAL BALLET, Gail Grant. Defines, explains, comments on steps, movements, poses and concepts. 15-page pictorial section. Basic book for student, viewer. 127pp. 5⅜ x 8½.
21843-0 Pa. $4.95

BRASS INSTRUMENTS: Their History and Development, Anthony Baines. Authoritative, updated survey of the evolution of trumpets, trombones, bugles, cornets, French horns, tubas and other brass wind instruments. Over 140 illustrations and 48 music examples. Corrected and updated by author. New preface. Bibliography. 320pp. 5⅜ x 8½. 27574-4 Pa. $9.95

HOLLYWOOD GLAMOR PORTRAITS, John Kobal (ed.). 145 photos from 1926-49. Harlow, Gable, Bogart, Bacall; 94 stars in all. Full background on photographers, technical aspects. 160pp. 8⅜ x 11¼. 23352-9 Pa. $12.95

MAX AND MORITZ, Wilhelm Busch. Great humor classic in both German and English. Also 10 other works: "Cat and Mouse," "Plisch and Plumm," etc. 216pp. 5⅜ x 8½. 20181-3 Pa. $6.95

THE RAVEN AND OTHER FAVORITE POEMS, Edgar Allan Poe. Over 40 of the author's most memorable poems: "The Bells," "Ulalume," "Israfel," "To Helen," "The Conqueror Worm," "Eldorado," "Annabel Lee," many more. Alphabetic lists of titles and first lines. 64pp. 5³⁄₁₆ x 8¼. 26685-0 Pa. $1.00

PERSONAL MEMOIRS OF U. S. GRANT, Ulysses Simpson Grant. Intelligent, deeply moving firsthand account of Civil War campaigns, considered by many the finest military memoirs ever written. Includes letters, historic photographs, maps and more. 528pp. 6⅛ x 9¼. 28587-1 Pa. $12.95

AMULETS AND SUPERSTITIONS, E. A. Wallis Budge. Comprehensive discourse on origin, powers of amulets in many ancient cultures: Arab, Persian Babylonian, Assyrian, Egyptian, Gnostic, Hebrew, Phoenician, Syriac, etc. Covers cross, swastika, crucifix, seals, rings, stones, etc. 584pp. 5⅜ x 8½. 23573-4 Pa. $12.95

RUSSIAN STORIES/PYCCKNE PACCKA3bl: A Dual-Language Book, edited by Gleb Struve. Twelve tales by such masters as Chekhov, Tolstoy, Dostoevsky, Pushkin, others. Excellent word-for-word English translations on facing pages, plus teaching and study aids, Russian/English vocabulary, biographical/critical introductions, more. 416pp. 5⅜ x 8½. 26244-8 Pa. $9.95

PHILADELPHIA THEN AND NOW: 60 Sites Photographed in the Past and Present, Kenneth Finkel and Susan Oyama. Rare photographs of City Hall, Logan Square, Independence Hall, Betsy Ross House, other landmarks juxtaposed with contemporary views. Captures changing face of historic city. Introduction. Captions. 128pp. 8¼ x 11. 25790-8 Pa. $9.95

AIA ARCHITECTURAL GUIDE TO NASSAU AND SUFFOLK COUNTIES, LONG ISLAND, The American Institute of Architects, Long Island Chapter, and the Society for the Preservation of Long Island Antiquities. Comprehensive, well-researched and generously illustrated volume brings to life over three centuries of Long Island's great architectural heritage. More than 240 photographs with authoritative, extensively detailed captions. 176pp. 8¼ x 11. 26946-9 Pa. $14.95

NORTH AMERICAN INDIAN LIFE: Customs and Traditions of 23 Tribes, Elsie Clews Parsons (ed.). 27 fictionalized essays by noted anthropologists examine religion, customs, government, additional facets of life among the Winnebago, Crow, Zuni, Eskimo, other tribes. 480pp. 6⅛ x 9¼. 27377-6 Pa. $10.95

FRANK LLOYD WRIGHT'S HOLLYHOCK HOUSE, Donald Hoffmann. Lavishly illustrated, carefully documented study of one of Wright's most controversial residential designs. Over 120 photographs, floor plans, elevations, etc. Detailed perceptive text by noted Wright scholar. Index. 128pp. 9¼ x 10¾. 27133-1 Pa. $11.95

THE MALE AND FEMALE FIGURE IN MOTION: 60 Classic Photographic Sequences, Eadweard Muybridge. 60 true-action photographs of men and women walking, running, climbing, bending, turning, etc., reproduced from rare 19th-century masterpiece. vi + 121pp. 9 x 12. 24745-7 Pa. $10.95

1001 QUESTIONS ANSWERED ABOUT THE SEASHORE, N. J. Berrill and Jacquelyn Berrill. Queries answered about dolphins, sea snails, sponges, starfish, fishes, shore birds, many others. Covers appearance, breeding, growth, feeding, much more. 305pp. 5¼ x 8¼. 23366-9 Pa. $8.95

GUIDE TO OWL WATCHING IN NORTH AMERICA, Donald S. Heintzelman. Superb guide offers complete data and descriptions of 19 species: barn owl, screech owl, snowy owl, many more. Expert coverage of owl-watching equipment, conservation, migrations and invasions, etc. Guide to observing sites. 84 illustrations. xiii + 193pp. 5⅜ x 8½. 27344-X Pa. $8.95

MEDICINAL AND OTHER USES OF NORTH AMERICAN PLANTS: A Historical Survey with Special Reference to the Eastern Indian Tribes, Charlotte Erichsen-Brown. Chronological historical citations document 500 years of usage of plants, trees, shrubs native to eastern Canada, northeastern U.S. Also complete identifying information. 343 illustrations. 544pp. 6½ x 9¼. 25951-X Pa. $12.95

STORYBOOK MAZES, Dave Phillips. 23 stories and mazes on two-page spreads: Wizard of Oz, Treasure Island, Robin Hood, etc. Solutions. 64pp. 8¼ x 11. 23628-5 Pa. $2.95

NEGRO FOLK MUSIC, U.S.A., Harold Courlander. Noted folklorist's scholarly yet readable analysis of rich and varied musical tradition. Includes authentic versions of over 40 folk songs. Valuable bibliography and discography. xi + 324pp. 5⅜ x 8½. 27350-4 Pa. $9.95

MOVIE-STAR PORTRAITS OF THE FORTIES, John Kobal (ed.). 163 glamor, studio photos of 106 stars of the 1940s: Rita Hayworth, Ava Gardner, Marlon Brando, Clark Gable, many more. 176pp. 8⅜ x 11¼. 23546-7 Pa. $12.95

BENCHLEY LOST AND FOUND, Robert Benchley. Finest humor from early 30s, about pet peeves, child psychologists, post office and others. Mostly unavailable elsewhere. 73 illustrations by Peter Arno and others. 183pp. 5⅜ x 8½. 22410-4 Pa. $6.95

YEKL and THE IMPORTED BRIDEGROOM AND OTHER STORIES OF YIDDISH NEW YORK, Abraham Cahan. Film Hester Street based on Yekl (1896). Novel, other stories among first about Jewish immigrants on N.Y.'s East Side. 240pp. 5⅜ x 8½. 22427-9 Pa. $6.95

SELECTED POEMS, Walt Whitman. Generous sampling from *Leaves of Grass*. Twenty-four poems include "I Hear America Singing," "Song of the Open Road," "I Sing the Body Electric," "When Lilacs Last in the Dooryard Bloom'd," "O Captain! My Captain!"–all reprinted from an authoritative edition. Lists of titles and first lines. 128pp. 5³⁄₁₆ x 8¼. 26878-0 Pa. $1.00

THE BEST TALES OF HOFFMANN, E. T. A. Hoffmann. 10 of Hoffmann's most important stories: "Nutcracker and the King of Mice," "The Golden Flowerpot," etc. 458pp. 5⅜ x 8½. 21793-0 Pa. $9.95

FROM FETISH TO GOD IN ANCIENT EGYPT, E. A. Wallis Budge. Rich detailed survey of Egyptian conception of "God" and gods, magic, cult of animals, Osiris, more. Also, superb English translations of hymns and legends. 240 illustrations. 545pp. 5⅜ x 8½. 25803-3 Pa. $13.95

FRENCH STORIES/CONTES FRANÇAIS: A Dual-Language Book, Wallace Fowlie. Ten stories by French masters, Voltaire to Camus: "Micromegas" by Voltaire; "The Atheist's Mass" by Balzac; "Minuet" by de Maupassant; "The Guest" by Camus, six more. Excellent English translations on facing pages. Also French-English vocabulary list, exercises, more. 352pp. 5⅜ x 8½. 26443-2 Pa. $9.95

CHICAGO AT THE TURN OF THE CENTURY IN PHOTOGRAPHS: 122 Historic Views from the Collections of the Chicago Historical Society, Larry A. Viskochil. Rare large-format prints offer detailed views of City Hall, State Street, the Loop, Hull House, Union Station, many other landmarks, circa 1904-1913. Introduction. Captions. Maps. 144pp. 9⅜ x 12¼. 24656-6 Pa. $12.95

OLD BROOKLYN IN EARLY PHOTOGRAPHS, 1865-1929, William Lee Younger. Luna Park, Gravesend race track, construction of Grand Army Plaza, moving of Hotel Brighton, etc. 157 previously unpublished photographs. 165pp. 8⅞ x 11¾. 23587-4 Pa. $13.95

THE MYTHS OF THE NORTH AMERICAN INDIANS, Lewis Spence. Rich anthology of the myths and legends of the Algonquins, Iroquois, Pawnees and Sioux, prefaced by an extensive historical and ethnological commentary. 36 illustrations. 480pp. 5⅜ x 8½. 25967-6 Pa. $10.95

AN ENCYCLOPEDIA OF BATTLES: Accounts of Over 1,560 Battles from 1479 B.C. to the Present, David Eggenberger. Essential details of every major battle in recorded history from the first battle of Megiddo in 1479 B.C. to Grenada in 1984. List of Battle Maps. New Appendix covering the years 1967-1984. Index. 99 illustrations. 544pp. 6½ x 9¼. 24913-1 Pa. $16.95

SAILING ALONE AROUND THE WORLD, Captain Joshua Slocum. First man to sail around the world, alone, in small boat. One of great feats of seamanship told in delightful manner. 67 illustrations. 294pp. 5⅜ x 8½. 20326-3 Pa. $6.95

ANARCHISM AND OTHER ESSAYS, Emma Goldman. Powerful, penetrating, prophetic essays on direct action, role of minorities, prison reform, puritan hypocrisy, violence, etc. 271pp. 5⅜ x 8½. 22484-8 Pa. $7.95

MYTHS OF THE HINDUS AND BUDDHISTS, Ananda K. Coomaraswamy and Sister Nivedita. Great stories of the epics; deeds of Krishna, Shiva, taken from puranas, Vedas, folk tales; etc. 32 illustrations. 400pp. 5⅜ x 8½. 21759-0 Pa. $12.95

BEYOND PSYCHOLOGY, Otto Rank. Fear of death, desire of immortality, nature of sexuality, social organization, creativity, according to Rankian system. 291pp. 5⅜ x 8½. 20485-5 Pa. $8.95

A THEOLOGICO-POLITICAL TREATISE, Benedict Spinoza. Also contains unfinished Political Treatise. Great classic on religious liberty, theory of government on common consent. R. Elwes translation. Total of 421pp. 5⅜ x 8½. 20249-6 Pa. $9.95

MY BONDAGE AND MY FREEDOM, Frederick Douglass. Born a slave, Douglass became outspoken force in antislavery movement. The best of Douglass' autobiographies. Graphic description of slave life. 464pp. 5⅜ x 8½. 22457-0 Pa. $8.95

FOLLOWING THE EQUATOR: A Journey Around the World, Mark Twain. Fascinating humorous account of 1897 voyage to Hawaii, Australia, India, New Zealand, etc. Ironic, bemused reports on peoples, customs, climate, flora and fauna, politics, much more. 197 illustrations. 720pp. 5⅜ x 8½. 26113-1 Pa. $15.95

THE PEOPLE CALLED SHAKERS, Edward D. Andrews. Definitive study of Shakers: origins, beliefs, practices, dances, social organization, furniture and crafts, etc. 33 illustrations. 351pp. 5⅜ x 8½. 21081-2 Pa. $8.95

THE MYTHS OF GREECE AND ROME, H. A. Guerber. A classic of mythology, generously illustrated, long prized for its simple, graphic, accurate retelling of the principal myths of Greece and Rome, and for its commentary on their origins and significance. With 64 illustrations by Michelangelo, Raphael, Titian, Rubens, Canova, Bernini and others. 480pp. 5⅜ x 8½. 27584-1 Pa. $9.95

PSYCHOLOGY OF MUSIC, Carl E. Seashore. Classic work discusses music as a medium from psychological viewpoint. Clear treatment of physical acoustics, auditory apparatus, sound perception, development of musical skills, nature of musical feeling, host of other topics. 88 figures. 408pp. 5⅜ x 8½. 21851-1 Pa. $11.95

THE PHILOSOPHY OF HISTORY, Georg W. Hegel. Great classic of Western thought develops concept that history is not chance but rational process, the evolution of freedom. 457pp. 5⅜ x 8½. 20112-0 Pa. $9.95

THE BOOK OF TEA, Kakuzo Okakura. Minor classic of the Orient: entertaining, charming explanation, interpretation of traditional Japanese culture in terms of tea ceremony. 94pp. 5⅜ x 8½. 20070-1 Pa. $3.95

LIFE IN ANCIENT EGYPT, Adolf Erman. Fullest, most thorough, detailed older account with much not in more recent books, domestic life, religion, magic, medicine, commerce, much more. Many illustrations reproduce tomb paintings, carvings, hieroglyphs, etc. 597pp. 5⅜ x 8½. 22632-8 Pa. $12.95

SUNDIALS, Their Theory and Construction, Albert Waugh. Far and away the best, most thorough coverage of ideas, mathematics concerned, types, construction, adjusting anywhere. Simple, nontechnical treatment allows even children to build several of these dials. Over 100 illustrations. 230pp. 5⅜ x 8½. 22947-5 Pa. $8.95

DYNAMICS OF FLUIDS IN POROUS MEDIA, Jacob Bear. For advanced students of ground water hydrology, soil mechanics and physics, drainage and irrigation engineering, and more. 335 illustrations. Exercises, with answers. 784pp. 6⅛ x 9¼. 65675-6 Pa. $19.95

SONGS OF EXPERIENCE: Facsimile Reproduction with 26 Plates in Full Color, William Blake. 26 full-color plates from a rare 1826 edition. Includes "The Tyger," "London," "Holy Thursday," and other poems. Printed text of poems. 48pp. 5¼ x 7. 24636-1 Pa. $4.95

OLD-TIME VIGNETTES IN FULL COLOR, Carol Belanger Grafton (ed.). Over 390 charming, often sentimental illustrations, selected from archives of Victorian graphics—pretty women posing, children playing, food, flowers, kittens and puppies, smiling cherubs, birds and butterflies, much more. All copyright-free. 48pp. 9¼ x 12¼. 27269-9 Pa. $7.95

PERSPECTIVE FOR ARTISTS, Rex Vicat Cole. Depth, perspective of sky and sea, shadows, much more, not usually covered. 391 diagrams, 81 reproductions of drawings and paintings. 279pp. 5⅜ x 8½. 22487-2 Pa. $7.95

DRAWING THE LIVING FIGURE, Joseph Sheppard. Innovative approach to artistic anatomy focuses on specifics of surface anatomy, rather than muscles and bones. Over 170 drawings of live models in front, back and side views, and in widely varying poses. Accompanying diagrams. 177 illustrations. Introduction. Index. 144pp. 8⅜ x11¼. 26723-7 Pa. $8.95

GOTHIC AND OLD ENGLISH ALPHABETS: 100 Complete Fonts, Dan X. Solo. Add power, elegance to posters, signs, other graphics with 100 stunning copyright-free alphabets: Blackstone, Dolbey, Germania, 97 more–including many lower-case, numerals, punctuation marks. 104pp. 8⅛ x 11. 24695-7 Pa. $8.95

HOW TO DO BEADWORK, Mary White. Fundamental book on craft from simple projects to five-bead chains and woven works. 106 illustrations. 142pp. 5⅜ x 8. 20697-1 Pa. $4.95

THE BOOK OF WOOD CARVING, Charles Marshall Sayers. Finest book for beginners discusses fundamentals and offers 34 designs. "Absolutely first rate . . . well thought out and well executed."–E. J. Tangerman. 118pp. 7¾ x 10⅝. 23654-4 Pa. $6.95

ILLUSTRATED CATALOG OF CIVIL WAR MILITARY GOODS: Union Army Weapons, Insignia, Uniform Accessories, and Other Equipment, Schuyler, Hartley, and Graham. Rare, profusely illustrated 1846 catalog includes Union Army uniform and dress regulations, arms and ammunition, coats, insignia, flags, swords, rifles, etc. 226 illustrations. 160pp. 9 x 12. 24939-5 Pa. $10.95

WOMEN'S FASHIONS OF THE EARLY 1900s: An Unabridged Republication of "New York Fashions, 1909," National Cloak & Suit Co. Rare catalog of mail-order fashions documents women's and children's clothing styles shortly after the turn of the century. Captions offer full descriptions, prices. Invaluable resource for fashion, costume historians. Approximately 725 illustrations. 128pp. 8⅜ x 11¼. 27276-1 Pa. $11.95

THE 1912 AND 1915 GUSTAV STICKLEY FURNITURE CATALOGS, Gustav Stickley. With over 200 detailed illustrations and descriptions, these two catalogs are essential reading and reference materials and identification guides for Stickley furniture. Captions cite materials, dimensions and prices. 112pp. 6½ x 9¼. 26676-1 Pa. $9.95

EARLY AMERICAN LOCOMOTIVES, John H. White, Jr. Finest locomotive engravings from early 19th century: historical (1804–74), main-line (after 1870), special, foreign, etc. 147 plates. 142pp. 11⅜ x 8¼. 22772-3 Pa. $10.95

THE TALL SHIPS OF TODAY IN PHOTOGRAPHS, Frank O. Braynard. Lavishly illustrated tribute to nearly 100 majestic contemporary sailing vessels: Amerigo Vespucci, Clearwater, Constitution, Eagle, Mayflower, Sea Cloud, Victory, many more. Authoritative captions provide statistics, background on each ship. 190 black-and-white photographs and illustrations. Introduction. 128pp. 8⅞ x 11¾. 27163-3 Pa. $14.95

EARLY NINETEENTH-CENTURY CRAFTS AND TRADES, Peter Stockham (ed.). Extremely rare 1807 volume describes to youngsters the crafts and trades of the day: brickmaker, weaver, dressmaker, bookbinder, ropemaker, saddler, many more. Quaint prose, charming illustrations for each craft. 20 black-and-white line illustrations. 192pp. 4⅝ x 6. 27293-1 Pa. $4.95

VICTORIAN FASHIONS AND COSTUMES FROM HARPER'S BAZAR, 1867–1898, Stella Blum (ed.). Day costumes, evening wear, sports clothes, shoes, hats, other accessories in over 1,000 detailed engravings. 320pp. 9⅜ x 12¼.
22990-4 Pa. $15.95

GUSTAV STICKLEY, THE CRAFTSMAN, Mary Ann Smith. Superb study surveys broad scope of Stickley's achievement, especially in architecture. Design philosophy, rise and fall of the Craftsman empire, descriptions and floor plans for many Craftsman houses, more. 86 black-and-white halftones. 31 line illustrations. Introduction 208pp. 6½ x 9¼. 27210-9 Pa. $9.95

THE LONG ISLAND RAIL ROAD IN EARLY PHOTOGRAPHS, Ron Ziel. Over 220 rare photos, informative text document origin (1844) and development of rail service on Long Island. Vintage views of early trains, locomotives, stations, passengers, crews, much more. Captions. 8⅞ x 11¾. 26301-0 Pa. $13.95

THE BOOK OF OLD SHIPS: From Egyptian Galleys to Clipper Ships, Henry B. Culver. Superb, authoritative history of sailing vessels, with 80 magnificent line illustrations. Galley, bark, caravel, longship, whaler, many more. Detailed, informative text on each vessel by noted naval historian. Introduction. 256pp. 5⅜ x 8½.
27332-6 Pa. $7.95

TEN BOOKS ON ARCHITECTURE, Vitruvius. The most important book ever written on architecture. Early Roman aesthetics, technology, classical orders, site selection, all other aspects. Morgan translation. 331pp. 5⅜ x 8½. 20645-9 Pa. $8.95

THE HUMAN FIGURE IN MOTION, Eadweard Muybridge. More than 4,500 stopped-action photos, in action series, showing undraped men, women, children jumping, lying down, throwing, sitting, wrestling, carrying, etc. 390pp. 7⅞ x 10⅝.
20204-6 Clothbd. $27.95

TREES OF THE EASTERN AND CENTRAL UNITED STATES AND CANADA, William M. Harlow. Best one-volume guide to 140 trees. Full descriptions, woodlore, range, etc. Over 600 illustrations. Handy size. 288pp. 4½ x 6⅜.
20395-6 Pa. $6.95

SONGS OF WESTERN BIRDS, Dr. Donald J. Borror. Complete song and call repertoire of 60 western species, including flycatchers, juncoes, cactus wrens, many more–includes fully illustrated booklet. Cassette and manual 99913-0 $8.95

GROWING AND USING HERBS AND SPICES, Milo Miloradovich. Versatile handbook provides all the information needed for cultivation and use of all the herbs and spices available in North America. 4 illustrations. Index. Glossary. 236pp. 5⅜ x 8½.
25058-X Pa. $7.95

BIG BOOK OF MAZES AND LABYRINTHS, Walter Shepherd. 50 mazes and labyrinths in all–classical, solid, ripple, and more–in one great volume. Perfect inexpensive puzzler for clever youngsters. Full solutions. 112pp. 8⅛ x 11.
22951-3 Pa. $4.95

PIANO TUNING, J. Cree Fischer. Clearest, best book for beginner, amateur. Simple repairs, raising dropped notes, tuning by easy method of flattened fifths. No previous skills needed. 4 illustrations. 201pp. 5⅜ x 8½.   23267-0 Pa. $6.95

A SOURCE BOOK IN THEATRICAL HISTORY, A. M. Nagler. Contemporary observers on acting, directing, make-up, costuming, stage props, machinery, scene design, from Ancient Greece to Chekhov. 611pp. 5⅜ x 8½.   20515-0 Pa. $12.95

THE COMPLETE NONSENSE OF EDWARD LEAR, Edward Lear. All nonsense limericks, zany alphabets, Owl and Pussycat, songs, nonsense botany, etc., illustrated by Lear. Total of 320pp. 5⅜ x 8½. (USO)   20167-8 Pa. $7.95

VICTORIAN PARLOUR POETRY: An Annotated Anthology, Michael R. Turner. 117 gems by Longfellow, Tennyson, Browning, many lesser-known poets. "The Village Blacksmith," "Curfew Must Not Ring Tonight," "Only a Baby Small," dozens more, often difficult to find elsewhere. Index of poets, titles, first lines. xxiii + 325pp. 5⅜ x 8½.   27044-0 Pa. $8.95

DUBLINERS, James Joyce. Fifteen stories offer vivid, tightly focused observations of the lives of Dublin's poorer classes. At least one, "The Dead," is considered a masterpiece. Reprinted complete and unabridged from standard edition. 160pp. 5³⁄₁₆ x 8¼.   26870-5 Pa. $1.00

THE HAUNTED MONASTERY and THE CHINESE MAZE MURDERS, Robert van Gulik. Two full novels by van Gulik, set in 7th-century China, continue adventures of Judge Dee and his companions. An evil Taoist monastery, seemingly supernatural events; overgrown topiary maze hides strange crimes. 27 illustrations. 328pp. 5⅜ x 8½.   23502-5 Pa. $8.95

THE BOOK OF THE SACRED MAGIC OF ABRAMELIN THE MAGE, translated by S. MacGregor Mathers. Medieval manuscript of ceremonial magic. Basic document in Aleister Crowley, Golden Dawn groups. 268pp. 5⅜ x 8½.
          23211-5 Pa. $9.95

NEW RUSSIAN-ENGLISH AND ENGLISH-RUSSIAN DICTIONARY, M. A. O'Brien. This is a remarkably handy Russian dictionary, containing a surprising amount of information, including over 70,000 entries. 366pp. 4½ x 6⅛.
          20208-9 Pa. $9.95

HISTORIC HOMES OF THE AMERICAN PRESIDENTS, Second, Revised Edition, Irvin Haas. A traveler's guide to American Presidential homes, most open to the public, depicting and describing homes occupied by every American President from George Washington to George Bush. With visiting hours, admission charges, travel routes. 175 photographs. Index. 160pp. 8¼ x 11.   26751-2 Pa. $11.95

NEW YORK IN THE FORTIES, Andreas Feininger. 162 brilliant photographs by the well-known photographer, formerly with *Life* magazine. Commuters, shoppers, Times Square at night, much else from city at its peak. Captions by John von Hartz. 181pp. 9¼ x 10¾.   23585-8 Pa. $12.95

INDIAN SIGN LANGUAGE, William Tomkins. Over 525 signs developed by Sioux and other tribes. Written instructions and diagrams. Also 290 pictographs. 111pp. 6⅛ x 9¼.   22029-X Pa. $3.95

CATALOG OF DOVER BOOKS

ANATOMY: A Complete Guide for Artists, Joseph Sheppard. A master of figure drawing shows artists how to render human anatomy convincingly. Over 460 illustrations. 224pp. 8⅜ x 11¼. 27279-6 Pa. $11.95

MEDIEVAL CALLIGRAPHY: Its History and Technique, Marc Drogin. Spirited history, comprehensive instruction manual covers 13 styles (ca. 4th century thru 15th). Excellent photographs; directions for duplicating medieval techniques with modern tools. 224pp. 8⅜ x 11¼. 26142-5 Pa. $12.95

DRIED FLOWERS: How to Prepare Them, Sarah Whitlock and Martha Rankin. Complete instructions on how to use silica gel, meal and borax, perlite aggregate, sand and borax, glycerine and water to create attractive permanent flower arrangements. 12 illustrations. 32pp. 5⅜ x 8½. 21802-3 Pa. $1.00

EASY-TO-MAKE BIRD FEEDERS FOR WOODWORKERS, Scott D. Campbell. Detailed, simple-to-use guide for designing, constructing, caring for and using feeders. Text, illustrations for 12 classic and contemporary designs. 96pp. 5⅜ x 8½. 25847-5 Pa. $3.95

SCOTTISH WONDER TALES FROM MYTH AND LEGEND, Donald A. Mackenzie. 16 lively tales tell of giants rumbling down mountainsides, of a magic wand that turns stone pillars into warriors, of gods and goddesses, evil hags, powerful forces and more. 240pp. 5⅜ x 8½. 29677-6 Pa. $6.95

THE HISTORY OF UNDERCLOTHES, C. Willett Cunnington and Phyllis Cunnington. Fascinating, well-documented survey covering six centuries of English undergarments, enhanced with over 100 illustrations: 12th-century laced-up bodice, footed long drawers (1795), 19th-century bustles, 19th-century corsets for men, Victorian "bust improvers," much more. 272pp. 5⅝ x 8¼. 27124-2 Pa. $9.95

ARTS AND CRAFTS FURNITURE: The Complete Brooks Catalog of 1912, Brooks Manufacturing Co. Photos and detailed descriptions of more than 150 now very collectible furniture designs from the Arts and Crafts movement depict davenports, settees, buffets, desks, tables, chairs, bedsteads, dressers and more, all built of solid, quarter-sawed oak. Invaluable for students and enthusiasts of antiques, Americana and the decorative arts. 80pp. 6½ x 9¼. 27471-3 Pa. $8.95

HOW WE INVENTED THE AIRPLANE: An Illustrated History, Orville Wright. Fascinating firsthand account covers early experiments, construction of planes and motors, first flights, much more. Introduction and commentary by Fred C. Kelly. 76 photographs. 96pp. 8¼ x 11. 25662-6 Pa. $8.95

THE ARTS OF THE SAILOR: Knotting, Splicing and Ropework, Hervey Garrett Smith. Indispensable shipboard reference covers tools, basic knots and useful hitches; handsewing and canvas work, more. Over 100 illustrations. Delightful reading for sea lovers. 256pp. 5⅜ x 8½. 26440-8 Pa. $7.95

FRANK LLOYD WRIGHT'S FALLINGWATER: The House and Its History, Second, Revised Edition, Donald Hoffmann. A total revision–both in text and illustrations–of the standard document on Fallingwater, the boldest, most personal architectural statement of Wright's mature years, updated with valuable new material from the recently opened Frank Lloyd Wright Archives. "Fascinating"–*The New York Times*. 116 illustrations. 128pp. 9¼ x 10¾. 27430-6 Pa. $12.95

PHOTOGRAPHIC SKETCHBOOK OF THE CIVIL WAR, Alexander Gardner. 100 photos taken on field during the Civil War. Famous shots of Manassas Harper's Ferry, Lincoln, Richmond, slave pens, etc. 244pp. 10⅝ x 8¼.   22731-6 Pa. $9.95

FIVE ACRES AND INDEPENDENCE, Maurice G. Kains. Great back-to-the-land classic explains basics of self-sufficient farming. The one book to get. 95 illustrations. 397pp. 5⅜ x 8½.   20974-1 Pa. $7.95

SONGS OF EASTERN BIRDS, Dr. Donald J. Borror. Songs and calls of 60 species most common to eastern U.S.: warblers, woodpeckers, flycatchers, thrushes, larks, many more in high-quality recording.   Cassette and manual 99912-2 $9.95

A MODERN HERBAL, Margaret Grieve. Much the fullest, most exact, most useful compilation of herbal material. Gigantic alphabetical encyclopedia, from aconite to zedoary, gives botanical information, medical properties, folklore, economic uses, much else. Indispensable to serious reader. 161 illustrations. 888pp. 6½ x 9¼. 2-vol. set. (USO)   Vol. I: 22798-7 Pa. $9.95
Vol. II: 22799-5 Pa. $9.95

HIDDEN TREASURE MAZE BOOK, Dave Phillips. Solve 34 challenging mazes accompanied by heroic tales of adventure. Evil dragons, people-eating plants, blood-thirsty giants, many more dangerous adversaries lurk at every twist and turn. 34 mazes, stories, solutions. 48pp. 8¼ x 11.   24566-7 Pa. $2.95

LETTERS OF W. A. MOZART, Wolfgang A. Mozart. Remarkable letters show bawdy wit, humor, imagination, musical insights, contemporary musical world; includes some letters from Leopold Mozart. 276pp. 5⅜ x 8½.   22859-2 Pa. $7.95

BASIC PRINCIPLES OF CLASSICAL BALLET, Agrippina Vaganova. Great Russian theoretician, teacher explains methods for teaching classical ballet. 118 illustrations. 175pp. 5⅜ x 8½.   22036-2 Pa. $5.95

THE JUMPING FROG, Mark Twain. Revenge edition. The original story of The Celebrated Jumping Frog of Calaveras County, a hapless French translation, and Twain's hilarious "retranslation" from the French. 12 illustrations. 66pp. 5⅜ x 8½.   22686-7 Pa. $3.95

BEST REMEMBERED POEMS, Martin Gardner (ed.). The 126 poems in this superb collection of 19th- and 20th-century British and American verse range from Shelley's "To a Skylark" to the impassioned "Renascence" of Edna St. Vincent Millay and to Edward Lear's whimsical "The Owl and the Pussycat." 224pp. 5⅜ x 8½.
27165-X Pa. $5.95

COMPLETE SONNETS, William Shakespeare. Over 150 exquisite poems deal with love, friendship, the tyranny of time, beauty's evanescence, death and other themes in language of remarkable power, precision and beauty. Glossary of archaic terms. 80pp. 5³⁄₁₆ x 8¼.   26686-9 Pa. $1.00

BODIES IN A BOOKSHOP, R. T. Campbell. Challenging mystery of blackmail and murder with ingenious plot and superbly drawn characters. In the best tradition of British suspense fiction. 192pp. 5⅜ x 8½.   24720-1 Pa. $6.95

THE WIT AND HUMOR OF OSCAR WILDE, Alvin Redman (ed.). More than 1,000 ripostes, paradoxes, wisecracks: Work is the curse of the drinking classes; I can resist everything except temptation; etc. 258pp. 5⅜ x 8½.   20602-5 Pa. $5.95

SHAKESPEARE LEXICON AND QUOTATION DICTIONARY, Alexander Schmidt. Full definitions, locations, shades of meaning in every word in plays and poems. More than 50,000 exact quotations. 1,485pp. 6½ x 9¼. 2-vol. set.
Vol. 1: 22726-X Pa. $17.95
Vol. 2: 22727-8 Pa. $17.95

SELECTED POEMS, Emily Dickinson. Over 100 best-known, best-loved poems by one of America's foremost poets, reprinted from authoritative early editions. No comparable edition at this price. Index of first lines. 64pp. 5³⁄₁₆ x 8¼.
26466-1 Pa. $1.00

CELEBRATED CASES OF JUDGE DEE (DEE GOONG AN), translated by Robert van Gulik. Authentic 18th-century Chinese detective novel; Dee and associates solve three interlocked cases. Led to van Gulik's own stories with same characters. Extensive introduction. 9 illustrations. 237pp. 5⅜ x 8½.   23337-5 Pa. $7.95

THE MALLEUS MALEFICARUM OF KRAMER AND SPRENGER, translated by Montague Summers. Full text of most important witchhunter's "bible," used by both Catholics and Protestants. 278pp. 6⅝ x 10.   22802-9 Pa. $12.95

SPANISH STORIES/CUENTOS ESPAÑOLES: A Dual-Language Book, Angel Flores (ed.). Unique format offers 13 great stories in Spanish by Cervantes, Borges, others. Faithful English translations on facing pages. 352pp. 5⅜ x 8½.
25399-6 Pa. $8.95

THE CHICAGO WORLD'S FAIR OF 1893: A Photographic Record, Stanley Appelbaum (ed.). 128 rare photos show 200 buildings, Beaux-Arts architecture, Midway, original Ferris Wheel, Edison's kinetoscope, more. Architectural emphasis; full text. 116pp. 8¼ x 11.   23990-X Pa. $9.95

OLD QUEENS, N.Y., IN EARLY PHOTOGRAPHS, Vincent F. Seyfried and William Asadorian. Over 160 rare photographs of Maspeth, Jamaica, Jackson Heights, and other areas. Vintage views of DeWitt Clinton mansion, 1939 World's Fair and more. Captions. 192pp. 8⅞ x 11.   26358-4 Pa. $12.95

CAPTURED BY THE INDIANS: 15 Firsthand Accounts, 1750-1870, Frederick Drimmer. Astounding true historical accounts of grisly torture, bloody conflicts, relentless pursuits, miraculous escapes and more, by people who lived to tell the tale. 384pp. 5⅜ x 8½.   24901-8 Pa. $8.95

THE WORLD'S GREAT SPEECHES, Lewis Copeland and Lawrence W. Lamm (eds.). Vast collection of 278 speeches of Greeks to 1970. Powerful and effective models; unique look at history. 842pp. 5⅜ x 8½.   20468-5 Pa. $14.95

THE BOOK OF THE SWORD, Sir Richard F. Burton. Great Victorian scholar/adventurer's eloquent, erudite history of the "queen of weapons"—from prehistory to early Roman Empire. Evolution and development of early swords, variations (sabre, broadsword, cutlass, scimitar, etc.), much more. 336pp. 6⅛ x 9¼.
25434-8 Pa. $9.95

AUTOBIOGRAPHY: The Story of My Experiments with Truth, Mohandas K. Gandhi. Boyhood, legal studies, purification, the growth of the Satyagraha (nonviolent protest) movement. Critical, inspiring work of the man responsible for the freedom of India. 480pp. 5⅜ x 8½. (USO)   24593-4 Pa. $8.95

CELTIC MYTHS AND LEGENDS, T. W. Rolleston. Masterful retelling of Irish and Welsh stories and tales. Cuchulain, King Arthur, Deirdre, the Grail, many more. First paperback edition. 58 full-page illustrations. 512pp. 5⅜ x 8½.   26507-2 Pa. $9.95

THE PRINCIPLES OF PSYCHOLOGY, William James. Famous long course complete, unabridged. Stream of thought, time perception, memory, experimental methods; great work decades ahead of its time. 94 figures. 1,391pp. 5⅜ x 8½. 2-vol. set.
Vol. I: 20381-6 Pa. $13.95
Vol. II: 20382-4 Pa. $14.95

THE WORLD AS WILL AND REPRESENTATION, Arthur Schopenhauer. Definitive English translation of Schopenhauer's life work, correcting more than 1,000 errors, omissions in earlier translations. Translated by E. F. J. Payne. Total of 1,269pp. 5⅜ x 8½. 2-vol. set.
Vol. 1: 21761-2 Pa. $12.95
Vol. 2: 21762-0 Pa. $12.95

MAGIC AND MYSTERY IN TIBET, Madame Alexandra David-Neel. Experiences among lamas, magicians, sages, sorcerers, Bonpa wizards. A true psychic discovery. 32 illustrations. 321pp. 5⅜ x 8½. (USO)   22682-4 Pa. $9.95

THE EGYPTIAN BOOK OF THE DEAD, E. A. Wallis Budge. Complete reproduction of Ani's papyrus, finest ever found. Full hieroglyphic text, interlinear transliteration, word-for-word translation, smooth translation. 533pp. 6½ x 9¼.
21866-X Pa. $11.95

MATHEMATICS FOR THE NONMATHEMATICIAN, Morris Kline. Detailed, college-level treatment of mathematics in cultural and historical context, with numerous exercises. Recommended Reading Lists. Tables. Numerous figures. 641pp. 5⅜ x 8½.
24823-2 Pa. $11.95

THEORY OF WING SECTIONS: Including a Summary of Airfoil Data, Ira H. Abbott and A. E. von Doenhoff. Concise compilation of subsonic aerodynamic characteristics of NACA wing sections, plus description of theory. 350pp. of tables. 693pp. 5⅜ x 8½.   60586-8 Pa. $14.95

THE RIME OF THE ANCIENT MARINER, Gustave Doré, S. T. Coleridge. Doré's finest work; 34 plates capture moods, subtleties of poem. Flawless full-size reproductions printed on facing pages with authoritative text of poem. "Beautiful. Simply beautiful."—*Publisher's Weekly.* 77pp. 9¼ x 12.   22305-1 Pa. $7.95

NORTH AMERICAN INDIAN DESIGNS FOR ARTISTS AND CRAFTSPEOPLE, Eva Wilson. Over 360 authentic copyright-free designs adapted from Navajo blankets, Hopi pottery, Sioux buffalo hides, more. Geometrics, symbolic figures, plant and animal motifs, etc. 128pp. 8⅜ x 11. (EUK)   25341-4 Pa. $8.95

SCULPTURE: Principles and Practice, Louis Slobodkin. Step-by-step approach to clay, plaster, metals, stone; classical and modern. 253 drawings, photos. 255pp. 8⅛ x 11.
22960-2 Pa. $11.95

THE INFLUENCE OF SEA POWER UPON HISTORY, 1660–1783, A. T. Mahan. Influential classic of naval history and tactics still used as text in war colleges. First paperback edition. 4 maps. 24 battle plans. 640pp. 5⅜ x 8½. 25509-3 Pa. $14.95

THE STORY OF THE TITANIC AS TOLD BY ITS SURVIVORS, Jack Winocour (ed.). What it was really like. Panic, despair, shocking inefficiency, and a little heroism. More thrilling than any fictional account. 26 illustrations. 320pp. 5⅜ x 8½. 20610-6 Pa. $8.95

FAIRY AND FOLK TALES OF THE IRISH PEASANTRY, William Butler Yeats (ed.). Treasury of 64 tales from the twilight world of Celtic myth and legend: "The Soul Cages," "The Kildare Pooka," "King O'Toole and his Goose," many more. Introduction and Notes by W. B. Yeats. 352pp. 5⅜ x 8½. 26941-8 Pa. $8.95

BUDDHIST MAHAYANA TEXTS, E. B. Cowell and Others (eds.). Superb, accurate translations of basic documents in Mahayana Buddhism, highly important in history of religions. The Buddha-karita of Asvaghosha, Larger Sukhavativyuha, more. 448pp. 5⅜ x 8½. 25552-2 Pa. $12.95

ONE TWO THREE . . . INFINITY: Facts and Speculations of Science, George Gamow. Great physicist's fascinating, readable overview of contemporary science: number theory, relativity, fourth dimension, entropy, genes, atomic structure, much more. 128 illustrations. Index. 352pp. 5⅜ x 8½. 25664-2 Pa. $8.95

ENGINEERING IN HISTORY, Richard Shelton Kirby, et al. Broad, nontechnical survey of history's major technological advances: birth of Greek science, industrial revolution, electricity and applied science, 20th-century automation, much more. 181 illustrations. ". . . excellent . . ."–*Isis.* Bibliography. vii + 530pp. 5⅜ x 8¼. 26412-2 Pa. $14.95

DALÍ ON MODERN ART: The Cuckolds of Antiquated Modern Art, Salvador Dalí. Influential painter skewers modern art and its practitioners. Outrageous evaluations of Picasso, Cézanne, Turner, more. 15 renderings of paintings discussed. 44 calligraphic decorations by Dalí. 96pp. 5⅜ x 8½. (USO) 29220-7 Pa. $4.95

ANTIQUE PLAYING CARDS: A Pictorial History, Henry René D'Allemagne. Over 900 elaborate, decorative images from rare playing cards (14th–20th centuries): Bacchus, death, dancing dogs, hunting scenes, royal coats of arms, players cheating, much more. 96pp. 9¼ x 12¼. 29265-7 Pa. $12.95

MAKING FURNITURE MASTERPIECES: 30 Projects with Measured Drawings, Franklin H. Gottshall. Step-by-step instructions, illustrations for constructing handsome, useful pieces, among them a Sheraton desk, Chippendale chair, Spanish desk, Queen Anne table and a William and Mary dressing mirror. 224pp. 8⅛ x 11¼. 29338-6 Pa. $13.95

THE FOSSIL BOOK: A Record of Prehistoric Life, Patricia V. Rich et al. Profusely illustrated definitive guide covers everything from single-celled organisms and dinosaurs to birds and mammals and the interplay between climate and man. Over 1,500 illustrations. 760pp. 7½ x 10⅛. 29371-8 Pa. $29.95

Prices subject to change without notice.

Available at your book dealer or write for free catalog to Dept. GI, Dover Publications, Inc., 31 East 2nd St., Mineola, N.Y. 11501. Dover publishes more than 500 books each year on science, elementary and advanced mathematics, biology, music, art, literary history, social sciences and other areas.